T0248801

Natural Language Processing and Computational Linguistics

Natural Language Processing and Computational Linguistics

Edited by
Martin Whitehead

www.willfordpress.com

Published by Willford Press,
118-35 Queens Blvd., Suite 400,
Forest Hills, NY 11375, USA

ISBN: 978-1-68285-841-7

Cataloging-in-Publication Data

Natural language processing and computational linguistics / edited by Martin Whitehead.
   p. cm.
Includes bibliographical references and index.
ISBN 978-1-68285-841-7
1. Natural language processing (Computer science). 2. Computational linguistics.
3. Multilingual computing. 4. Applied linguistics. 5. Cross-language information retrieval.
I. Whitehead, Martin.
QA76.9.N38 N38 2020
006.35--dc23

For information on all Willford Press publications
visit our website at www.willfordpress.com

Contents

Preface

Natural language processing is a field of research which deals with the interactions between human languages and computer. It also deals with the process of programming computers to analyze and process natural language data on a large scale. It is considered to be a subfield of several different fields such as artificial intelligence, computer science and linguistics. Computational linguistics is an inter-disciplinary field which uses a computational perspective to deal with statistical modeling of natural language. It has two main components, namely theoretical and applied. Theoretical computational linguistics is devoted to the study of issues in cognitive science. Applied computational linguistics, on the other hand, deals with the practical outcome of modeling human language use. This book discusses the fundamentals as well as modern approaches of natural language processing and computational linguistics. Those in search of information to further their knowledge will be greatly assisted by this book. It is appropriate for students seeking detailed information in this area as well as for experts.

All of the data presented henceforth, was collaborated in the wake of recent advancements in the field. The aim of this book is to present the diversified developments from across the globe in a comprehensible manner. The opinions expressed in each chapter belong solely to the contributing authors. Their interpretations of the topics are the integral part of this book, which I have carefully compiled for a better understanding of the readers.

At the end, I would like to thank all those who dedicated their time and efforts for the successful completion of this book. I also wish to convey my gratitude towards my friends and family who supported me at every step.

Editor

Computational modelling of Yorùbá numerals in a number-to-text conversion system

Olúgbénga O. Akinadé and Ọdẹ́túnjí A. Ọdẹ́jọbí
Computing and Intelligent Systems Research Group
Department of Computer Science and Engineering
Ọbáfẹ́mi Awólọ́wọ̀ University
Ilé-Ifẹ̀, Nigeria

Keywords: Analysis of numerals, Yorùbá numerals, numbers to text, text normalisation

ABSTRACT

In this paper, we examine the processes underlying the Yorùbá numeral system and describe a computational system that is capable of converting cardinal numbers to their equivalent Standard Yorùbá number names. First, we studied the mathematical and linguistic basis of the Yorùbá numeral system so as to formalise its arithmetic and syntactic procedures. Next, the process involved in formulating a Context-Free Grammar (CFG) to capture the structure of the Yorùbá numeral system was highlighted. Thereafter, the model was reduced into a set of computer programs to implement the numerical to lexical conversion process. System evaluation was done by ranking the output from the software and comparing the output with the representations given by a group of Yorùbá native speakers. The result showed that the system gave correct representation for numbers and produced a recall of 100% with respect to the collected corpus. Our future study is focused on developing a text normalisation system that will produce number names for other numerical expressions such as ordinal numbers, date, time, money, ratio, etc. in Yorùbá text.

1   INTRODUCTION

The use of numbers and their power in capturing concepts makes them indispensable in effective communication (Goyvaerts 1980). In any society, the use of numbers is firmly anchored to numerous beliefs and perceived usefulness of the significant philosophy underlying numerical messages (Abímbọ́lá 1977). In fact, key advancement in civilisation can be traced to the conception, invention, representation, and manipulation of numbers to facilitate accurate rendering of measurable objects. This has made the use of numbers an important tool within the society, where it is used in trade, cosmology, mathematics, divination, music, medicine, etc. Early cultures devised various means of number representation, which include body/finger counting (Zaslavsky 1973; Saxe 1981), object counting, Egyptian numerals, Babylonian numerals, Greek numerals, Chinese numerals, Roman numerals, Mayan numerals, Hindu-Arabic numerals, etc. The Hindu-Arabic numeral system, which is considered to be the greatest mathematical discovery (Bailey and Borwein 2011), is still the most commonly used symbolic representation of numbers due to its simplicity and the fact that it requires little memorisation to represent practically any number.

Naming numbers in human languages requires various mathematical and linguistic processes. For example, the number 74 is represented as 70 (7×10) increased by 4 in English, whereas it is represented as 60 (6×10) increased by 14 ($4 + 10$) in French. In Logo, the number 74 is represented as 10 added to 60 (20×3) increased by 4. In Yorùbá, in turn, the same number is derived in a more complex way by adding 4 to 80 (20×4) reduced by 10. Table 1 shows the representation of the number 74 in the four languages.

The analysis of number names is important but understudied in human language processing. While it may seem trivial to compute number names in languages like English, it may be difficult to get it

Table 1: Derivation of the number 74 in four languages

Language	Name	Derivation
English	*seventy four*	$(7 \times 10) + 4$
French	*soixante-quatorze*	$60 + 14$
Logo	*nyaɓa na drya mudri drya su*	$(20 \times 3) + 10 + 4$
Yorùbá	*ẹ̀rìnlélảảdọ́rin*	$4 + (-10 + (20 \times 4))$

right in many other languages, particularly in the Yorùbá language. In this paper, we present a formal description of the Yorùbá numeral system; specifically, the problem of Yorùbá number name transcription is addressed from an engineering perspective, by applying standard theories and techniques to an understudied language. This is part of a wider interest in the development of Text-To-Speech (TTS) synthesis and Machine Translation (MT) systems for the Yorùbá language. In TTS and related applications, text normalisation is often the first task, in which Non-Standard Words (NSW) such as numbers, abbreviations, acronyms, time, date, etc. are correctly identified and expanded into their textual forms (Sproat 1996). The expansion of numerical expressions in text is thus a key task in such applications because numbers occur more frequently in varying forms within a block of text. These forms include cardinal numbers, ordinal numbers, telephone numbers, date, time, percentages, monetary value, address, etc.

The rest of this paper is structured as follows: Section 2 gives an analysis of the Yorùbá numeral system and its associated number naming rules. Section 3 discusses the system design and implementation, while Section 4 discusses the results. Section 5 presents the system evaluation and Section 6 concludes the paper with areas of further study.

2 THE YORÙBÁ NUMERALS

The Yorùbá language (ISO 639.3 yor), which belongs to the West Benue-Congo branch of the Niger-Congo African languages family, is spoken by about 19,000,000 speakers in the South-Western Nigeria (Owolabi 2006). The language is also spoken in other West African countries such as Central Togo, the East-Central part of the Republic of Benin, and Creole population of Sierra Leone. Outside Africa, Yorùbá (called Nagô, Aku, or Lukumi; Lovejoy and Trotman 2003) is spoken in Brazil, Cuba, and Trinidad and Tobago.

Without a formal method of documenting literature, the Yorùbá community developed a complex numeral system that extensively uses subtraction throughout its system (Verran 2001). This has attracted many linguistic scholars to investigate the reasons why this community has developed an intricate numeral system. Certainly, knowledge of the Yorùbá numeral system has been passed from generation to generation by means of oral literature. Young language learners, in particular, are made to undergo drills of reciting rhymes with numbers ranging from 1 to 10.

In an early study of the Yorùbá numeral system, Mann (1887) shows how large numbers could be represented as an arithmetic combination of the basic number units and reveals that the subtraction operation plays an important role in number naming. The peculiarity in the Yorùbá numerals was highlighted as follows:

> "Very different is the framework of the Yorùbá, it can boast of a greater number of radical names of numerals, and to a large extent makes use of subtraction..." (Mann 1887, p. 60)

A fact worth noting is that some systems illustrate a pervasive use of the subtractive techniques. Examples of such systems are the clock system and the Roman numeral system. In the conventional clock system, when the minute part of time is greater than 30 minutes, the spoken representation can be derived by employing the subtractive technique. For instance, four canonical representations of 2:30 PM are:

(i) Half two (half hour past two)
(ii) Two thirty (2 o'clock + 30 min)
(iii) Thirty minutes after two (2 o'clock + 30 min)
(iv) Thirty minutes to three (3 o'clock − 30 min)

All four representations in (i) to (iv) are acceptable and none has precedence over the other. The form in (iv) is used to a large extent in our daily lives without any difficulty. Similarly, *halb zwei* in German means 'half of the second hour', which is 'half one'. So, the Yorùbá's use of subtraction is not completely exceptional, but its extensive usage may seem unusual, especially when it is preferred over the simpler addition operation.

Another observable feature of the Yorùbá numeral system is the use of base 20 (vigesimal), which likely stems from the counting of cowry shells as described by Mann:

> "Here we may explain the origin of this somewhat cumbersome system; it springs from the way in which the large sum of money (cowries) are counted. When a bagful is cast on the floor, the

counting person sits or kneels down beside it, takes 5 and 5
cowries and counts silently, 1, 2, up to 20, thus 100 are counted
off, this is repeated to get a second 100, these little heaps each of
100 cowries are united, and a next 200 is, when counted, swept
together with the first" (Mann 1887, p. 63)

However, there are vigesimal systems that do not have any relation to cowry shells. A more obvious reason for vigesimal systems
could be that humans have 10 fingers and 10 toes. The use of 20 as a
base may seem cumbersome, however, it is not entirely exceptional. In
many languages, especially in Europe and Africa, 20 is a base with respect to the linguistic structure of the names of certain numbers. Even
so, a consistent vigesimal system based on the powers of 20, i.e.: 20,
400, 8000, etc. is not generally used. Examples of a strict vigesimal numeral system are those of Maya and Dzongkha (the national language
of Bhutan). The numeral systems of the Ainu language of Japan and
Kaire language of Sudan also rely, to an extent, on base 20 for the representation of numbers. Apart from Yorùbá, other African languages
with vigesimal numeral system are: Madingo, Mundo, Logone, Nupe,
Mende, Bongo, Efik, Vei, Igbo, and Affadeh (Conant 1896). The study
by Conant (1896) highlighted the extent of the mental computation
required in the expression and conception of the Yorùbá numerals,
and concluded that the Yorùbá numeral system is the most peculiar
numeral system in existence. One might then begin to wonder why
the Yorùbá language, with a simple syllabic structure, will use such a
complex numeral system. The reason for this may not be too clear.

Johnson (1921) conducted an analysis of the Yorùbá numerals
by focusing on the derivation processes and the morphophonological
rules required, and showed how large numbers are calculated in multiples of 20,000. The study by Abraham (1958) examined the arithmetic skills employed in different Yorùbá numeral groups, and provided a guide into their syntactic representation. A profound study on
Yorùbá numerals was done by Ẹkúndayọ̀ (1977), where the derivational breakdown of the Yorùbá numerals was discussed and the structural representation of Yorùbá numerals was illustrated. In the study,
16 basic number lexemes which serve as the basic building blocks of
the Yorùbá numeral system were identified as presented in Section 2.1.

2.1   *Basic numbers in Yorùbá*

The Yorùbá counting system has lexemes for basic numbers from 1 to 10 and six higher numerals (i.e.: 20, 30, 200, 300, 400, and 20,000). These 16 basic number lexemes are:

> *ọ̀kan* (1), *èjì* (2), *ẹ̀ta* (3), *ẹ̀rin* (4), *àrún-ún* (5), *ẹ̀fà* (6), *èje* (7), *ẹ̀jọ* (8), *ẹ̀sán-án* (9), *ẹ̀wá* (10), *ogún* (20), *ogbọ̀n* (30), *igba* (200), *ọ̀dúnrún* (300), *irínwó* (400), *ọ̀kẹ́* (20,000) (Ẹkúndayọ̀ 1977)

Abraham (1958) and Ẹkúndayọ̀ (1977) also highlighted another set of basic numerals which are multiples of 20 from 20 to 80. These include:

> *okòó* (20), *òjì* (40), *ọ̀tà* (60), and *ọ̀rìn* (80).

These forms of lexemes are used with multiples of 100 between 200 and 20,000. The lexical representation of 20 has two values, i.e., *ogún* or *okòó*, which are used in different contexts. *Okòó* is the only form used in initial word positions when it is added to (*ó lé*) or subtracted from (*ó dín*) a vigesimal, while *ogún* is used with the multiplication formatives in numerical derivation. To illustrate this, 220 may either be expressed as *igba ó lé ogún* (200 increased by 20) or *okòólérúgba* (20 added to 200) but not as *igba ó lé okòó* or *ogúnlérúgba* although they would represent the same quantity.

Numbers are generated using syntactic combination of these lexemes, and only three of the basic mathematical operators are required to represent an infinite set of numbers within the Yorùbá language. These operators are represented by special position words like *lé* for addition, *dín* for subtraction, and *ọ̀nà* for multiplication. However, it should be pointed out that subtraction has an unusually higher functional load than addition. An exponential represented as *ìlọpo* may be required to express very large numerals as powers of 20,000 (Ọdéjọbí 2003) but this is not generally used in the Yorùbá numeral system.

2.2   *Overcounting in Yorùbá numerals*

We have mentioned the use of three of the standard arithmetic operations (i.e., multiplication, subtraction, and addition) in the Yorùbá numeral system. However, it is important to discuss a special mode of subtraction depicted by *ẹẹdín* and its variant, *aadín*. The *ẹẹdín* phenomenon was well articulated in Ẹkúndayọ̀ (1977), where a detailed explanation of this concept was given. Overcounting (Menninger 1969) occurs when a numeral is expressed in relation to a higher numeral. Overcounting, thus, becomes inevitable within any numeral system employing subtraction operation in number representation.

In the Yorùbá numerals system, when *ẹẹdín* is used with a number, it implies that the number must be reduced by a certain value. The use of *ẹẹdín* or *aadín* is context-dependent; hence, the value deducted varies depending on the numeral to which it is attached. This is shown in Table 2. When *ẹẹdín'* is used with numbers 20 and 30, 5 is deducted from them to produce 15 (*ẹẹdín ogún = èèdógún*) and 25 (*ẹẹdín ogbòn = èèdógbòn*) respectively. But if *ẹẹdín* is used with 600, 100 is deducted to produce 500 (*ẹẹdín ẹgbèta = èèdégbèta*).

Table 2: '*ẹẹdin*' mode of subtraction

Variant	Number	Reduction
ẹẹdín	20 and 30	5 (half of 10)
aadín	60, 80, ..., 200	10 (half of 20)
ẹẹdín	600, 800, ..., 2000	100 (half of 200)
ẹẹdín	4000, 6000, ..., 20000	1000 (half of 2000)

The concept of overcounting is also noticeable in the numeral systems of Ainu and Maya. Danish, an essentially Germanic language, also exhibits a related subtractive phenomenon (Conant 1896) as illustrated below:

a) 50 = *halvtredsindstyve* = half (of 20) from 3 × 20
b) 70 = *halvfierdsindstyve* = half (of 20) from 4 × 20
c) 90 = *halvfemsindstyve* = half (of 20) from 5 × 20

Notably, the process of naming numbers in Danish is similar to Yorùbá. Now, we present the rules used in naming numbers in Yorùbá.

2.3   *Yorùbá number naming rules*

There are basic rules that hold in the generation of an infinite set of number names in the Yorùbá language as captured in Figure 1. As observed by Hurford (2001), numeral sequences in human languages show several discontinuities in their patterns of representation. Therefore, it is important to identify numeral groups that exhibit similar derivative process within the Yorùbá numeral system. This is to

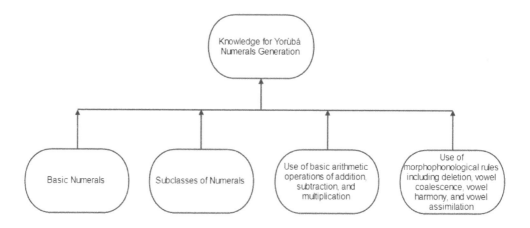

Figure 1: Knowledge for Yorùbá numerals generation

achieve the design of an effective computational model to handle the mathematical and syntactic structure of each group. The groups are:

a) **Basic numbers:** The canonical lexemes in the Yorùbá language have been discussed in Subsection 2.1. This set of lexemes cannot be broken down to simpler forms, and other number names are generated using arithmetic combinations of these lexemes.

b) **Numbers from 11 to 200:** The addition operation is used for deriving numbers from one to four above multiples of 10, while numbers from five to one below such points are obtained through subtraction as illustrated in Figure 2. The Yorùbá lexical representation of number 11 is formed as an additive concatenation of the terms for numbers 1 and 10. This also applies to numbers 12, 13, and 14 as :

   i) $11 = (1 + 10) =$ ọkan lé ẹwá $=$ ọ̀kànlá
   ii) $12 = (2 + 10) =$ èjì lé ẹwá $=$ èjìlá
   iii) $13 = (3 + 10) =$ ẹta lé ẹwá $=$ ẹ̀tànlá
   iv) $14 = (4 + 10) =$ ẹ̀rìn lé ẹwá $=$ ẹ̀rìnlá

Note that the lexical representation of '+ 10', i.e., lé ẹwá is contracted to lá. The Numbers from 15 to 19 are represented as 5 to 1 deducted from 20, respectively.

   i) $15 = 5$ from $20 =$ àrún-úndínlógún
   ii) $16 = 4$ from $20 =$ ẹ̀rindínlógún
   iii) $17 = 3$ from $20 =$ ẹ̀tadínlógún

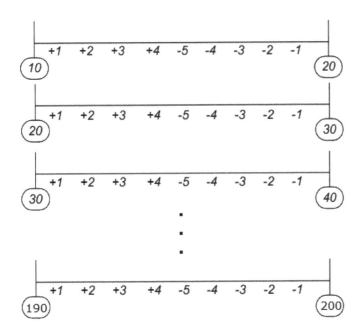

Figure 2: Yorùbá number scale

    iv) 18 = 2 from 20 = *èjìdínlógún*

    v) 19 = 1 from 20 = *ọ̀kàndínlógún*

Multiples of 20 from 40 to 180 are expressed as such in succes-
sive elision and vowel harmony. Numerals 50, 70, 90, 110, 130,
150 and 170 are expressed as 10 deducted (*aadín*) from the next
multiple of 20. Again, this is illustrated below:

    i) 40 = (20 × 2) = *ogún èjì* = *ogójì*

    ii) 50 = 10 less (20 × 3) = *aadín (ogún ẹ̀ta)* = *ààdọ́ta*

    iii) 110 = 10 less (20 × 6) = *aadín (ogún ẹ̀fà)* = *ààdọ́fà*

    iv) 180 = 20 × 9 = *ogún ẹ̀sàn-án* = *ọgọ́sàn-án*

Notably, a possible representation of 30 is *ààdóji*, which means
10 deducted from 2 twenties ((20 × 2) − 10), but 30 is referred to
as *ogbọ̀n*, which is a generic term in the Yorùbá numeral system.

c) **Numbers From 200 to 2000:** Apart from 400, numbers which
are multiples of 200 are derived in multiples of *igba* and the numbers 500, 700, 900, 1100, 1300, 1500, 1700, and 1,900 are derived by 100 deducted (*ẹẹdín*) from the next multiple of 200.

    i) 600 = (200 × 3) = *igba ẹ̀ta* = *ẹgbẹ̀ta*

    ii) 1000 = (200 × 5) = *igba àrùn-ún* = *ẹgbẹ̀rún-ún*

  iii) $1400 = (200 \times 7) = igba$ *èje* $= egbèje$

  iv) $1500 = (1600 - 100) = (200 \times 8) - 100 = $ *ẹẹdín igba èjọ* $=$ *èẹdégbèjọ*

  v) $2000 = (200 \times 10) = igba$ *èwá* $= egbèwá = egbàá$

d) **Numbers Between 2,000 and 20,000:** Numbers in this sub-group are formed from 2,000 as the root word. The multiples of 2,000 within this range are expressed as multiples of *egbàá* and intermediate numbers are formed with the *eedín* that shows a subtraction of 1,000.

  i) $6,000 = (2,000 \times 3) = $ *ẹgbàá ẹ̀ta* $=$ *ẹgbààta*

  ii) $10,000 = (2,000 \times 5) = $ *ẹgbàá àrún-ún* $=$ *ẹgbààrún-ún*

  iii) $15,000 = (16,000 - 1000) = (2,000 \times 8) - 1000 = $ *eedín ẹgbàá èjọ* $=$ *ẹẹdẹgbààjọ*

  iv) $20,000 = (2,000 \times 10) = $ *ẹgbàá ẹ̀wá* $=$ *ẹgbààwá*. This number is also expressed as *ọ̀kẹ́ kan*.

e) **Numbers 20,000 and above:** Numerals greater than 20,000 are derived as a multiple of 20,000 (*ọ̀kẹ́ kan* = twenty thousand in one place).

  i) $40,000 = (20,000 \times 2) = $ *ọ̀kẹ́ méjì*

  ii) $1,000,000 = (20,000 \times 50) = $ *ààdọ́ta ọ̀kẹ́*

  iii) $800,000,000 = (20,000 \times 20,000 \times 2) = $ *ọ̀kẹ́ ona ọ̀kẹ́ méjì*

  iv) $8,000,000,000,000 = 20,000 \times 20,000 \times 20,000 = $ *ọ̀kẹ́ ọ̀nà ọ̀kẹ́ ọ̀nà ọ̀kẹ́ kan*

Once the number groups are identified, Yorùbá numerals can be represented as a combination of members from each group using the addition and subtraction operations. For example, the number 45,678 will be represented as:

$$45,678 = 40,000 + 5,000 + 600 + 70 + 8 \tag{1}$$

A close observation of these groups shows that certain numbers occur as reference points in the Yorùbá numeral system as proposed by Pollmann and Jansen (1996). An observable trend is that the numbers 20 and 10 play important roles within the Yorùbá numeral system.

2.4   *The linguistic structure of numerals*

In this section, we review two important bibliographic references on the syntactic structure of numerals. The first one is Hurford (1975), which is an extensive study of various numeral systems. The other one is the study conducted by Ẹkúndayọ̀ (1977), in which phrase structure rules were proposed for the Yorùbá numeral system.

2.4.1   Hurford's generative numeral grammar

A notable work on the application of generative grammar to numerals is the work of Hurford (1975), where the universal phrase structure rules for deriving numerals were presented. A modified version of the phrase structure rules was presented in Hurford (2007), being a significant improvement with respect to well-formed numerals. In this extensive study of numerals, Hurford considered numerals as syntactic structural constructs and proposed a universal constraint on numerals, which he called the packing strategy. The packing strategy helps to make the right choice for a number name from different structural constructs derived by the production rules presented in Definition 1. The packing strategy guides the general constraints on the well-formed nature of numerals and any structure containing an ill-formed structure is itself ill-formed.

Definition 1 (Hurford's production rules for Yorùbá numerals)
Hurford's production rules for the Yorùbá numeral system are as follows:

$$NUM \quad \rightarrow \quad \left\{ \begin{array}{c} DIGIT \\ NP \end{array} \right\} (NUM) \tag{2}$$

$$NP \quad \rightarrow \quad (M) \; NUM \tag{3}$$

$$M \quad \rightarrow \quad 10 \left(\left\{ \begin{array}{c} 2 \\ M \end{array} \right\} \right) \tag{4}$$

Where DIGIT is a set of basic number lexemes, M is a set of multiplicative base lexemes, NUM is a numeral and the start symbol, and NP is a Number Phrase. Rule (2) is interpreted as addition/subtraction, and it can occur in reverse order, i.e., NUM → NUM NP. Rules (3) and (4) are interpreted as multiplication when two constituents are chosen. The curly brace in the production rules shows alternative productions, while parenthesis indicates an optional item. For example, an NP can be formed from a single NUM or a multiplicative combination of M NUM.

Hurford's generative framework provides an adequate account for the numeral system of most languages including English. However, the grammar was structurally inadequate for the Yorùbá numeral system. It is worth noting that the grammar does not provide an adequate mechanism to differentiate between the addition and subtraction operations in Rule (2). For example, Hurford (1975) presented structures for 46 and 4,600, as shown in Figure 3. In the structure in Figure 3(a), 46 (*èrindínlààdóta*) was derived by deducting 4 (*èrin*) from 50 (*ààdóta*) and 50 was derived by deducting 10 from 60 (*ògóta*). In Figure 3(b) and (c), representing structures for 4,600, i.e., *egbètalélogún* (200 × 23) and *egbà) àjì ó lé egbèta* (4,000+600) respectively, 23 (*ètalélogún*) was derived by adding 3 (*èta*) to 20 (*ogún*) and 4,600 was derived by 4,000 plus 600. Rule *NUM → NUM NP* is interpreted as subtraction in Figure 3(a), whereas, it is interpreted as addition in Figures 3(b) and (c). This means that the structure in Figure 3(a) could be misinterpreted as 54, and structures in Figure 3(b) and (c) as 3,400. Therefore, this introduces ambiguity in interpretation. It is also important to point out that Rule (4) results in an incorrect interpretation of the structures of *M*. To illustrate this, the rule represents 20 (*ogún*) as a combination of 10 (*èwá*) and 2 (*èjì*), which is structurally incorrect. This is because *ogún* is not formed, by any means, from the combination of *èwá* and *èjì*.

The study also acknowledged that multiple structures may exist for some numbers like 4,600, as shown in Figures 3(b) and 3(c), but concluded that the structure in 3(c) was ill-formed, whereas it is a valid structure in Yorùbá. This conclusion could result from a limited expert knowledge in verifying the correctness of these structures, as noted:

> *"Despite the difficulty in finding crucial information in the sources, it is conceivable that some complete account of Yorùbá numerals can be given that is soundly motivated. This language certainly presents the weightiest challenge for a general theory of numerals that we have encountered." (Hurford 1975, p. 232)*

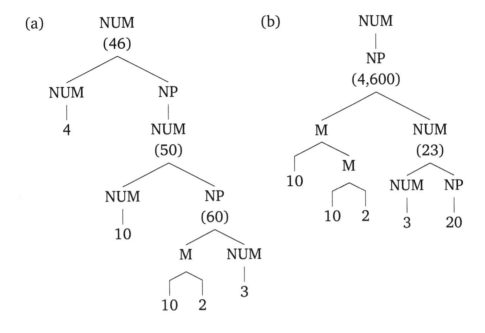

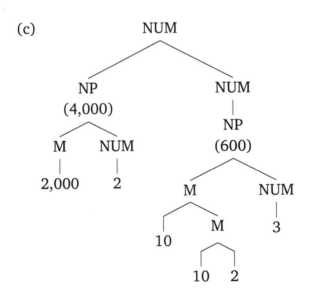

Figure 3: Parse tree for (a) 46 derived by 4 deducted from (10 deducted from (20 × 3))(b) 4,600 derived by 200 × (3 + 20) (c) 4,600 derived by (2,000 × 2) + (200 × 3)

2.4.2   Ẹkúndayọ̀'s phrase structure rules

The study conducted by Ẹkúndayọ̀ (1977) reveals that there exist similarities between the mechanism used in the Yorùbá language for constructing an infinite number of sentences from a finite set of building blocks and constructing an infinite set of numerals from a limited set of basic numbers. This proposition was corroborated into 3 different concepts as shown in Table 3. This shows that all Yorùbá numerals can be sententially represented through the addition, subtraction, and multiplication operators. The study also shows that some numbers have multiple representations in the Yorùbá language, but constraints of correctness are imposed on these representations. These constraints include linguistic and structural plausibilities.

Apart from the concept of infinity, creativity, and paraphrasable representation of numerals, Ẹkúndayọ̀ (1977) demonstrated that a recursive grammar is needed for numeral derivation and representation. It was observed that the recursive rules are not easily established for the Yorùbá numerals, however, a set of phrase structure (PS) rules for the Yorùbá numeral system was given as shown in Definition 2.

Table 3: Comparison of sentence construction and number naming in Yorùbá

No.	Concept	Language	Yorùbá numerals
1	**Infinity**	There is no longest sentence. Any sentence, however long, can be expanded. So with the use of recursive rules, an infinite number of sentences can be constructed.	Numerals are infinitely enumerable. This means that there is no longest numeral. Any numeral, however large can still be increased. So, the concept of recursive rules can be adopted in numerals.
2	**Creativity**	It is possible to construct and perceive an entirely new sentence that has never been heard before.	Yorùbá numerals also require a high level of creativity as higher numerals must be recreated every time they are used.
3	**Paraphrase**	A single idea could be represented in several ways.	A single number may also be represented in different forms in Yorùbá numerals.

Definition 2 (Ẹkúndayọ̀'s PS rules for Yorùbá numerals)

Ẹkúndayọ̀ phrase structure rules for the Yorùbá numeral system are as follows:

$$NUM \rightarrow NP \tag{5}$$

$$NP \rightarrow \left\{ \begin{array}{l} NP \ S \\ N \\ PRON \end{array} \right\} \tag{6}$$

$$S \rightarrow NP \ VP \tag{7}$$

$$VP \rightarrow V \ NP \tag{8}$$

Where NUM is a numeral and the start symbol, NP is a noun phrase, VP is a verb phrase, S is a sentence, N is the set of 16 basic number lexemes, PRON is the formative ó ('it'), and V is a verb represented as the operating formatives ọ̀nà (for multiplication), dín (for subtraction), and lé (for addition). NOTE: Rule (8) was presented as V → V NP in the original article but it was modified to make the grammar complete.

The point of interest here is that verbs are used in number naming, and that numbers are sententially represented in their surface structure. This allows for a distinction between addition and subtraction operations. This is illustrated by the structure of *ẹ̀rinlélááðọta* (54), shown in Figure 4, where the operating formative (*V*) is explicitly represented. Although these PS rules proved useful in the derivation of Yorùbá numerals, they are mostly arithmetic rather than syntactic rules as the positions of the basic lexical numerals and operatives do not correspond to their positions in the surface structure. An example would be the surface structure of *ẹ̀rinlélááðọta* (54) represented in Figure 4 as ((ọ̀gún ọ̀nà mẹ́ta) ó dín ẹ̀wá) ó lé ẹ̀rin rather than *ẹ̀rin ó lé (aadín (ọ̀gún ọ̀nà mẹ́ta))*, thereby leading to a misrepresentation of numerals.

Another problem with Ẹkúndayọ̀'s PS rules is that multiplicative bases (*M*) in Hurford's grammar are not captured. The multiplicative bases help to understand which numbers are important milestones in a numeral system. Hence, in this paper, we used knowledge from these two models to capture the essential components of the Yorùbá numerals. The grammar developed captures the multiplicative bases and treats Yorùbá numerals as both arithmetic and syntactic constructs.

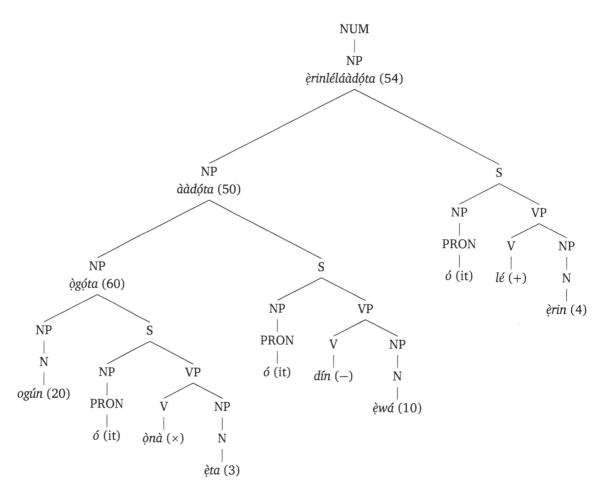

Figure 4: Parse tree for *èrinléláàdóta* (54)

3   SYSTEM DESIGN AND IMPLEMENTATION

It has been shown that the Yorùbá numeral system is very methodical, thus, an efficient computational system is required to gain accuracy in number representation. Figure 5 presents the block diagram of number transcription in the Yorùbá language. There are four important processes in this model. First, there is the number decomposition process, where numbers are expressed as a sum of smaller numbers in harmony with the sub-grouping discussed in Section 2.3. The output of this process is the magnitude stack. Next, there is a process that generates the possible forms of a single number. This is done by careful combinations of neighbouring elements of the magnitude stack and parsing them with the designed numeral grammar. This is done by using

Figure 5: Number to Yorùbá text transcription system. The figure shows the processes involved in converting a cardinal number to Yorùbá text.

the packing strategy to verify whether the structures are well-formed. The third process is where tokens of the number forms are converted to their equivalent lexical forms, and the final process is where the morphophonological rules employed in Yorùbá naming numbers are applied.

3.1 *Number decomposition to vigesimal*

Within the Yorùbá numeral system, every number can be represented using a combination of five different smaller terms, each drawn from the possible groups of the Yorùbá numeral system. So, the first process is to generate the magnitude stack from the given number. This generates five new numbers $(d_0, d_1, d_2, d_3, d_4)$ from the given number. So that

$$number = d_4 + d_3 + d_2 + d_1 + d_0 \qquad (9)$$

where

a) d_0 is 0 or a member of subgroup (a), i.e.,
d_0 takes values from 0 to 9, i.e., $d_0 \in DIGIT = \{0, 1, 2, ..., 9\}$.

b) d_1 is 0 or a member of subgroup (b), i.e.,
d_1 is a multiple of 20 ($d_1 = 20 \times n \mid 0 \leq n < 10$) **or** 10 deducted from a multiple of 20 ($d_1 = (20 \times n) - 10 \mid 2 \leq n \leq 10$).

c) d_2 is 0 or a member of subgroup (c), i.e.,
d_2 is a multiple of 200 ($d_2 = 200 \times n \mid 0 \leq n < 10$) **or** 100 deducted from a multiple of 200 ($d_2 = (200 \times n) - 100 \mid 2 \leq n \leq 10$).

d) d_3 is 0 or a member of subgroup (d), i.e.,
d_3 is a multiple of 2,000 ($d_3 = 2,000 \times n \mid 0 \leq n < 10$), **or** 1,000 deducted from a multiple of 2,000 ($d_3 = (2,000 \times n) - 1,000 \mid 2 \leq n \leq 10$).

e) d_4 is 0 or a member of subgroup (e), i.e.,
d_4 is a multiple of 20,000 ($d_4 = 20000 \times n \mid 0 \leq n < \infty$).

Table 4: Magnitude stack of some numbers

Number	Magnitude stack
23	[20, 3]
167	[160, 7]
3,459	[3,000, 400, 50, 9]
19,669	[19,000, 600, 60, 9]
412,987	[400,000, 12,000, 900, 80, 7]
1,876,234	[1,860,000, 16,000, 200, 30, 4]

These new numbers can be derived using Algorithm 1. Any of d_4, d_3, d_2, d_1, d_0 that is equal to zero is removed from the magnitude stack. The magnitude stacks of some numbers are presented in Table 4. For example, the magnitude stack generated for number 1,876,234 was:

$$[d_4, d_3, d_2, d_1, d_0] = [1,860,000,\ 16,000,\ 200,\ 30,\ 4]$$

In the next section, we discuss how the representations of single numbers are generated.

3.2   *Generating forms of a number*

Once the magnitude stack has been computed, the next task is to generate the possible forms of the number in Yorùbá. All the possible Yorùbá forms of a number are derived by some combinations of neighbouring elements of the magnitude stack. The possible forms for a number with magnitude stack of $[d_4, d_3, d_2, d_1, d_0]$ are listed in Table 5. For example, the magnitude stack for 19,669 is $[d_3, d_2, d_1, d_0] =$ [19,000, 600, 60, 9], and the possible forms are shown in Table 6. All possible forms are then stored in the form stack. However, not all numbers exhibit all these forms. The number of forms largely depends on the values of d_4, d_3, d_2, d_1, and d_0.

Thereafter, the elements of the form stack are expanded to a form containing only the symbols representing the basic lexical items. The expanded form stack for number 19,669 is presented in Table 7. In these forms, '×' represents multiplication, '−' and '+' represent subtraction and addition within a number phrase respectively; '——' and '++' represent subtraction and addition between number phrases respectively, as discussed in Section 3.3 b(ii). It should be noted that

---

Algorithm 1: Magnitude generator algorithm

Data: *number*: Input number

Result: *magnitudeStack*: The magnitude stack

1 **procedure GenerateMagnitude(*number*)**

2      $d_0, d_1, d_2, d_3, d_4 = 0$;

3   *divisor* $= 10$;

4   *magnitudeStack* $= [\ ]$;

5   **while** *number* $\neq 0$ **do**

6   *remainder* $=$ *number* $\%$ *divisor*;

7   **if** *remainder* $\neq 0$ **then**

8   *magnitudeStack*.**push**(*remainder*);

9   **end if**

10   *number* $=$ *number* $-$ *remainder*;

11   *divisor* $=$ *divisor* $\times 10$;

12   **end**

13   **for** *mag* **in** *magnitudeStack* **do**

14   **if** *mag* < 10 **then**

15              $d_0 = d_0 + mag$;

16   **else if** *mag* < 200 **then**

17              $d_1 = d_1 + mag$;

18   **else if** *mag* < 2000 **then**

19              $d_2 = d_2 + mag$;

20   **else if** *mag* < 20000 **then**

21              $d_3 = d_3 + mag$;

22   **else**

23              $d_4 = d_4 + mag - (mag \% 20000)$;

24              $d_3 = d_3 + (mag \% 20000)$;

25   **end if**

26   **end**

27   *magnitudeStack* $= [d_0, d_1, d_2, d_3, d_4]$;

28   **return** *magnitudeStack.reverse*();

29 **end procedure**

---

arithmetic is mostly done from right to left in the Yorùbá numeral system, i.e., $2-20$ implies 2 removed from 20, which gives 18. In the same way, $(10-(20\times4))$ implies 10 deducted from (20×4) to give 70.

Table 5: Forms of Yorùbá number

	Derivation
1	$[d_4, d_3, d_2 + d_1, d_0]$
2	$[d_4, d_3, d_2 + d_1 + 20, d_0 - 20]$
3	$[d_4, d_3, d_2 + d_1 - 20, d_0 + 20]$
4	$[d_4, d_3, d_2, d_1 + d_0]$
5	$[d_4, d_3, d_2 + 100, d_1 + d_0 - 100]$
6	$[d_4, d_3 + 1000, d_2 - 1000, d_1 + d_0]$
7	$[d_4, d_3 + 1000, d_2 - 1000 + 100, d_1 + d_0 - 100]$
8	$[d_4, d_3 + 1000, d_2 + d_1 - 1000, d_0]$
9	$[d_4, d_3 + d_2, d_1 + d_0]$
10	$[d_4, d_3 + d_2 + 100, d_1 + d_0 - 100]$

Table 6: Generation of the forms of 19,669. Item d_4 is discarded because $d_4 = 0$

	Derivation	Form Stack
1	$[d_3, d_2 + d_1, d_0]$	[19,000, 660, 9]
2	$[d_3, d_2 + d_1 + 20, d_0 - 20]$	[19,000, 680, −11]
3	$[d_3, d_2 + d1 - 20, d_0 + 20]$	[19,000, 640, 29]
4	$[d_3, d_2, d_1 + d_0]$	[19,000, 600, 69]
5	$[d_3, d_2 + 100, d_1 + d_0 - 100]$	[19,000, 700, −31]
6	$[d_3 + 1000, d_2 - 1000, d_1 + d_0]$	[20,000, −400, 69]
7	$[d_3 + 1000, d_2 - 1000 + 100, d_1 + d_0 - 100]$	[20,000, −300, −31]
8	$[d_3 + 1000, d_2 + d1 - 1000, d_0]$	[20,000, −340, 9]
9	$[d_3 + d_2, d_1 + d_0]$	[19,600, 69]
10	$[d_3 + d_2 + 100, d_1 + d_0 - 100]$	[19,700, −31]

3.3   *Context-free grammar for Yorùbá numerals*

We studied the structures of the five numeral groups discussed in Section 2.3, from which some patterns became apparent. We started the design of the CFG by identifying the set of terminal symbols which are:

a) The set of lexemes listed in Section 2.1.

     i) *DIGIT* = {ọ̀kan (1), èjì (2), ẹ̀ta (3), ẹ̀rin (4), àrún-ún (5), ẹ̀fà (6), èje (7), ẹ̀jọ (8), ẹ̀sán-án (9), ẹ̀wá (10), ogbọ̀n (30), ọ̀dún-rún (300), irínwó (400), okòó (20), òjì (D40), ọ̀tà (D60), ọ̀rìn (D80)}, and

     ii) The set of multiplicative bases i.e., *M* = {ogún (20), igba (200), ọ̀kẹ́ (20,000)}

b) The sets of lexical affixes depicting arithmetic operations in Yorùbá numerals. These three sets of operators are:

Table 7: Expanded forms of number 19,669. '++' and '——' are operation formatives found between phrases, while $D40$, $D60$, and $D80$ are multiples of 20 as mentioned in Section 2.1

No	Form Stack
1	$[(1{,}000-(2{,}000\times10))++(D60+(200\times3))++9]$
2	$[(1{,}000-(2{,}000\times10))++(D80+(200\times3))--(1+10)]$
3	$[(1{,}000-(2{,}000\times10))++(D40+(200\times3))++(1-30)]$
4	$[(1{,}000-(2{,}000\times10))++(200\times3)++(1-(10-(20\times4)))]$
5	$[(1{,}000-(2{,}000\times10))++(100-(200\times4))--(1+30)]$
6	$[20{,}000--400++(1-(10-(20\times4)))]$
7	$[20{,}000--300--(1+30)]$
8	$[20{,}000--(D40+300)++9]$
9	$[(200\times(2-(20\times5)))++(1-(10-(20\times4)))]$
10	$[(100-(200\times(1-(20\times5))))--(1+30)]$

i) A set of operators that occur within a phrase. This includes *lé ní* (+) for addition and *dín ní* (−) for subtraction. Multiplication within a phrase is implied, which means it is not explicitly represented. Hence, V = *{lé ní, dín ní}*.

ii) A set of operators that occur between phrases. This includes *ó lé* (++) for addition, *ó dín* (——) for subtraction and *ònà* (×) for multiplication. So we say VV = *{ó lé, ó dín, ònà}*.

iii) A set of implied subtraction operators represented by the prefixes *aadín* (reduction by 10) and *ẹẹdín* (reduction by 5, 100, and 1,000), i.e., *REDUCE* = *{aadín, ẹẹdín}*.

Thus the set of terminal symbols, T, is made up of all elements in: *DIGIT*, M, V, VV, and *REDUCE*.

The start symbol is a numeral which is denoted by *NUM*. Since a CFG is the union of simpler grammars (Sipser 2007), we started by constructing rules for structures of numerals that could occur as a number phrase.

A phrase could be formed as a single *DIGIT* (Ẹkúndayọ̀ 1977) or from the multiplication of M and *DIGIT*. A phrase formed by multiplication is denoted by *MP* (Hurford 2007), i.e.,

$$NP \quad \rightarrow \quad DIGIT \mid MP \tag{10}$$

$$MP \quad \rightarrow \quad M \mid MP\ NP \tag{11}$$

MP is formed by a single multiplicative base M, or recursively by multiplying *MP* by a number phrase *NP*, e.g. *ọgóta* is formed by multiplying an *MP* (20 – formed by *MP* → M) and an *NP* (3 – formed

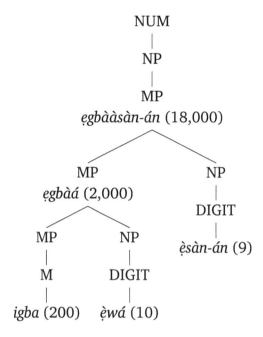

Figure 6: Parse tree of *ẹgbààsàn-án* (18,000)

by *NP → DIGIT*). Also, Rule (11) is recursive to handle multiple levels of multiplication. For example, 18,000 (*ẹgbààsán*) is represented as 2,000 multiplied by 9, and 2,000 is subsequently represented as 200 multiplied by 10, as shown in the parse tree in Figure 6.

We then added a rule to make allowance for the *ẹẹdín/aadín* type of subtraction. The phrase *ẹẹdín/aadín* can only occur as a prefix to a number derived from a multiplication operation. When this is done, the value deducted depends on the number to which it is prefixed (discussed in Subsection 2.2). A further example is 50 (*ààdọ́ta*), which is derived by deducting 10 from 60 (*ọgọ́ta*). Rule (12) captures this as shown in the structure in Figure 7.

$$NP \rightarrow REDUCE\ MP \qquad\qquad (12)$$

With the inclusion of this rule, it should be pointed out that it has some obvious consequences. The rule overgenerates, that is, it allows the use of *ẹẹdín* or *aadín* without respecting Table 2. We shall devise means of filtering out ill-formed structures using the packing strategy.

The next stage refers to how the operators *V* (Verbs) are represented within a phrase. Within a phrase, the Yorùbás start number presentation with the smaller number (Addend/Subtrahend) rather than the larger number (Augend/Minuend). For instance, number 21

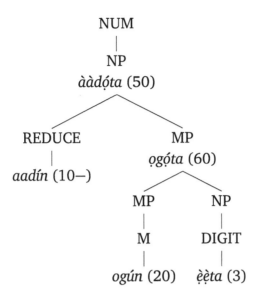

Figure 7: Parse tree of ààdọ́ta (50)

(twenty one) is represented as ọ̀kànelélógún (1+20) in Yorùbá. We then considered '1 +' as a verb phrase (*VP*), which is made up of a *DIGIT* and a *V* as presented in Rule (13):

$$VP \rightarrow DIGIT \ V \qquad (13)$$

A *VP* can then be combined with an *NP* to make up an *NP*, i.e.:

$$NP \rightarrow VP \ NP \qquad (14)$$

Also, the order in Rule (11) can be reversed to capture the structure of numbers like 600,000 (ọgbọ̀n ọ̀kẹ́), which is represented as 30 times 20,000. The multiplicative base now is positioned at the end of the rule, and can only take ọ̀kẹ́ (20,000) as a value. The outcome of this new rule is a phrase (*NP*), since it cannot be used as a multiplicand (*MP*) to derive higher numerals. For example, 1,200,000 cannot be represented as ọgbọ̀n ọ̀kẹ́ ọ̀nà mẹ́wàá ((30 × 20,000) × 10), but as ọ̀dúnrún ọ̀kẹ́ (300 × 20,000). So we added Rule (15). The structure of number 600,000 is shown in Figure 8.

$$NP \rightarrow NP \ M \qquad (15)$$

Next, we created rules to connect these phrases together to form a number. So, a number could be formed from a phrase, i.e.:

$$NUM \rightarrow NP \qquad (16)$$

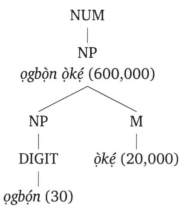

Figure 8: Parse tree of *ọgbọ̀n ọ̀kẹ́* (600,000)

Also, a number could be formed by combining an existing number with a phrase using the lexical operatives in the set *VV*. We added two rules to capture this as follows:

$$NUM \quad \rightarrow \quad NUM \ S \tag{17}$$

$$S \quad \rightarrow \quad VV \ NP \tag{18}$$

Although multiplication plays an important role in Yorùbá numerals, its lexical representation, *ọ̀nà* does not occur in number names except when more than one 20,000 (*ọ̀kẹ́*) occur within a number phrase. For example, 400,000,000 is represented as 20,000 × 20,000, i.e., *ọ̀kẹ́ ọ̀nà ọ̀kẹ́ kan*, and the structure is also captured using Rule (18) as shown in Figure 9.

Finally, all these rules were merged to make up the production rules of the Yorùbá numeral grammar, as presented in Definition 3.

Definition 3 (Production rules of the Yorùbá numeral grammar)
The production rules for the Yorùbá numeral system are as follows:

$$NUM \quad \rightarrow \quad NP \mid NUM \ S \tag{19}$$

$$S \quad \rightarrow \quad VV \ NP \tag{20}$$

$$NP \quad \rightarrow \quad DIGIT \mid MP \mid VP \ NP \tag{21}$$

$$NP \quad \rightarrow \quad REDUCE \ MP \mid NP \ M \tag{22}$$

$$MP \quad \rightarrow \quad M \mid MP \ NP \tag{23}$$

$$VP \quad \rightarrow \quad DIGIT \ V \tag{24}$$

These phrase structure rules include the verbs which are operating formatives (V and VV) proposed by (Ẹkúndayọ̀ 1977). These rules pro-

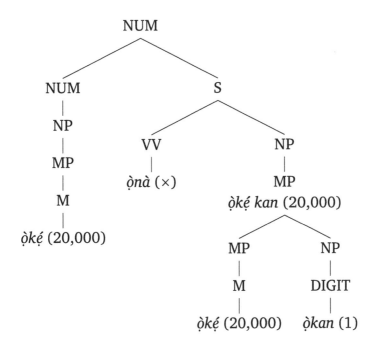

Figure 9: Parse tree of *ọ̀kẹ́ ọ̀nà ọ̀kẹ́ kan* (400,000,000)

duce a single and correct structure for most Yorùbá numerals, how-ever, the rules overgenerate with some numerals. For example, the number 1,000,000 produces 3 structures as presented in Figure 10, but the valid structure is determined using a single packing strategy defined in Definition 4.

Definition 4 (Packing strategy for the Yorùbá numeral system)
The following metarules govern well-formed Yorùbá numeral structures:

(i) *Whenever a phrase MP is formed by a multiplicative combination of two numerals, the multiplicand (MP) must be greater than the multiplier (NP).*

(ii) *Whenever the rule NP → REDUCE MP is used, the lexical item of REDUCE must correspond to the appropriate MP, as shown in Table 2.*

(iii) *Whenever the rule S → VV NP is used and the VV has the value of ọ̀nà, then NP can only take a value of ọ̀kẹ́, and the resulting S must be used with a multiple of ọ̀kẹ́. (see Figure 9).*

Using the packing strategy for Yorùbá numerals, the well-formed-ness of the structures in Figure 10 was investigated and only the struc-ture in (c) was well-formed. The analysis is as follows:

(i) In the structure in Figure 10(b), the formation of *MP* from *ogún* (20) disagrees with metarule (i), thereby making the structure in Figure 10(b) ill-formed.

(ii) The structure in Figure 10(a) is not well-formed as *REDUCE* (*aadín* (10−)) is applied to a multiple of *ọ̀kẹ́* (20,000), which

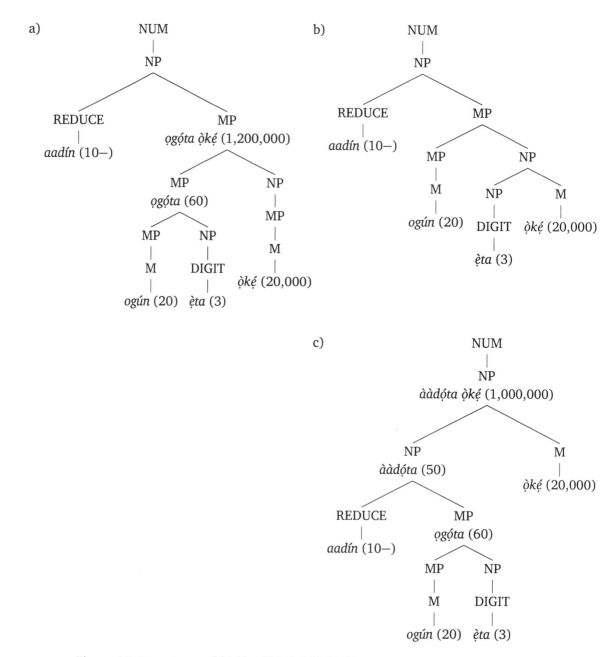

Figure 10: Parse trees of *ààdọ́ta ọ̀kẹ́* (1,000,000)

disagrees with metarule (ii). Hence, only the structure in Figure 10(c) is well-formed.

Once a parse tree is generated, we then convert the tokens to their lexical equivalences followed by the application of morphophonological rules.

3.4   *Morphophonological rules in Yorùbá numeral system*

The representation of numbers in Yorùbá is cumbersome due to the fact that a high level of linguistic processing is involved. Therefore, the speakers are required to have adequate knowledge of some morphophonological rules in the Yorùbá language. These morphophonological rules include deletion, vowel coalescence, vowel harmony, and vowel assimilation. These rules will be discussed to show how they are useful in number naming.

3.4.1   Deletion

Deletion is a process by which a phrase or word is shortened by completely deleting a segment. Both vowels and consonants can be deleted in Yorùbá. The most commonly deleted consonants are *w* (when it is part of the last syllable) and *g*. Deletion is notable in the contracted form of phrases *dín ní* (less than) and *lé ní* (more than), where *i* is completely deleted and *n* is converted to *l*. This conversion is possible because *n* and *l* are allophones of the same phoneme. For example, the expression for 28, which is derived as 2 from 30 (*èjì dín ní ọgbọ̀n*), is *èjìdínlọ́gbọ̀n*.

A deletion also occurs in naming numbers between 11 and 14. For example, *ókànlá* (11) is formed by adding 1 to 10, i.e., *òkan lé ẹwá*, which is contracted to form *òkanléẹ̀wá* by deleting the vowel *é*. The consonant *w* and vowel *ẹ* are then deleted to form *òkànlá*. Another example is *ẹ̀ẹ̀dégbẹ̀ta*, which is formed from *ẹẹdín ẹgbẹ̀ta*. This is achieved by completely deleting the vowel *ín*.

3.4.2   Vowel coalescence

Coalescence is a phonological process whereby two adjoining segments converge or fuse into one element such that the new segment is phonologically distinct from the input segments (Bámiṣilẹ̀ 1994). This is illustrated by Equation 25, where V_1 is the vowel that ends the first morpheme, V_2 is the vowel that begins the second morpheme, '+' is the morpheme boundary, and V_3 is the resulting morpheme.

$$V_1 + V_2 \rightarrow V_3 \qquad (25)$$

In coalescence, the combining vowels may be phonologically distinct from each other but the resulting vowel must be distinct from the combining vowels, i.e., $V_1 \neq V_3$ and $V_2 \neq V_3$ (Awóbùlúyì 1987).

Vowel coalescence is most notable when two nouns are next to each other. And since Yorùbá numerals are mostly treated as nominal entities, they also use vowel coalescence in naming numbers. For example, vowel coalescence is used in the formation of *ogóji* (40) derived from 20 multiplied by 2, i.e., *ogún èjì*. The vowels *ún* and *e* are combined by coalescence to become *o*. Table 8 shows the possible occurrence of vowel coalescence in the Yorùbá numeral system.

Table 8: Vowel coalescence in Yorùbá numerals. V_1 is the vowel that ends the first morpheme, V_2 is the vowel that begins the second morpheme, + is the morpheme boundary, and → stands for 'rewritten as'

V_1	V_2	V_3	Example
un	a	ọ	ogún + àrùn-ún → ọgórùn-ún
un	e	o	ogún + èjì → ọgóji
un	ẹ	ọ	ogún + ẹ̀ta → ọgóta
i	i	u	èjì dín ní + igba → èjìdínlúgba

3.4.3   Vowel harmony

Standard Yorùbá has 7 oral vowels, which are: *a, e, ẹ, i, o, ọ, u*. Vowel harmony places a constraint on the occurrence of vowel sequence in words. Archangeli and Pulleyblank (1989) discussed the two classes of Standard Yorùbá oral vowels which are:

i) Advanced Tongue Root (ATR), which are vowels *i, e, o,* and *u*,

ii) Non-ATR, which are vowels *a, ẹ,* and *ọ*

ATR vowels involve drawing forward the root of the tongue so that the pharynx is expanded. In simple Yorùbá words, the last vowel in the word determines the other vowels in the word (Akinlabí 2004). So, if the last vowel in a word is an ATR, the immediately preceding vowel must be an ATR. The high vowels (*i* and *u*) do not participate in the vowel harmony at all, and they can occur with any vowel. Only the mid vowels (*e, o, ẹ,* and *ọ*) are fully involved in the vowel harmony (Akinlabí 2004). The chart presented in Table 9 shows the permissible and non-permissible sequences of vowels in the Yorùbá language.

Table 9: Sequence of vowels in Yorùbá bisyllabic words. The symbols + and Ø indicate the permissible and non-permissible vowel sequence, respectively. V_2 is the second oral vowel in the word and V_1 indicates the vowel that may precede V_2.

		i	e	ẹ	a	ọ	o	u
	i	+	+	+	+	+	+	+
	e	+	+	Ø	Ø	Ø	+	+
V_1	ẹ	+	Ø	+	+	+	Ø	+
	a	+	+	+	+	+	+	+
	ọ	+	Ø	+	+	+	Ø	+
	o	+	+	Ø	Ø	Ø	+	+
	u*	+	+	+	+	+	+	+

The top row is labeled V_2.

(Adapted from Archangeli and Pulleyblank (1989))
*The letter u cannot start a word in the Standard Yorùbá language.

These rules also apply to number naming in Yorùbá as illustrated with the following example: The number *ọgọ́ta* (120) is derived as 20 (*ogún*) multiplied by 3 (*ẹ̀ta*), i.e., *ogún ẹ̀ta*. The vowels *ún* and *ẹ̀* are then changed to vowel *ọ́* to form *ogọ́ta* by means of vowel coalescence. Since the last vowel in the last two syllables is *a*, which is a non-ATR, therefore, the immediately preceding vowels must be non-ATR. We will then proceed to check for harmony between the first two sylla-bles. The second vowel *ọ́* is non-ATR, therefore, the first vowel *o* must also be a non-ATR. This will transform *o* to *ọ* by means of the vowel harmony.

3.4.4   Vowel assimilation

Vowel assimilation is a process whereby a vowel becomes completely or partially like another vowel (Akinlabí 2004). Vowel assimilation is most notable in Yorùbá numerals when a consonant separating 2 vowels is deleted. This can be illustrated by number 2,000 (*ẹgbàá*). The number 2,000 is actually formed from 200 × 10, i.e., *igba ẹ̀wá*, which will produce *ẹgbẹ̀wá* by vowel deletion. *ẹgbàá* is then formed by deleting the consonant *w* and allowing the vowel *ẹ* to assimilate the form of vowel *a*.

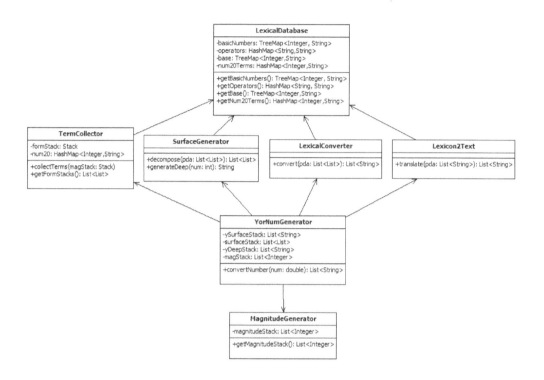

Figure 11: UML class diagram

Vowel assimilation can also occur between vowels separated by a consonant as in the expression for 800 (ẹgbẹ̀rin). This expression is derived as 200 (igba) multiplied by 4 (ẹ̀rin), i.e., igba ẹ̀rin. igbẹ̀rin is then formed by deleting a. The vowel i then assimilates ẹ to form ẹgbẹ̀rin.

3.5   *System and implementation*

An object oriented programming (OOP) approach with 7 classes was used during the system design. The UML class diagram and the sequence diagram for the software are as shown in Figure 11 and Figure 12 respectively.

The software implementation was done using Python and Java. The software was implemented following the specifications in the system design. The following software pieces were developed to demonstrate the conversion of numbers to Standard Yorùbá text:

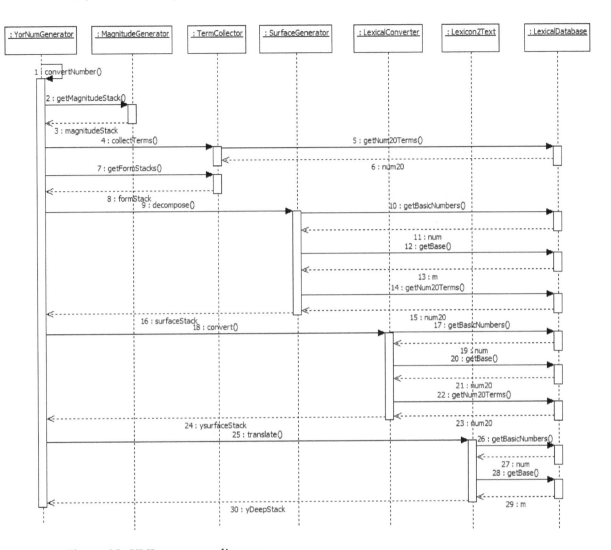

Figure 12: UML sequence diagram

a) **Desktop application:** The desktop application was implemented using PyQt in the Python programming language environment. The combination of Python and Qt makes possible the development of applications that are platform-independent (Summerfield 2008). NLTK (Loper and Bird 2002) was used to implement the grammar designed for the Yorùbá numeral system. It was also used to generate the parse trees of the number forms. The screenshot is as shown in Figure 13 and the software is available for download at http://www.ifecisrg.org/yorubanumerals.

b) **Web application:** The web application was implemented using the Google App Engine Python API. The screenshot is as shown in

Figure 14. The application is available at `http://www.num2yor.appspot.com`

c) **Mobile application on Android OS:** The mobile application was ported to Android using Java and the Android Application Development Toolkit (ADT). The screenshot is as shown in Figure 15.

The desktop application has a single document interface with toolbars for all tasks on top, a menu bar duplicating toolbar tasks, and a dockable history and analysis widgets. The analysis widget shows the computational details of a numeral structure. The Onka software has the following features:

a) The history can be saved for future usage.

b) Users can copy the output text to the computer's clipboard and paste it into an editing program or word processor.

c) The output of the software can be printed or saved in Unicode text format.

d) LATEX users can copy or save the output in the LATEX format. Also, the parse trees generated can be copied in the qtree (Siskind and Dimitriadis 2008) bracketed syntax for inclusion in TEX documents.

4   DISCUSSION

The software produces the correct lexical transcription for numbers in the Yorùbá language. In the following subsections, analysis will be carried out on the structure, computation, and forms of certain numbers. The numbers that will be considered are 240, 969, 19,669, and 40,000,000.

4.1   *The number 240*

The software processing of 240 produced two different forms, which are:

a. *òjìléígba*: This number is computed by the addition of digit 40 to 200, i.e., [D40 + 200]. This representation uses only one addition operation. The parse tree of this representation is shown in Figure 16. This representation contains three terminal symbols, and the depth of the parse tree is 6.

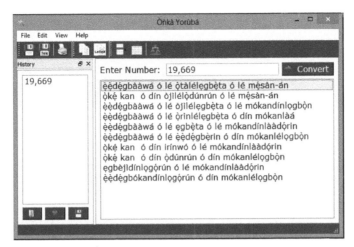

Figure 13: Screenshot of Òǹ kà desktop application

Figure 14: Screenshot of Òǹ kà web application hosted on Google App engine

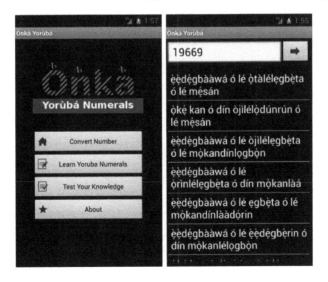

Figure 15: Screenshot of Òǹ kà Android application

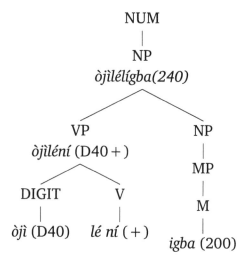

Figure 16: Parse tree of *òjìlélígba* (240 = 40 added to 200) – representation 1

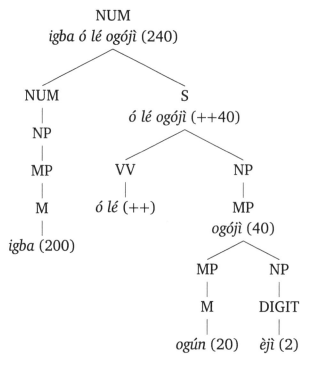

Figure 17: Parse tree of *igba ó lé ogóji* (240 = 200 increased by 40)⁻
representation 2

   b. *igba ó lé ogóji*: This representation is presented as a phrase containing two number phrases. The parse tree of this representation
   is shown in Figure 17. This representation contains four terminal
   symbols, and the depth of the parse tree is 7.

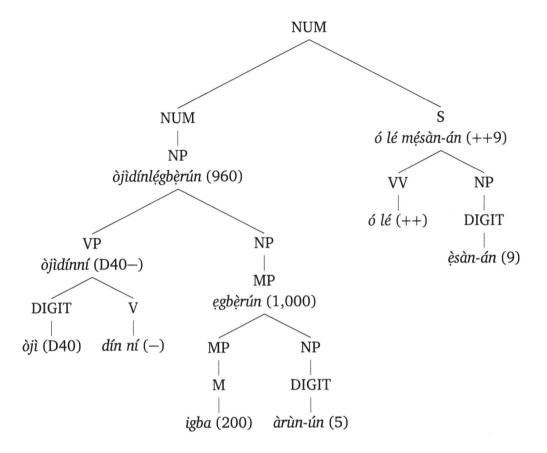

Figure 18: Parse tree for *òjìdínlẹ́gbẹ̀rún ó lé mẹ́sán* (969)

4.2   *The number 969*

The software gives 5 representations for number 969 as shown in Table 10. All these representations are valid and none has preference over others. The choice of a representation depends on the mental dexterity of the speaker. The parse tree for the first representation is shown in Figure 18.

Table 10: Representations of number 969

No	Representation	Derivation
1	*òjìdínlẹ́gbẹ̀rún ó lé mẹ́sàn-án*	$((200 \times 5) - 40) + 9$
2	*ọ̀tàdínlẹ́gbẹ̀rún ó lé mókandínlọgbọ̀n*	$((200 \times 5) - 60) + (-1 + 30)$
3	*okòódínlẹgbẹ̀rún ó dín mókanláà*	$((200 \times 5) - 20) - 11$
4	*ẹ̀ẹ̀dẹ́gbẹ̀rún ó lé mókandínlààdọ́rin*	$((200 \times 5) - 100) + (((20 \times 4) - 10) - 1)$
5	*ẹgbẹ̀rún ó dín mókanlélọgbọ̀n*	$(200 \times 5) - (1 + 30)$

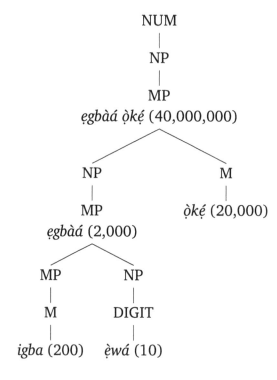

Figure 19: Parse tree of *ẹgbàá ọ̀kẹ́* (40,000,000)

4.3   *The number 19,669*

The output of the software for number 19,669 is shown in Figure 14. Representations 1 to 7 were presented by Ẹkúndayọ̀ (1977) and the developed software produced three more representations (8–10) that are structurally valid.

4.4   *The number 40,000,000*

The software gave one representation for 40,000,000 (*ẹgbàá ọ̀kẹ́*), which is derived as a multiple of 20,000 (i.e., 2,000 × 20,000). Next, 2,000 was derived as 200 in 10 places, i.e., 200 × 10. The parse tree is shown in Figure 19.

5   SYSTEM EVALUATION

In order to determine the accuracy of the system, we analysed and evaluated the output generated using the qualitative evaluation method. However, in these circumstances, it becomes expedient to rank the output of the software when multiple representations are produced. The aim is to order the representations according to the economy of computation.

5.1   *Number name ranking*

Although all representations produced are valid, we proposed some heuristic measures for ranking the representations when there are multiple correct expressions for a number. Once the parse tree had been generated for each representation, we computed the values to determine the computational economy of the numeral structure in the following order:

i) **The total number of terminal nodes** (t)**:** This represents the number of basic lexical items that make up a Yorùbá numeral. The fewer the number of terminal nodes, the more economical the numeral structure is.

ii) **The height of the parse tree** (h)**:** The height of the generated parse tree was determined by using the *height()* function of the package *nltk.tree*. The parse tree with the least height is thus considered the most suitable representation for a number.

iii) **The relative number of subtractions** (r)**:** The most natural operations in most numeral systems are addition and multiplication, yet, the Yorùbá numeral system places a higher functional load on subtraction.

The value of r is calculated by dividing the number of subtraction operations by the total number of arithmetic operations as shown in Equation 26. The two possible types of subtraction are the normal subtraction operation and the *ẹẹdín* type of subtraction.

$$r = \frac{\textit{Number of subtraction operations}}{\textit{Total number of arithmetic operations}} \qquad (26)$$

This means that a lower r implies a higher economy.

Once the first measure has been calculated and some structures have the same cost, the second measure, which checks the height of the parse tree in each structure, is used. But, if there is still a tie in values among any of the structures, the last measure (i.e., the relative number of subtraction) is used to determine the most suitable representation for a number. To illustrate this, we used these measures to decide which of the two representations for the number 240 discussed in Section 4.1 is more computationally economical. We started by picking the representation with the minimum number of terminals. The parse tree in Figure 16 has three terminal symbols compared to four in Figure 17. Thus, the structure in Figure 16 is more computationally economical.

Also, the analysis of the ten representations for the number 19,669 is presented in Table 11. This shows the number of terminal symbols, the depth of the parse tree, and the arithmetic complexity. The computational cost was calculated based on these criteria, and it was used to rank the representations. The representations with the lowest number of terminal symbols and least height are representations 2 and 8 (with 8 terminal symbols and height of 8), however, representation 2 has the lesser relative number of subtractions. Hence, representation 2 (Figure 20) is the most computationally economical. Table 12 presents the most economical representations of selected numbers derived from the software.

Table 11: Representations for the number 19,669 and their ranks. **t** is the number of terminal symbols, **h** is the height of the parse tree as generated by the software, and **r** is the relative number of subtraction operations in the representation

No	Rank	Yorùbá Text	t	h	r
2	1	ọkẹ ó dín ojìlélọdúnrún ó lé mẹsán-án	8	8	0.250
8	2	ọkẹ ó dín ọdúnrún ó dín mọkanlélọgbọn	8	8	0.500
7	3	ọkẹ ó dín irínwó ó lé mọkandínlaadọrin	10	8	0.500
10	4	ẹẹdégbọkandínlọgọrún ó dín mọkanlélọgbọn	10	10	0.500
1	5	ẹẹdegbààwá ó lé ọtalélẹgbẹta ó lé mẹsán	11	9	0.143
9	6	egbèjìdínlọgọrún ó lé mọkandínlaadọrin	11	10	0.429
6	7	ẹẹdegbààwá ó lé ẹẹdegbẹrin ó dín mọkanlélọgbọn	12	9	0.375
3	8	ẹẹdegbààwá ó lé ójìlélẹgbẹta ó lé mọkandínlọgbọn	13	9	0.250
4	9	ẹẹdegbààwá ó lé ọrinélẹgbẹta dín mọkanlàá	13	9	0.250
5	10	ẹẹdegbààwá ó lé egbẹta ó lé mọkandínlaadọrin	13	9	0.333

5.2   *Qualitative evaluation*

The Mean Opinion Score (MOS) was used for the qualitative evaluation of the system. Chosen members of the staff of Ọbáfẹ́mi Awólọ́wọ̀ University, who are Yorùbá native speakers with adequate knowledge of the Yorùbá language and its orthography, were asked to provide the textual equivalences of some numbers in Yorùbá. Afterwards, their responses were compared to the output from the software.

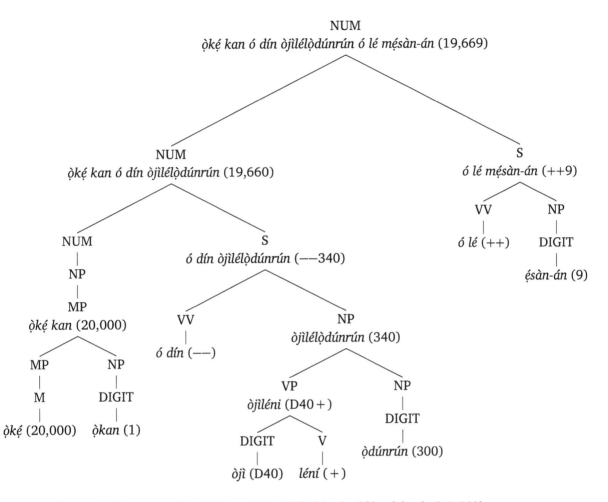

Figure 20: Parse tree for *òkẹ́ kan ó dín òjìlélọ̀dúnrún ó lé mẹ́sàn-án* (19,669)

Table 12: Software output for some numbers

Number	Yorùbá Text
182	*ọgọ́sán ó lé méjì*
187	*ọgọ́sán ó lé méje*
365	*irinwó ó dín márùndínlógójí*
595	*ẹgbẹ̀ta ó dín márùn-ún*
666	*òtàlélẹgbẹ̀ta ó lé mẹfà*
760	*òjìdínlẹ́gbẹ̀rin*
777	*èèdégbẹ̀rin ó lé mẹ́tàdínlógọ́rin*
815	*ẹgbẹ̀rin ó lé márùndínlógún*
840	*òjìlélẹ́gbẹ̀rin*
905	*èèdégbẹ̀rún ó lé márùn-ún*
1,247	*òjìlélẹ́gbèfà ó lé méje*
600,000	*ọgbọ̀n òkẹ́*

A questionnaire was designed and administered to the selected group of 32 respondents. The numbers in the questionnaire were 25, 67, 132, 750, 969, 2,400, 3,000, 19,669, 20,000, 30,000, 1,000,000, and 400,000,000. The MOS evaluation was carried out to capture two important aspects of the Yorùbá numeral system. The first one was the ability of the respondents to give an accurate representation of the numbers in terms of value and orthography, and the second one was to obtain the most suitable representation for the numbers as provided by the respondents.

The numbers used in the questionnaires were chosen based on the following criteria:

i)   Numbers 25, 67, and 132 were included to confirm that numbers between 1 and 200 have one standard lexical form.

ii) Numbers 750, 969, 2,400, and 19,669 were included to check whether the respondents are aware that there are multiple representations for these Yorùbá numerals.

iii) The number 20,000 was included to check whether the respondents find 20,000 as a single lexical item or think it is derived from the number 200.

iv) Numbers higher than 20,000 (30,000, 1,000,000, 400,000,000) were included to see if the respondents represent these numbers as multiples of 20,000 or in some other way.

v)   Some structurally complex numbers (969 and 19,669) were added to see the most convenient combination of basic lexical numerals used by the respondents to derive these numbers.

The results of the analysis revealed that:

• For numbers 25, 67, and 132, all the respondents gave one correct representation, which matched up with the output from the software. This shows that numbers below 200 have one standard lexical form and that the skills needed to name these numbers are well understood.

• Ten respondents gave a representation for 19,669 but only two of them gave a correct number name (ẹẹdẹgbàáwá ó lé ọtalélẹgbẹta ó lé mẹsán and ẹẹdẹgbàáwá ó lé ẹgbẹta ó lé mọkandínlaadọrin). The other eight respondents provided number names that do not in any way evaluate to the number 19,669. Twenty two (22) of the respondents did not give any representation for number 19,669. This shows that few respondents understand that 19,669 needs to be reconstructed and only two respondents were able to carry out the required computations. This result also shows that none of the respondents realised that multiple representations exist for the number 19,669.

- Seven of the respondents gave the correct number names for 20,000, with only two respondents using ọ̀kẹ́, and the remaining five using ẹgbàáwá. This shows that few respondents were able to represent 20,000 in Yorùbá.

- Only three respondents gave the correct names for 1,000,000 (àádọ́ta ọ̀kẹ́), and none of the respondents gave the correct representation for 400,000,000 (ọ̀kẹ́ ọ̀nà ọ̀kẹ́). This shows thatYorùbá native speakers may find the computations underlying naming large numbers cumbersome.

From these results, we conclude that the respondents were able to produce correct representations for numbers that are frequently used (number 1 to 200), although most of them were not able to produce names for higher numbers. After comparing the responses of the human evaluators with the system output, we recognise that the software out-performed the human evaluators. This affirms that most native-speakers know the terminologies needed for large numbers but are not familiar with the expression skills required for computing their number names. Without a doubt, modern Yorùbá speakers are losing the numeral generation skills embedded in their language. An obvious reason for this is the overwhelming use of the English numerals within the Yorùbá community.

6   CONCLUSION

In this paper, we discussed extensively the computational analysis of the Yorùbá numerals. We started by identifying the basic lexical numerals and the numeral groups. Then, we designed a CFG that was able to capture the structure of the Yorùbá numerals. Furthermore, we implemented a software for converting numbers to their textual equivalences in the Yorùbá language and generating their corresponding parse trees.

In this study, we are able to show that:

1. The Yorùbá number system has a systematic concept underlying it and that this concept can be articulated using modern computing tools and techniques.

2. The Yorùbá numeral system is not fully vigesimal. Elements of decimal (base 10) and quinary (base 5) are used in numeral representation.

3. The system's recall is 100% with respect to the corpus used in this study. This implies that, with carefully constructed computational model, the generation of the Yorùbá numeral system can be fully automated.

4. All the forms of number names produced were valid and the most computationally suitable representation are those in which : (a) the least number of terminal nodes is used, (b) the least height of the parse tree is generated, and (c) the least relative number of subtraction operations is involved. Though these measures are computationally reasonable, an interesting study will be to verify why Yorùbá native speakers sometimes prefer to adopt more complex methods, particularly when generating numerals greater that 200.

The results of this study can be applied in Yorùbá TTS. In any TTS system, numbers must be expanded into their textual forms before the actual speech synthesis is carried out. Thus, the system developed can serve as a sub-system of a Yorùbá TTS to handle the expansion of numbers to their textual equivalences. However, additional heuristic strategies must be employed by the TTS listeners to understand the number being spoken. Without a doubt, an increased usage of the Yorùbá numerals in communication could reduce the mental task needed for number conception.

The software developed in this study has a place in effective teaching and learning of the Yorùbá language. The software can be used in classes to teach the Yorùbá numeral system and its structure. This will allow the students to see the various forms possible for a single number and to visualise the structure (parse tree) of the numerals.

There are certain areas related to this study which we cannot explore. By pointing out these areas, we hope to focus our future study on them. There is a need to carry out the contextual analysis of the Yorùbá numeral systems which will establish the relationships between numerals and their surrounding words. This will ensure that the expansion of numbers is carried out based on the context (cardinal, ordinal, nominal, currency, percentage, ratio, date, time, etc.) they represent. Also, there is a need to carry out a study on how the textual forms of the Yorùbá numerals could be recognised and converted to numbers. Definitely, the results of these studies could be applied in Yorùbá MT and information retrieval.

ACKNOWLEDGEMENT

This work is supported by TETFUND Grant TETF/DESS/NRF/OAU/STI /VOL.1/B1.13.9. We would like to thank the editor and anonymous reviewers for their useful comments and suggestions to enhance the quality of the paper.

REFERENCES

Wándé ABÍMBỌ́LÁ (1977), *Ifa Divinity Poetry*, Traditional African Literature, Nok Pub Intl, New York.

Roy Clive ABRAHAM (1958), *Dictionary of Modern Yorùbá*, University of London Press, London.

Akinbiyi AKINLABÍ (2004), *Understanding Yorùbá Life and Culture*, chapter The Sound System of Yorùbá, pp. 453–468, Africa World Press, Trenton, NJ 08607.

Diana ARCHANGELI and Douglas PULLEYBLANK (1989), Yorùbá Vowel Harmony, *Linguistic Inquiry*, 20(2):173–218.

Ọládélé AWÓBÙLÚYÌ (1987), Towards a Typology of Coalescence, *Journal of West African Languages*, 17(2):5–22.

David BAILEY and Jonathan BORWEIN (2011), The Greatest Mathematical Discovery, *manuscript: Available online: http://escholarship.org/uc/item/0sp6t6h5*.

Rèmí BÁMIṢILȨ̀ (1994), Justification for the Survival of Vowel Coalescence as a Phonological Process in Yorùbá, *African Languages and Cultures*, 7(2):133–142.

Levi Leonard CONANT (1896), *The Number Concept: Its Origin and Development*, MacMillan, New York.

Samuel ẸKÚNDAYỌ̀ (1977), Vigesimal Numeral Derivational Morphology: Yorùbá Grammatical Competence Epitomized, *Anthropological Linguistics*, 19(9):436–453, http://www.jstor.org/stable/30027551.

Didier GOYVAERTS (1980), Counting in Logo, *Anthropological Linguistics*, 22(8):pp. 317–328, ISSN 00035483, http://www.jstor.org/stable/30027492.

James HURFORD (1975), *The Linguistic Theory of Numerals*, Cambridge University Press, Cambridge, ISBN 9780521133685.

James HURFORD (2001), Numeral Systems, in *International Encyclopedia of the Social & Behavioral Sciences*, pp. 10756–10761, Elsevier Science Ltd.

James HURFORD (2007), A Performed Practice Explains a Linguistic Universal: Counting Gives the Packing Strategy, *Lingua*, 117(5):773–783, doi:10.1016/j.lingua.2006.03.002, http://www.isrl.uiuc.edu/~amag/langev/paper/hurford06packingStrategy.html.

Samuel JOHNSON (1921), *The History of the Yorùbás: From the Earliest Times to the Beginning of the British Protectorate*, Routledge and Kegan Paul, London, reprinted 1966.

Edward LOPER and Steven BIRD (2002), NLTK: The Natural Language Toolkit, in *Proceedings of the ACL02 Workshop on Effective tools and methodologies for teaching natural language processing and computational linguistics*, volume 1, p. 8, http://arxiv.org/abs/cs/0205028.

Paul LOVEJOY and David TROTMAN (2003), *Trans-Atlantic Dimensions of Ethnicity in the African Diaspora*, Continuum: New York.

Adolphus MANN (1887), Notes on the Numeral System of the Yorùbá Nation, *The Journal of the Anthropological Institute of Great Britain and Ireland*, 16:59–64, available online: http://www.jstor.org/stable/2841738.

Karl MENNINGER (1969), *Number Words and Number Symbols: A Cultural History of Numbers*, MIT Press, Cambridge, translated by Paul Broneer for the revised German edition.

Ọdẹ́túnjí Àjàdí ỌDẸ́JỌBÍ (2003), Towards a Formal Specification of Some Computational Concepts in Yorùbá Thoughts, *ODU: Ifẹ̀ Journal of the Institute of Cultural Studies*, 8:87–110.

Kola OWOLABI (2006), Yoruba, *Encyclopedia of Language & Linguistics (Second Edition)*, pp. 735–738.

Thijs POLLMANN and Carel JANSEN (1996), The Language User as an Arithmetician, *Cognition*, 59:219–237.

Geoffrey SAXE (1981), Body Parts as Numerals: A Developmental Analysis of Numeration among the Oksapmin in Papua New Guinea, *Child Development*, 51(1):306–316, Blackwell Publishing on behalf of the Society for Research in Child Development.

Michael SIPSER (2007), *Introduction to the Theory of Computation*, Thomas Course Technology, India, 2nd edition, ISBN 81-315-0162-0.

Jeffrey Mark SISKIND and Alexis DIMITRIADIS (2008), Qtree, a LaTeX Tree-drawing Package, Available online: http://www.ling.upenn.edu/advice/latex/qtree/ (Accessed 19 September 2011).

Richard SPROAT (1996), Multilingual Text Analysis for Text-to-Speech Synthesis, in W. WAHLSTER, editor, 12th *European Conference on Artificial Intelligence*, pp. 75–80, John Wiley & Sons, Ltd.

Mark SUMMERFIELD (2008), *Rapid GUI Programming with Python and Qt*, Prentice Hall, New Jersey, 1st edition.

Helen VERRAN (2001), *Science and an African Logic*, University of Chicago Press, Chicago.

Claudia ZASLAVSKY (1973), *Africa Counts: Number and Pattern in African Cultures*, Lawrence Hill Books, 3rd edition.

2

Individuation, reliability, and the mass/count distinction

Peter R. Sutton and Hana Filip
Heinrich Heine University Düsseldorf

Keywords: *mass/count distinction, probabilistic semantics, individuation, reliability, semantic learning, information theory, context-sensitivity, Type Theory with Records*

ABSTRACT

Counting in natural language presupposes that we can successfully identify what counts as *one*, which, as we argue, relies on how and whether one can balance two pressures on learning nominal predicates, which we formalise in probabilistic and information theoretic terms: INDIVIDUATION (establishing a schema for judging what counts as one with respect to a predicate); and RELIABILITY (establishing a reliable criterion for applying a predicate). This hypothesis has two main consequences. First, the mass/count distinction in natural language is a complex phenomenon that is partly grounded in a theory of individuation, which we contend must integrate particular qualitative properties of entities, among which a key role is played by those that rely on our spatial perception. Second, it allows us to predict when we can expect the puzzling variation in mass/count lexicalization, cross- and intralinguistically: namely, exactly when the two learning pressures of INDIVIDUATION and RELIABILITY conflict.

1   INTRODUCTION

This paper attempts to combine state of the art research on the mass/count distinction in formal semantics with the cutting edge research in Type Theory with Records that provides a unified representation of cognitive, perceptual, and linguistic information. This allows

*This research was funded by the German Research Association (DFG), CRC 991, project C09. We would like to thank the attendees of the TYTLES workshop at ESSLLI 2015 and the CLASP research seminar. In particular, Robin Cooper, Simon Dobnik, and Shalom Lappin for many helpful discussions.

us not only to unify two largely separate strands of research and enrich both with our novel contributions, but also, and most importantly, to further our understanding of the concept of *individuation* (what counts as one) relative to a predicate, which, as we argue, is the fundamental concept in countability research. The account proposed here covers a number of the complex and puzzling data that pertain to cross- and intralinguistic mass/count variation, which resist an adequate account within the extant theories of the mass/count distinction in formal semantics, to the best of our knowledge.

The outline of this paper is as follows. In Section 2, we introduce the basis for our semantic formalism: Type Theory with Records (TTR, Cooper 2012) and probabilistic type theory with records (prob-TTR Cooper *et al.* 2015). In Section 3, we outline some of the most influential recent theories of the mass/count distinction in formal mereological semantics, which are largely driven by the concept of individuation (what counts as one). Sections 4–7 focus on our new proposal. In Section 4, we enrich prob-TTR with mereological assumptions (probM-TTR). We then show how this formalism can represent, in detail, both qualitative and quantitative criteria for the application of nominal predicates (inspired by Krifka (1989)).

Novelly, building on Dobnik *et al.* (2012), we model how representations of spatial perceptual information in a given context can inform and affect judgements about what counts as an individual (as one) relative to a predicate. In Section 5, we relate the quantitative and qualitative criteria to probabilistic learning and argue that the ability to successfully individuate entities relative to a predicate, and thereby establish a basis for counting, is essentially tied to how one balances two learning pressures. The first is to establish a disjoint individuation schema for a predicate (INDIVIDUATION), the second is to establish reliable criteria for applying a predicate (RELIABILITY). In Section 6, we give a schema for the lexical entries of concrete nouns.

In Section 7, we show how mass and count encoding arises from the balancing of individuation and reliability with respect to nominal predicate learning. One of the advantages of our proposal over merely mereological ones is that the interaction of these two learning pressures also allows us to delimit the range of cases where one should expect to find cross- and intralinguistic mass/count variation in natural language.

2   BACKGROUND: PROBABILISTIC TYPE THEORY WITH RECORDS

2.1   *Type Theory with Records*

TTR integrates rich lexical semantic frame-based representations in the sense of Fillmore (1975, 1976) (and elsewhere) with a compositional semantics in the Frege-Montague tradition. As such, it is an ideal theoretical framework to investigate the lexical semantics of nouns as well as compositional (formal) properties of complex expressions. TTR also integrates the insights of situation semantics insofar as situation types (RECORD TYPES) are taken to be true of situations (RECORDS), rather than being true at possible worlds. The idea is that an agent judges whether a situation *s*, is of type *T*. Such judgements correspond to type theoretic objects, namely *Austinian propositions* (Barwise and Etchemendy 1987) inspired by Austin's (1950/1979) idea that to say something true (in indicative, non-generic cases at least) is to refer to a particular situation with one's utterance that is of the type expressed by the sentence one uses. Sentences can be used to express situation types, and utterances can refer to particular situations.

In the following, we present TTR as presented in Cooper (2012). Record types, which are displayed in tabular format (1), are sets of fields, i.e., ordered pairs, whose first member is a LABEL (to the left of the colon in (1)) and whose second member is a TYPE (to the right of the colon in (1)):

$$(1) \qquad \begin{bmatrix} x & : & T_1 \\ \dots & & \\ y & : & T_n \end{bmatrix}$$

Records, which are displayed in tabular format (2), are sets of fields, i.e., ordered pairs, whose first member is a LABEL (to the left of the '=' in (2)) and whose second member is a VALUE for this label (to the right of the colon in (2)):

$$(2) \qquad \begin{bmatrix} x & = & v_1 \\ \dots & & \\ y & = & v_n \end{bmatrix}$$

An example of a record type is given in (3), which represents the type of situation in which a cat purrs.

$$
(3) \quad
\begin{bmatrix}
x & : & Ind \\
s_{cat} & : & \langle \lambda v.\mathrm{cat}(v), \langle x \rangle \rangle \\
s_{purr} & : & \langle \lambda v.\mathrm{purr}(v), \langle x \rangle \rangle
\end{bmatrix}
$$

In the record type in (3), the first field contains a label x and a basic type Ind. In TTR, there is a set of basic types, such as Ind for *individual*, *Time*, and *Loc* (location). Predicates are functions. This can be seen in the second field. The label s_{cat} is a label for a situation, and the type contains a predicate which is a function from a value v to the type of situation in which this value is a cat. It is important to note that these predicates do *not* take labels as arguments, but rather the *values* of labels. Labels function as pointers to values. We will use an abbreviated conventional notation in this work, as illustrated in (4) (Cooper 2012, p.11):

$$
(4) \quad
\begin{bmatrix}
x & : & Ind \\
s_{cat} & : & \mathrm{cat}(x) \\
s_{purr} & : & \mathrm{purr}(x)
\end{bmatrix}
$$

Records are the entities of which record types are true or false ('proofs' of propositions in type-theoretic terminology, 'witnesses' in a natural language setting). For example, (5) specifies a situation in which there is an individual, *felix*, and two witnesses p and q. Witnesses can be thought of as situations or parts of the world that make type judgements true or false.

$$
(5) \quad
\begin{bmatrix}
x & = & \mathrm{felix} \\
s_{cat} & = & p \\
s_{purr} & = & q
\end{bmatrix}
$$

Individuals in the domain are typed. The record in (5) will make the proposition in (3)/(4) true iff:

> felix is of type *Ind*,
> p is a witness of cat(felix),
> q is a witness of purr(felix).

An important aspect of TTR, however, is that it is a semantics that reserves a role for judgements made by agents (see Section 2.2). If the type in (3)/(4) is T_1 and the situation represented by (5) is s, an agent may judge s to be of type T_1, $(s : T_1)$. This judgement will be true iff the above conditions hold.

Finally, natural language predicates denote properties of type $[x : Ind] \rightarrow RecType$, a function from records containing individuals, to a record type. For example, a simplified representation of *cat* would be as in (6):

$$(6) \qquad \lambda r : [x : Ind].\left(\begin{bmatrix} r.x & : & Ind \\ s_{cat} & : & \text{cat}(r.x) \end{bmatrix} \right)$$

In (6), $r.x$ means that the value to be supplemented is the value of x in r. Hence, if provided with a record $[x = felix]$, (6) would, via β-conversion, yield the proposition that *felix is a cat* in (7):

$$(7) \qquad \begin{bmatrix} s_{cat} & : & \text{cat}(felix) \end{bmatrix}$$

2.2   *Probabilistic Type Theory with Records*

The following two subsections summarise some of the key details of probabilistic TTR from Cooper *et al.* (2014, 2015). The principal difference between prob-TTR and TTR is that judgements are graded as opposed to categorical. Instead of a judgement $s : T$, which is true or false, judgements hold with a probability $p(s : T) = k \in [0,1]$, or the probability that an agent will judge a situation s to be of type T. The reason for introducing probabilities is to be able to model the inherent gradience in the ways in which we classify parts of the world when we apply predicates of natural language to them. This type of gradedness is directly represented by the inherent gradedness in metalinguistic uncertainty within the range $[0,1]$.

A major advantage of prob-TTR is that one can model how probability values can be assigned, in a cognitively plausible way, and how probability distributions can be updated via observation and semantic learning. Witnessing how language is used provides localised information that, over time, helps language learners build a probability distribution that guides them how to use language and that approximates the 'true' distribution which underpins how competent speakers use language. This is in contrast to top-down probabilistic approaches that assign (global) probability distributions over sets of possible worlds. This issue is discussed in more depth in Cooper *et al.* (2015).

Meet types and join types in prob-TTR respect the Kolmogorov axioms for probability (Kolmogorov 1950):

(8) $p(a : T_1 \wedge T_2) = p(a : T_1) \times p(a : T_2 | a : T_1)$

(9) $p(a : T_1 \vee T_2) = p(a : T_1) + p(a : T_2) - p(a : T_1 \wedge a : T_2)$

2.3   *Bayesian learning in prob-TTR*

Assuming that agent–learners continually receive new evidence with respect to how to correctly apply types to aspects of the world, this can be modelled, in line with Bayesian approaches to cognition, as continuous updates of the probability distributions in the light of new evidence. The probability distributions of learners will gradually come to be close to those of competent speakers. The way this is modelled in prob-TTR is that agents maintain judgement sets.

In simple and intuitive terms, when an agent makes a judgement about a given situation, an entry in the agent's judgement set is made. Entries in judgement sets record the probability that the encountered situation is of some type. Members of judgement sets are what Cooper *et al.* (2015) refer to as *probabilistic Austinian propositions*.[1] For example, the probabilistic Austinian proposition involving a cat purring, judged with a probability of 0.9 would be:

(10)
$$
\begin{bmatrix}
\text{sit} & = & s_1 \\
\text{sit-type} & = & \begin{bmatrix} x & : & Ind \\ s_{cat} & : & \text{cat}(x) \\ s_{purr} & : & \text{purr}(x) \end{bmatrix} \\
\text{prob} & = & 0.9
\end{bmatrix}
$$

Proposition (10) records a situation, a type and a probability value for the judgement that the situation is of that type. The set of such judgements, i.e., the set of probabilistic Austinian propositions, for

---

[1] Cooper *et al.* (2015) present a naive Bayesian learning model, a picture that is highly simplified. (They state an intention to develop a more sophisticated learning model.) On the simple model, agents are presented with discrete situations, probabilistic judgements are made and the situation, situation type and judgement value are recorded in the judgement set. A more plausible model would have to incorporate the dynamic development of situations and how judgements will very often be implicit.

an agent A will be the set $\mathfrak{J}$. For a type T, $\mathfrak{J}_T$ is the set of Austinian propositions j such that j.sit-type $\sqsubseteq T$:

(11) $\mathfrak{J}_T = \{j | j \in \mathfrak{J}, j.\text{sit-type} = T\}$

The sum of probabilities associated with that type T in $\mathfrak{J}$ is:

(12) $$\|T\|_\mathfrak{J} = \sum_{j \in \mathfrak{J}_T} j.\text{prob}$$

Priors are calculated from sums over entries in the judgement set:

(13) $\text{prior}_\mathfrak{J}(T) = \dfrac{\|T\|_\mathfrak{J}}{\sum(\mathfrak{J})}$ if $\sum(\mathfrak{J}) > 0$ and 0 otherwise.

It is worth contrasting this approach with more top-down models in terms of possible worlds. What this system provides, in contrast to more top-down models, is an explanation of how priors are set. In probabilistic possible worlds-based approaches such as that of Eijck and Lappin (2012), one must assume a set of priors over possible worlds from which priors for particular sentences/propositions are calculated. On top of issues of computational tractability (discussed in Cooper *et al.* (2015)), this approach leaves it unexplained on what basis the priors for possible worlds are calculated.

The judgement set also provides a simple way to estimate conditional probabilities such as likelihoods and posteriors. For example, suppose $\mathfrak{J}$ were to contain the record in (10) and the record in (14):

(14) $\begin{bmatrix} \text{sit} & = & s_2 \\ \text{sit-type} & = & \begin{bmatrix} x & : & Ind \\ s_{cat} & : & \text{cat}(x) \end{bmatrix} \\ \text{prob} & = & 0.9 \end{bmatrix}$

We could then calculate the probability of there being a situation in which something purrs given it is a cat. $p_{\mathfrak{J},A}$ is a probability function with respect to a judgement set $\mathfrak{J}$, and an agent A. Conditional probabilities are calculated in terms of a type theoretic version of Bayes' Rule:

(15) $p_{\mathfrak{J},A}(s : T_1 | s : T_2) = \dfrac{\|T_1 \wedge T_2\|_\mathfrak{J}}{\|T_2\|_\mathfrak{J}}$

For the case in hand, this yields:

$$(16) \quad p_{\mathfrak{I},A}\left(s : \begin{bmatrix} x & : Ind \\ s_{cat} & : \mathrm{cat}(x) \\ s_{purr} & : \mathrm{purr}(x) \end{bmatrix} \;\middle|\; s : \begin{bmatrix} x & : Ind \\ s_{cat} & : \mathrm{cat}(x) \end{bmatrix}\right) = \frac{0.9}{0.9 + 0.9}$$

$$= 0.5$$

which follows given that:

$$\begin{bmatrix} x & : Ind \\ s_{cat} & : \mathrm{cat}(x) \\ s_{purr} & : \mathrm{purr}(x) \end{bmatrix} \sqsubseteq \begin{bmatrix} x & : Ind \\ s_{cat} & : \mathrm{cat}(x) \end{bmatrix}$$

and that if $T \sqsubseteq T'$, then $p(a : T \wedge T') = p(a : T')$. Intuitively, if two situations involving cats are observed with equal probability, but only one is a situation involving purring, then the probability of a situation involving a purring cat, given it involves a cat should be 0.5.

3   BACKGROUND: VAGUENESS, OVERLAP, MASS/COUNT VARIATION AND INDIVIDUATION

In this section, we briefly introduce some of the state of the art semantic accounts of the mass/count distinction in concrete nouns.[2] The accounts we discuss here are all based on enriching formal semantics with mereology (first proposed by Link (1983)). In mereological semantics, domains of entities form a Boolean semilattice closed under sum ($\sqcup$). That is to say: domains of entities are populated not just with individuals (a, b, c), but also with sums of entities ($a, \sqcup b, a \sqcup b \sqcup c$ etc.) which are of the same semantic type. The use of mereology has, since Link (1983), proved highly fruitful in analysing both plurality and the count/mass distinction.

We highlight two key factors that have been proposed to play a role in the mass/count distinction as part of a mereological semantics: (i) vagueness (understood in terms of a kind of context-sensitivity) (Chierchia 2010); (ii) disjointness vs. overlap at a context in a noun's denotation (Rothstein 2010; Landman 2011).

---

[2] For a more thorough critical analysis, see Sutton and Filip (2016a,b).

3.1   *Context sensitivity: vagueness and overlap*

Chierchia's (2010) main claim is that mass nouns are *vague* in a way that count nouns are not. Mass nouns are uncountable, because they lack *stable atoms*. Stable atoms are the entities in the denotation of a noun that are atoms in every context relative to a *ground context*. Ground contexts determine the entities that are denotations of a noun at every context (but are not necessarily atoms). If a noun lacks stable atoms (has only unstable individuals), then there is no entity that is an atom in the denotation of the predicate at all contexts.

Nouns such as *rice* are vague in so far as the minimal entities in the denotation of *rice* may vary depending on context. Sometimes they are sums of a few grains, sometimes single grains, half grains, or even rice flour dust. Thus these quantities of rice are in the vagueness band of *rice*. Chierchia (2010) models this vagueness with a supervaluationist semantics. At some total precisifications of a ground context, c, single grains are rice atoms. Where $c \propto c'$ means that c' precisifies c; then at some c' such that $c \propto c'$, half grains are rice atoms. At some c'' such that $c' \propto c''$, rice dust particles are rice atoms. There is, therefore, no entity that is a rice atom at every total precisification of rice. The denotation of *rice* lacks stable atoms, but counting is counting stable atoms, and so *rice* is mass.

Rothstein (2010) focuses on providing a formal model of how nouns such as *fence* and *wall* – which fail to denote entities with "natural units" in the sense of Krifka (1989) – nonetheless behave like ordinary count nouns.[3] Rothstein (2010) coins the term *counting context*, and defines count nouns as typally distinct from mass nouns. Mass nouns are of type $\langle e, t \rangle$. Count nouns, which are of type $\langle e \times k, t \rangle$, denote sets of entity-context pairs (the entity denoted and the context in which it counts as one). To take Rothstein's example, suppose that a square field is encircled by fencing. The question 'How many fences are there?' has no determinate answer, but rather the answer depends on what counts as one disjoint fence in a given context. In some con-

---

[3] However, Filip and Sutton (2017) argue that nouns such as *fence* are not bona fide count nouns, since they are felicitous as bare singulars in some measure constructions, for example, *"You will need about 150 yards of fence per acre"* (BNC). Bona fide count nouns are much less felicitous in such constructions. For example, *#I read 10cm of book.*

texts, it would be natural to answer 'four': namely, one for each side of the field. In other contexts, it would be more natural to answer 'one': namely, one fence encircling the whole field. By indexing count nouns to contexts, Rothstein can explain how there can be one single answer to the question of how many fences there are in any particular context, despite *fence* lacking natural atoms in its denotation, i.e., atoms that are independent of counting-contexts. Countability, in Rothstein's view, is a matter of what might be dubbed *disjointness at a counting ccontext.*

In Landman (2011), counting is a matter of *non-overlap in a given context.* He defines a set of generators which contains "the things that we would want to count as one" (Landman 2011, p. 26) relative to a context. Formally, generator sets generate a noun's whole denotation under sum. If the elements in the generator set are non-overlapping, as in the case of count nouns, then counting is sanctioned: counting is counting elements in the generator set and there is only one way to count. However, if generators overlap, as in the case of mass nouns, counting goes wrong, because it leads to a number of different simultaneous counting results. Formally, this is modelled as maximally disjoint subsets which generate the superset under sum (variants). In the above, "a number of different simultaneous counting results" equates to a variation in cardinality across variants. One of Landman's innovations is to provide a new delimitation of the two cases when this happens: *mess* mass nouns like *mud,* and *neat* mass nouns like *kitchenware* (a.k.a. 'object' or 'fake' mass nouns). A noun is a *mess* mass noun if, at every world, its intension determines a regular generator set whose set of minimal elements is overlapping. A noun is a *neat* mass noun if its intension at every world specifies a regular generator set whose set of minimal elements is non-overlapping.

Landman offers an ingenious solution to the perennial problems posed by mass nouns like *kitchenware, furniture, silverware* and the like. Let us take his paradigm example *kitchenware*:

> "The teapot, the cup, the saucer, and the cup and saucer all count as kitchenware and can all count as one simultaneously in the same context. ... In other words: the denotations of *neat nouns* are sets in which the distinction between *singular individuals* and *plural individuals* is not properly articulated." (Landman 2011, pp. 34–35)

The key idea here is that there are contexts which allow overlap in the denotation of a noun N with respect to what counts as 'one N'. In other words, there are contexts in which, either one simply does not apply an individuation schema, or, alternatively, the individuation schema one applies fails to resolve overlap; in either case, overlap is not made 'irrelevant', and therefore counting goes wrong.

3.2   *The puzzle of mass/count variation*

All three of the aforementioned analyses of the mass/count distinction make significant advances in accommodating the puzzling data that display cross- and intralinguistic mass/count variation. However, each account taken individually cannot accommodate the full range of such data. We take five broad classes of nouns as cases in point. Two of these, the prototypical cases, pose no problems for most accounts of the mass/count distinction:

Prototypical objects: Examples in English are *cat, car, boy, chair*. These nouns show a very strong intra- and crosslinguistic tendency towards being count.[4] They are not vague in Chierchia's sense, not counting context-sensitive in Rothstein's sense, and not overlapping in Landman's sense.

Substances: Examples in English are *mud, air, blood, slime*. These nouns show a very strong intra- and crosslinguistic tendency towards being mass.[5] They are vague in Chierchia's sense, not indexed to counting contexts in Rothstein's semantics, and have overlapping minimal generators (are mess mass) in Landman's sense.

Granulars: Examples in English are *lentils, rice, oats, beans*. These nouns show a significant amount of variation in mass/count encoding such as in (17) and (18):

(17)   *lentil-s*$_{+C,PL}$; *linse-n*$_{+C,PL}$ (German); *lešta*$_{-C}$ (Bulgarian); *čočka*$_{-C}$ (Czech).

(18)   *oat-s*$_{+C,PL}$, *oatmeal*$_{-C}$; *kaura*$_{-C}$ (Finnish); *kaurahiutale-et*$_{+C,PL}$ (Finnish, lit. oat. flake-s).

---

[4] There are some languages, such as Brazilian Portuguese, which also license a non-coerced mass reading of many count nouns. See Pires de Oliveira and Rothstein (2011) for discussion.

[5] There are some languages, such as Yudja, which also license a non-coerced count reading of many or even all mass nouns. See Lima (2014) for discussion.

Granulars are vague in the sense of Chierchia (2010), but if vagueness were the only factor in mass/count encoding, these data could not be accommodated.[6] Rothstein's account can introduce a typal difference between, for example, *rice* and *lentils*, but does not have the formal tools to explain why a typal distinction should arise commonly for these nouns, but not for, say, prototypical count nouns. Landman (2011) faces a challenge, given that it is unclear why the English *lentil*, for example, should be count, whereas its Bulgarian counterpart *lešta* ('lentil') would presumably come out as either a neat or a mess mass noun (depending on how Landman's theory is applied to this case). That is, it is unclear – given Landman's account – why granulars should license non-overlapping generators in some languages but overlapping generators in others.

Collective artifacts: These nouns, examples of which in English are *furniture, kitchenware, footwear, equipment*, show a significant amount of variation in mass/count encoding, such as we see in (19) and (20):

(19) *furniture$_{-C}$; huonekalu-t$_{+C,PL}$* (Finnish);
       meubel-s$_{+C,PL}$, meubilair$_{-C}$ (Dutch).

(20) *kitchenware$_{-C}$; Küchengerät-e$_{+C,PL}$* (German, lit. kitchen device-s).

Collective artifacts are recognised to be exceptions to a vagueness based analysis of the mass/count distinction and as requiring a separate source for their mass/count encoding (Chierchia 2010, pp. 136–139). For Landman, collective artifacts constitute the key data points for developing his theory, and to this goal, he focuses on Dutch examples like (19).

Although Landman's theory is not explicitly intended to account for cross-linguistic variation in mass/count encoding, it could be extended to do this job too. A possible line one could then adopt is that mass/count variation is only licensed for neat nouns which can have overlapping generators 'simultaneously in the same context'. If neat mass nouns have overlapping generators simultaneously in the same context, and overlap means MASS, then we may ask why the count noun counterparts of neat mass nouns are count nouns. In Landman's analysis, they have non-overlapping generator sets. However, presum-

---

[6] Chierchia (2010) is aware of this problem; however it is only informally addressed (Chierchia 2010, p.140).

ably, at different contexts, exactly what counts as one can vary. For example, in some contexts a vanity counts as one *huonekalu* (the Finnish count noun counterpart of the English neat mass *furniture*); in other contexts, it counts as at least two (the mirror and the table etc.).

If the count noun counterparts of neat mass nouns are context sensitive with respect to what counts as one across contexts, then arguably, the count nouns in (19) and (20) are counting context-sensitive in the sense of Rothstein (2010) (just like *fence*). A possible extension to Rothstein's account is that one tends to find cross- and intralinguistic mass counterparts of count nouns that are counting context sensitive. Indeed, the link between these two classes suggests, to us, that the explanation of why count/mass variation is found within them should have a common explanation. We develop these lines of thought in Section 7 in the light of the formal analysis we develop in Sections 4-6.

Non-bounded objects: Examples in English are *fence, wall*. These nouns are usually count in their morphologically simple form, but frequently have derived mass counterparts:

(21) *fence$_{+C}$ - fencing$_{-C}$; wall$_{+C}$ - walling$_{-C}$*

Chierchia (2010) argues that the count versions of these nouns are not vague (with respect to their minimal countable entities), given that the ground context is fixed (Chierchia 2010, pp. 122–123). As such, the mass counterparts provide a challenge to a vagueness-only based account.

Overlap/non-overlap based accounts may fare better when it comes to *non-bounded objects*. Indeed, Rothstein's and Landman's accounts could be extended in a similar way just outlined for collective artifacts. Namely, the mass counterparts of count non-bounded object nouns are neat mass (licensing a count counterpart), and the count counterparts (*fence*) of mass non-bounded object nouns (*fencing*) are counting context sensitive (licensing a mass counterpart). Indeed, the link between the non-bounded objects and collective artifacts classes suggests, to us, that the explanation of why count/mass variation is found within them should have a common explanation.[7] We pursue this in Section 7.

---

[7] See Sutton and Filip (2016a) for in-depth discussion.

In summary, two ways in which context is important emerge from these three accounts. First, the extension of a noun may vary across contexts with respect to its atomic elements (Chierchia 2010). Second, the entities that 'count as one' in the denotation of a noun may vary across contexts thereby yielding either a disjoint set of individuated entities (Rothstein 2010), or an overlapping set in which all possible individuated units appear simultaneously (Landman 2011).

3.3 *Individuation and two criteria of applicability for nouns*

Here we briefly review how both qualitative and quantitative criteria for the application of noun predicates have been highlighted as important for the semantics of the mass/count distinction and individuation. Specifying these two criteria originates in the work of Krifka (1989), but echoes of it percolate through his later work and that of others. The majority of responses to Krifka's work have focused on improving his representation of the quantitative criteria for the application of count predicates. We will also detail how these qualitative and quantitative criteria come together to feed into an account of individuation in the form of mereotopological properties (Grimm 2012).

Krifka (1989) proposed that the semantic representation of (concrete) count nouns involves two criteria of applicability: one qualitative, and one quantitative. For example, *one/a cow* has the following semantic representation: $\lambda n.\lambda x.[\mathbf{COW}(x) \wedge \mathbf{NU}(\mathbf{COW})(x) = n]$. Intuitively, the quantitative criterion yields what counts as one 'natural unit' in the denotation of a given predicate, and is represented by means of $\mathbf{NU}$, standing for a natural unit measure function. Natural unit functions are instances of extensive measure functions and are used to form quantized predicates from cumulative ones.[8] The qualitative criterion of applicability, which is represented by $\mathbf{COW}$, qualitatively distinguishes cows from, say, cats, dogs and other entities. In contrast, the semantic representation of (concrete) mass nouns only contains the qualitative criterion of application. For example, the semantic representation for *water* is: $\lambda x.[\mathbf{WATER}(x)]$. This amounts to the claim that there is a typal distinction between mass and count nouns, such that only count nouns involve $\mathbf{NU}$ a natural unit function. This is motivated by the fact that singular

---

[8] $\forall P[QUA(P) \leftrightarrow \forall x, y[P(x) \wedge P(y) \rightarrow \neg x < y]]$

count nouns, Krifka argues, have quantized reference, whereas mass nouns do not.

The main responses to Krifka's proposal (to be detailed below) have focused on criticisms of his **NU** function; however something akin to a distinction between qualitative and quantitative criteria remains in most leading accounts (even if the quantitative criterion is often given at a pretheoretical level). The position we will argue for, in line with Grimm (2012), is that a more satisfactory account of individuation requires specifying mereotopological properties.

Zucchi and White (1996, 2001) criticise Krifka's claim that count nouns are semantically quantized. Take, for example, *fence, twig, line*. They have entities in their denotation whose proper parts also fall under the denotation of *fence, twig, line*, hence they fail to be quantized. They have a solution in terms of a "maximal participant" relative to situation and a time. On their *Maximal Participant Approach*, determiners such as *a/an* encode a requirement that the entity bound by the existential quantifier is the largest sum individual in the denotation of the V predicate at the event time. On this view, *Alex broke a twig* translates loosely as, *a breaking event whose patient is maximal among the individuals in the denotation of twig broken at the reference time*. Crucially, this does not require that the maximal twig entity is maximal for other events and reference times. The effect, in simple terms, is to make sure that the denotation of the noun is quantized relative to an event and a time.

Whereas Zucchi and White (1996, 2001) emphasise the maximal participant relative to an event and reference time, Rothstein (2010) emphasises that what counts as one varies with *counting context* (Section 3.1). However, on Rothstein's account, what is 'one' is not defined in terms of maximality. Take, for example, fencing around a square field, where what counts as one *fence* need not be the whole enclosure, in each context. Furthermore, *fence* does not denote natural units, since what counts as one varies with context. However, how exactly the set of entities that can count as one are to be delimited remains at a pretheoretical level.

Similarly, as per Landman's account, as we saw in Section 3.2, the only formal restriction on the set of entities that count as one for a predicate is that this set generates the noun's whole denotation. But this means that the criteria deciding the membership of *the* set of entities that count as one also remain at a pretheoretical level.

What matters the most for our proposal is that these accounts converge on one key and valuable insight: namely, there is a non-trivial concept 'what counts as one' that underlies the mass/count distinction, albeit treated as pre-theoretical.[9] This insight in fact takes centre stage in Grimm (2012). Grimm argues that mereology is insufficient to define the notion of individual, and that mereology, therefore, must be enriched with topological notions. Mereotopological properties of concrete objects include their part-whole structure, spatial proximity, size, disjointness, adjacency, and shape. Grimm's *mereotopological* theory uses mereotopological predicates in the lexical entries of nouns. For example, for *dog*:

(22) $[\![dog]\!] := \lambda x_o[R(x_o, Dog) \wedge MSSC(x_o)]$

This states that entities in the denotation of the singular count noun *dog* are *Maximally Strongly Self-Connected* (MSSC). x_o is an object variable (as opposed to a kind variable). MSSC is a mereotopological property. An mereological individual "is Maximally Strongly Self-Connected relative to a property if (i) every (interior) part of the individual is connected to (overlaps) the whole (Strongly Self-Connected) and (ii) anything else which has the same property and overlaps it is once again part of it (Maximality))" (Grimm 2012, p. 135).

Our account takes inspiration from Grimm (2012), but we will connect mereotopological properties more directly to formal accounts of perception. In particular, we will address the problematic data of *granulars* like *rice* and *lentils* and argue that the conceptualisation of mereotopological properties can arise out of more domain general perceptual processes.

Instead, building on the suggestion in Krifka (1989) that the application criteria of nouns consist of both a qualitative and a quantitative criterion, we propose that qualitative criteria involve perceptual

---

[9] Although, arguably, Chierchia (2010) tries to derive 'counting as one' from his supervaluationist semantics, he still assumes a pre-theoretical setting of the 'ground context' which, among other things, ensures that nouns such as *mountain* and *fence* have stable atoms. On Chierchia's (2010) account, different answers to the question 'How many fences are there?' is attributed to their being different ground contexts (Chierchia 2010, pp. 122–123).

properties of objects, which subsume Grimm's mereotopological properties, and functional properties of objects. This is not to say that there
are not other properties relevant to individuation, but perceptual and
functional properties form the most salient aspects of entities in the
denotation of concrete nouns. Here we focus on perceptual properties that concern the spatial organisation entities in the world, and as
a case study we take granulars, since granulars present problems for
previous theories (Section 3.2). To model this with probM-TTR, we
take as a foundation work done by Dobnik *et al.* (2012), because they
link spatial knowledge gained by perception with semantic knowledge
in a single TTR representation.

4 PROPOSAL: COUNTABILITY AND PROBABILISTIC MEREOLOGICAL TYPE THEORY WITH RECORDS

4.1   *Probabilistic mereological Type Theory with Records*

Thus far, the structure of objects of basic types has been left unspecified. We assume a domain for physical entities that is structured as
a Boolean semi-lattice closed under sum. A part of such a domain is
given in Figure 1. As is standard in mereological semantics, we assume
the operation $\sqcup$ and the relations $<, \leq$.[10]

Figure 1: Boolean semi-lattice closed under join

$$a \sqcup b \sqcup c \sqcup d$$

$$a \sqcup b \sqcup c \quad a \sqcup b \sqcup d \quad a \sqcup c \sqcup d \quad b \sqcup c \sqcup d$$

$$a \sqcup b \quad a \sqcup c \quad a \sqcup d \quad b \sqcup c \quad b \sqcup d \quad c \sqcup d$$

$$a \qquad b \qquad c \qquad d$$

This means that, formally, our enrichment of (prob-)TTR regards
the structure of the domain. The principal divergence from TTR and
prob-TTR is that we do not assume a basic type *Ind*, but instead only a
basic type of *Stuff* for physical entities and individuals; i.e. the type for
the whole physical domain. In terms of mereological semantics, this is
comparable to adopting the approaches of Krifka (1989) and Landman
(2016) who assume a domain unspecified for atomicity (non-atomic).
This contrasts with Link's (1983) two domain approach (an atomic

---

[10] Part relation: $\leq$, where $x \leq y \leftrightarrow x \sqcup y = x$. Proper part relation $<$, where
$x < y \leftrightarrow x \leq y \wedge \neg y \leq x$.

domain for count nouns and a non-atomic domain for mass nouns), and also with, for example, Chierchia (2010) and Rothstein (2010) who assume a single atomic domain.

Upward closures of types are defined recursively:

Definition: $^*T$ (The upward closure of a type T under sum)
Where **Type** is the set of types:

1. for any $T \in$ **Type**, $^*T \in$ **Type**
2. for any $T \in$ **Type**, $a : {}^*T$ iff:
   (i) $a : T$
   (ii) or there is some $b, c : {}^*T$ such that $b \sqcup c = a$

For example, if $a, b : T$, then, by (i), $a, b : {}^*T$, and by (ii), $a \sqcup b : {}^*T$.

The advantage of using the tools of probM-TTR is that they will allow us to provide a more nuanced proposal of what it means to be an individual relative to a predicate than those which are found in most mereological approaches to the mass/count distinction. Individuals relative to a predicate are what count as one relative to that predicate (see Section 3.3). TTR provides us with the sufficient tools to combine perceptual, functional, spatial and semantic information within the same representational framework. This will allow us, for example, to show how the same entities can count as a plurality, an aggregate, or even be judged to count as an individual (as one). Such subtle cognitive and perceptual details at the level of our representations allow us to give a formal characterisation of individuation that captures intuitions which are left at the pre-theoretical level in other approaches.

4.2   *Qualitative types*

The qualitative criteria for applying concrete noun concepts will vary greatly from noun to noun not only in values for predicates (like COLOUR, SHAPE, SIZE) used to capture the criteria related to their perceptual properties, or in values for predicates (like USED-FOR-GRINDING) related to their functional properties, but they will also vary with respect to which kinds of criteria are relevant for their application in the first place. Take, for instance, the contrast between natural objects like apples, leaves, trees on the one hand, and artifacts like cars, chairs, buildings, on the other. Whereas *perceptual* properties (from the senses) may be relevant for identifying both natural objects and artifacts, *functional* properties will play a far bigger role in identifying artifacts. A pile of cushions can count as a chair and a cardboard box can function as a table if, in context, that pile of cushions can aptly function as a chair and the cardboard box can aptly function as a table. In contrast, it is harder to imagine a situation in which some natural object that is not a carrot could count as a carrot even if it fits the same functional role as a carrot does. For instance, even if one uses beetroot or courgette instead of carrot to moisten a cake, one has not, thereby, still made a carrot cake.[11]

We represent such perceptual and functional properties in terms of an all-encompassing type as the one schematised in (23) and exemplified for *rice* in (24). In this respect, we build on a previous proposal in Sutton and Filip (2016b). We assume a basic type *Stuff* that does not distinguish between substances and individuals. Entities of this type may or may not be a clearly demarcated and countable entity, i.e., an individual in our sense.

(23)
$$\begin{bmatrix} x & : & \textit{Stuff} \\ s_{P_{pptys}} & : & P_{pptys}(x) \end{bmatrix}$$

(24)
$$\begin{bmatrix} x & : & \textit{Stuff} \\ s_{rice_{pptys}} & : & rice_{pptys}(x) \end{bmatrix}$$

Instances of the predicate P_{pptys} are placeholders for a wider number of predicates that specify perceptual information such as colour, texture, and, especially for artifacts, functional information (e.g. what activities these items are used for).

Here we wish to expand somewhat on what kind of information the predicate P_{pptys} is a placeholder for, especially with respect to granular nouns such as *rice* and *lentil(s)*. To this end, for the rest of this section we will focus on how qualitative *perceptual* – in particular mereotopological – properties of concrete objects facilitate their classifications under concrete noun predicates (Grimm 2012). We will show how this information can be included in TTR frames, and to this goal, we will also make use of the work done in Dobnik, Cooper and

---

[11] It is quite plausible that our discussion of perceptual and functional properties mirrors distinctions made in Pustejovsky (1995). For example, Pustejovsky's *constitutive* and *formal* roles seem to approximate our perceptual properties and his *telic* and *agentive* roles seem to approximate our functional properties.

Larsson (Dobnik *et al.* 2012) on the linking of semantic, perceptual and world knowledge in a single TTR representation. Their focus is on the interaction of the inputs from robot perceptual sensors with higher level semantic representations of the robot's environment.

The robot uses a sensor to build a map of points where each point has been classified as being at a particular location in the robot's environment (a point map). Points, in this context, are minimal readings that the robot's sensor makes; the robot builds up a map of its environment by taking point readings. Point maps are represented along the lines of the schema in (25) (Dobnik *et al.* 2012, p. 54).

$$(25) \qquad PointMap = \begin{bmatrix} p_1 & : & Point \\ \cdot & & \cdot \\ \cdot & & \cdot \\ \cdot & & \cdot \\ p_n & : & Point \end{bmatrix}$$

Such point maps are then used as the inputs to functions to define bounded regions or volumes which envelop points. These are known as convex hulls, i.e., regions or volumes, and are classified as individuals. The convex hull of a set of points is the smallest convex region containing that set of points. A simple representation of a 2D convex hull of points is given in Figure 2.

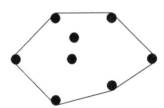

Figure 2: Simple example of a 2D convex hull of 8 points

Formally, this is represented in (26) (Dobnik *et al.* 2012, p. 55).

$$(26) \quad f : \lambda r : PointMap(\begin{bmatrix} a & : Ind \\ p_1 & : r.Point \\ \cdot & \cdot \\ \cdot & \cdot \\ \cdot & \cdot \\ p_n & : r.Point \\ c_{reg} & : region(a) \\ c_{inc} & : includes(a, \langle p_1, ..., p_n \rangle) \\ conv\text{-}hull & : \langle p_i, p_j, p_k \rangle \\ c_{hulled} & : hulled(\langle p_1, ..., p_n \rangle, conv\text{-}hull) \end{bmatrix})$$

It turns out that the above insights from Dobnik *et al.* (2012) allow us to analyse the problematic data of granulars such as *rice, lentils, peas,* which pose thorny problems for mereological accounts (Section 3).

The basic idea we pursue here is that stuff in the world can be conceptualised in different ways based in part on its perceptual properties. Entities such as, for example, grains of rice can be conceptualised in different ways; this reflects different ways of individuating or otherwise grouping stuff with the relevant rice properties. We highlight three such ways. Granular entities can be (i) individuated in terms of single grains; (ii) grouped in terms of *aggregates* of grains (of some amount or another); (iii) grouped in terms of *bounded aggregates* of grains (portions of grains that form a discrete bounded region or volume in space). Substances such as mud, in contrast, cannot be individuated in terms of anything like grains (mud does not come in clearly perceptible units such as grains). However, stuff like mud can, similar to aggregation, be *amassed* (stuff of some amount with the relevant properties) and conceived of in terms of *bounded amassments* (stuff with the relevant properties that forms some discrete bounded region or volume in space).

We now outline how aggregation and bounded aggregation can be represented in mereological TTR using representations inspired by the work of Dobnik *et al.* (2012). We use rice as a working example. Aggregates with respect to a predicate *rice* involve identifying some plurality of entities each of which has the relevant properties for being grains of rice and judging them to be an aggregate. Unlike Dobnik *et al.*'s convex hulled regions, aggregates need not be grouped into a single discrete region. This is outlined in (27).

$$(27) \quad f : \lambda r : \begin{bmatrix} x_1 : \textit{Stuff} \\ \vdots \quad \vdots \\ x_n : \textit{Stuff} \end{bmatrix} \left(\begin{bmatrix} c_{\text{rice\_agg}} : \text{rice}_{\text{agg}}(a) \\ r.x_1 \quad : \textit{Stuff} \\ c_{1\_col} \quad : \text{white}(r.x_1) \\ c_{1\_shape} : \text{grain\_shaped}(r.x_1) \\ \vdots \qquad \vdots \\ r.x_n \quad : \textit{Stuff} \\ c_{n\_col} \quad : \text{white}(r.x_n) \\ c_{n\_shape} : \text{grain\_shaped}(r.x_n) \\ c_{agg} \quad : \text{aggregate}(a) \\ c_{inc} \quad : \text{includes}(a, \langle r.x_1, ..., r.x_n \rangle) \end{bmatrix} \right)$$

The predicate *aggregate* is specified as containing some quantity of entities each of which has some relevant properties (such as white colour or being grain-shaped). This collection is then judged as being a rice aggregate ($rice_{agg}$). In other words, we can recast mereological sums in terms of an aggregation of, in this case, entities with the requisite rice-grain properties.

Alternatively, we can add extra restrictions on aggregates by requiring that aggregate entities form 'hulled regions'. That is to say that we use the notion of a hulled volume or region as a means of representing mereotopological sum entities. Our novel proposal is that something akin to hulling, namely, carving out chunks or regions out of the parts of the world and judging this region to be a *bounded aggregate* (or alternatively a *bounded amassment* for substance denoting nouns) could model a process of individuation that relies on the spatial (mereotopological) properties of concrete objects: namely, properties having to do with their spatial proximity, disjointness, adjacency, size and shape. This proposal not only capitalises on some insights in Grimm (2012), but is also reminiscent of the longstanding proposals in cognitive semantics (Jackendoff 1991; Talmy 2000) which emphasise spatial notions in the analysis of lexicalization patterns of mass and count nouns.

In the frame in (28), we assume that mereotopological sums of bounded entities may be represented via a similar mechanism to 'region hulling', namely, aggregating identified portions of stuff each of which have certain physical properties.

$$(28) \quad f : \lambda r : \begin{bmatrix} x_1 : Stuff \\ \vdots \quad \vdots \\ x_n : Stuff \end{bmatrix} \left(\begin{bmatrix} c_{rice\_agg} & : rice_{bounded}(a) \\ r.x_1 & : Stuff \\ c_{1\_col} & : white(r.x_1) \\ c_{1\_shape} & : grain\_shaped(r.x_1) \\ \vdots & \vdots \\ r.x_n & : Stuff \\ c_{n\_col} & : white(r.x_n) \\ c_{n\_shape} & : grain\_shaped(r.x_n) \\ c_{reg} & : region(a) \\ c_{inc} & : includes(a, \langle r.x_1, ..., r.x_n \rangle) \\ conv\text{-}agg & : \langle r.x_i, r.x_j, r.x_k, ... \rangle \\ c_{b\_agged} & : agg(\langle r.x_1, ..., r.x_n \rangle, conv\text{-}agg) \end{bmatrix} \right)$$

We can perceptually identify the collection of grains of rice as being comprised of individual grains; however, at the same time this collection can be viewed as a bounded entity in a manner akin to hulling. Importantly, just as with hulling collections of perceptual points to identify entities, there will be restrictions on what kinds of collections of entities will be identified as bounded aggregates. One such restriction will be that the entities that form the aggregate cannot be too dispersed and so must be relatively clustered together. Such intuitions also motivate how some of the mereotopological restrictions on granular and collective aggregates in Grimm (2012) can be represented.[12]

The function in (28) mirrors that in (26); however the function is from a record of a type of having more than one physical entity (or bit of stuff), rather than in terms of perceived points. The function determines a bounded aggregate then yields a new entity judged to be of type $rice_{bounded}$ that 'collates' the physical entities in this region. The bits of stuff have properties such as colour and shape. c_{inc} labels a function that selects which of these is to be included in the region. The conv-agg tuple determines the entities around which the boundaries of the convex aggregate will be 'drawn'. c_{b_agged} is the condition that all the entities in the region are within the bounds of the boundary.

So, similarly to defining a convex hull in terms of perceived points, this function defines a *bounded aggregate* in terms of entities that have already been classified as physical entities.[13] Intuitively, if a situation contains many small entities (such as lentils or grains of rice) that are in close proximity to one another, this function picks them out as a convex aggregate – an aggregate falling within what is judged to be a certain bounded area of space – and then classifies this as $rice_{bounded}$.

For substance denoting nouns such as *mud* or *blood*, a similar function could be defined. However, instead of aggregating grains into bounded aggregates, it would hull stuff with the relevant properties into a bounded amassment.

---

[12] Examples of collective aggregates in Grimm (2012) are names for insects (found in swarms or groups) and berries. Examples of granular aggregates are *rice* and *sand*.

[13] It will be that something akin to (26) is also needed to classify what, in a perceptual field, is to be identified as of the type *Stuff*, albeit at a 'lower' level.

4.3   *Quantitative functions relative to a predicate*

Given a representation of the qualitative properties of an entity or some collection of entities, we may assign some quantity value to the entities of that type. This is the role of a quantitative function, which is of the type in (29), a function from record types specifying qualitative criteria for applicability to real numbers.

(29) $f_{P_{quant}}$: $\left(\begin{bmatrix} x & : & \textit{Stuff} \\ s_{P_{pptys}} & : & P_{pptys}(x) \end{bmatrix} \rightarrow \mathbb{R} \right)$

Quantitative functions are relative to predicates (different functions are defined for different predicates), since the same entity or entities may count as 'one' relative to one predicate, but not another. For example, 52 playing cards could be judged to have a quantity of 1 with respect to a predicate *deck of cards*, but not with respect to the predicate *card* (Link 1983). However, because we are not assuming a pretheoretical notion of individuation, how some stuff will be quantified may depend on what counts as an individual relative to that predicate. Our strategy is to derive individuation from a special case in which a quantitative function outputs 1. Competing schemas for individuation will be represented as competing quantitative functions. These competing quantitative functions differ with respect to what perceptual and functional properties are required to measure 1 (count as one). For example, take the record type in the right hand side of (27) as compared to the one below in (30).

(30) $\begin{bmatrix} x_1 & : \textit{Stuff} \\ c_{1\_col} & : \text{white}(x_1) \\ c_{1\_shape} & : \text{grain\_shaped}(x_1) \end{bmatrix}$

There is more than one possible way to try to individuate the stuff or collections of stuff with rice-like properties (being white, grain shaped etc.). We give three cases by way of example.

Case 1: One possible quantitative function would output a value 1 for the type in (30). This function would individuate single grains. Applied to something like the type in (27), which contains multiple entities with the requisite properties that have been judged to be an aggregate, this function could use, for example, the approximate size of the aggregate to output an approximate quantity value. We do not assume that these functions are mere cardinality functions. In fact, it would be cognitively implausible to do so. Take the case of some collections of rice grains. For larger collections that have been judged to be aggregates (Section 4.2), we do not assume that the quantity value will reflect the number of rice grains exactly, since we are not in a position to know this without explicitly counting. However, for small numbers of grains, such as an aggregate entity comprised of three grains, this function could return a value where the output number of the function equals the number of grains. Whether the output of the quantitative function reflects the exact number of grains or some approximation, we suggest, could be grounded in the distinction found in psychology between the *approximate number system* (ANS) and the *parallel individuation system* (PI) (Hyde and Spelke 2011, and references therein). In brief, both of these systems are supposed to be developed pre-linguistically. The difference between them is that PI operates accurately in individuating entities, but is severely limited in terms of number. It operates accurately up to about four entities, and is assumed to involve the representation of all entities individually. ANS works on much larger numbers of entities but is assumed to represent entities as collections, not individually. ANS works effectively as a way of discerning differences in number between collections, but not as an accurate representation of cardinality. If the quantitative function is constrained by these systems, its numerical output would be an accurate measure of cardinality of pluralities up to about four entities, but only an approximation of cardinality for larger collections (about 5, about 10, ..., about 50, about 100). What the output of this function is, we suggest, could be modeled in relation to factors such as the size and density of the aggregate identified in the situation. So an output of e.g. 1 would indicate *exactly 1*, but an output of e.g. 10, would indicate *approximately 10*.

Case 2: An alternative quantitative function could individuate, not single grains, but clusters, such that any (sufficiently large) aggregates containing entities that are individually white, grain shaped, etc., would measure 1. This function, applied to the type in (27) would output 1, but applied to the type for a single grain in (30) would measure either a value less than one (or, alternatively, could be undefined). This would allow for the possibility that overlapping collections of rice grains could each be judged to be an aggregate and so each be measured by the quantitative function as one.

Case 3: Another alternative quantitative function could individuate, not single grains or aggregates, but bounded aggregates: any clusters of entities that are individually white, grain shaped etc., but also form a discrete bounded region would measure 1. This function, applied to the type in (28) would output 1. The additional boundedness condition, in effect, treats any discrete regions filled with rice grains as entities to be counted.

These cases represent different ways of individuating rice. The first quantitative function 'finds' individual grains, and if more than one is present approximates a quantity. The second function 'finds' collections of grains and groups them as an aggregate entity. The third function 'finds' bounded regions or clusters of grains and groups them as a bounded aggregate. In Sections 5–7, we will argue that the fact that there can be competing individuation schemas can be used in conjunction with information theoretic requirements, to explain count/mass lexicalization patterns cross- and intralinguistically.

The special case for the application of a quantitative function will therefore be where the output is 1. In the case of *cat* this would indicate a type of individual cats. For granular nouns such as *rice* or *lentils,* this could be the type for individual grains of rice or individual lentils.[14] In this sense, the special case where a quantitative function returns a value of 1 marks the INDIVIDUATION SCHEMA for a predicate. We introduce the following notational convention for the special case to act as both an abbreviation and as an mnemonic for this individuating role:

$$(31) \quad \begin{bmatrix} s_{\text{cat-ind}} : \begin{bmatrix} s_{\text{cat}_{qual}} & : \begin{bmatrix} s_{\text{cat}_{pptys}} & : \text{cat}_{pptys}(x) \end{bmatrix} \\ f_{\text{cat-quant}} & : (\begin{bmatrix} s_{\text{cat}_{pptys}} & : \text{cat}_{pptys}(x) \end{bmatrix} \to \mathbb{R}) \\ f_{\text{cat-quant}}(s_{\text{cat}_{qual}}) & : \mathbb{R}_1 \end{bmatrix} \end{bmatrix}$$

$$= [s_{\text{cat-ind}} : \text{cat}_{Ind}(x)]$$

In other words, the type of situation in which for some predicate P, a physical entity (or sum) is judged to have a quantity of 'one' is a type of situation in which one judges that thing to be a P-individual. To emphasise, this means that we do not take being an individual as a basic notion, but rather as a classification task. We assume a basic

---

[14] We discuss other nouns in detail in Section 7.

type of physical entities (and the upward closure of this type), but which of these (collections of) physical entities are individuals is both relative to a predicate and a non-trivial question.

An important restriction for any P_{Ind} predicate associated with a count noun is that the entities of this type are disjoint (do not overlap mereologically). In other words, an entity that is judged to be 'one' P-individual cannot also be judged to be of some larger quantity value with respect to P under the same individuation schema if that individuation schema is to form the basis for grammatical counting.

4.4 *Individuation schemas and learningto apply predicates in context*

It is important to note that there may be cases where individuating, relative to a predicate and a quantitative function, may not always guarantee felicitous application of the predicate. Chierchia (2010) points out that for many mass nouns, whether or not some entity falls under the denotation of that noun can depend on the context. For example, take a collection of around ten grains of rice. In the context of cooking dinner, one can truly say "We have no rice" when the ten grains are all that remains of a once full packet, and a child can felicitously say "I have eaten all the rice" when only ten grains remain on the plate. However, when around ten grains have fallen in the same context, we can felicitously and truthfully state "I spilled some rice on the floor". Stating "There is rice in this dish" is felicitous and truthful, when uttered by someone with a severe rice allergy, for example, even if it contains only about ten grains of rice.

Assuming a quantitative function (labeled $f_{P_{quant}}$) for a predicate P, this kind of context sensitivity can be represented as the calculation of conditional probabilities of the form in (32). The learner-agent A must identify which qualities (specified in the qualitative criterion type) and which quantities of these entities (relative to an individuation schema) maximise the probability of applying the predicate relative to her judgement set $\mathfrak{J}$.

$$
(32) \quad p_{\mathfrak{J},A}\left(r : \begin{bmatrix} x : Stuff \\ s_P : \mathrm{P}(x) \end{bmatrix} \middle| r : \begin{bmatrix} s_{P_{qual}} & : \begin{bmatrix} \text{qualitative} \\ \text{criterion type} \end{bmatrix} \\ f_{P_{quant}} & : (\begin{bmatrix} \text{qualitative} \\ \text{criterion type} \end{bmatrix}) \to \mathbb{N} \\ i & : \mathbb{N} \\ f_{P_{quant}}(s_{P_{qual}}) : \mathbb{N}_i \end{bmatrix}\right)
$$

We assume the data for these judgements come from, in part, witnessing competent speakers' judgements with regard to applying predicates. We now give a simple example for *rice*.

Suppose that a learner is exposed to two situations in which an adult speaker provides her with evidence for how to make *rice* judgements. Furthermore, the agent is employing a schema/quantitative function that individuates single grains. In $s_{\text{making dinner}}$, there are, by the agents' estimations, approximately 10 grains (say at the bottom of a packet). The adult speaker may say, looking at the packet, *Oh no! We have no rice left.* This constitutes evidence that the small quantity of around 10 grains is not sufficient to count as *rice*. In s_{allergy}, a similar quantity of grains falls into the soup. The soup is for someone with a rice allergy and the adult speaker says *Oh no! Rice fell into the soup.* This constitutes evidence that the small quantity of around 10 grains is sufficient to count as *rice*.

In terms of learning data, these utterances in context provide conflicting information as to whether or not a collection of around ten grains counts as *rice*. For the case we just informally described, this could result in a judgement set containing the probabilistic Austinian propositions in Figure 3. The figure itself contains judgements for different situations (labelled *sit*). These situations are meant to represent the contexts just described. The idea is that the quantity of grains

$$
j_1 = \begin{bmatrix} \text{sit} & =s_{\text{making dinner}} \\ \text{sit-type=} & \begin{bmatrix} x & :Stuff \\ s_{rice} & :\neg\text{rice}(x) \\ s_{rice_{qual}} & : \begin{bmatrix} s_{rice.col} : \text{white}(x) \\ ... \end{bmatrix} \\ f_{rice_{quant}}(s_{rice_{qual}}): \mathbb{N}_{10} \end{bmatrix} \\ \text{prob} & =0.9 \end{bmatrix}
$$

$$
j_2 = \begin{bmatrix} \text{sit} & =s_{\text{allergy}} \\ \text{sit-type=} & \begin{bmatrix} x & :Stuff \\ s_{rice} & :\text{rice}(x) \\ s_{rice_{qual}} & : \begin{bmatrix} s_{rice.col} : \text{white}(x) \\ ... \end{bmatrix} \\ f_{rice_{quant}}(s_{rice_{qual}}): \mathbb{N}_{10} \end{bmatrix} \\ \text{prob} & =0.9 \end{bmatrix}
$$

Figure 3: Possible (partial) judgement set for around 10 grains of rice.

to count as *rice* could vary across these contexts. The situation types assign a measure to stuff with the relevant rice properties (such as colour) and a condition that the stuff is rice. The probability values represent the extent to which the situations are of that type.

We assume that the learner has learned these judgements directly from the competent speaker and so attributed a high value (0.9) to all of them.[15] Using the prob-TTR version of Bayes' rule (15), these judgements then allow the calculation of the probability of something being rice, given that it has a quantitative function value (relative to *rice*) of 10. This is shown in (33).[16]

$$(33) \quad p_{\mathfrak{J},A}(s : [s_{rice} : \mathrm{rice}(x)] \mid s : \begin{bmatrix} s_{rice_{qual}} & : \begin{bmatrix} s_{rice.col} : \mathrm{white}(x) \\ \ldots \end{bmatrix} \\ f_{rice_{quant}}(s_{rice_{qual}}):\mathbb{N}_{10} \end{bmatrix}$$

$$= \frac{\left\| [s_{rice} : \mathrm{rice}(x)] \wedge \begin{bmatrix} s_{rice_{qual}} & : \begin{bmatrix} s_{rice.col} : \mathrm{white}(x) \\ \ldots \end{bmatrix} \\ f_{rice_{quant}}(s_{rice_{qual}}):\mathbb{N}_{10} \end{bmatrix} \right\|_{\mathfrak{J}}}{\left\| \begin{bmatrix} s_{rice_{qual}} & : \begin{bmatrix} s_{rice.col} : \mathrm{white}(x) \\ \ldots \end{bmatrix} \\ f_{rice_{quant}}(s_{rice_{qual}}):\mathbb{N}_{10} \end{bmatrix} \right\|_{\mathfrak{J}}}$$

$$= \frac{0.9}{0.9 + 0.9}$$

$$= 0.5$$

Given the judgements in Figure 3, the result is 0.5. A gloss on the importance of this value is that the learner has as much reason to believe that the predicate *rice* can be applied to around 10 grains of rice as she does for not thinking so, given her judgement set. By "around 10", we mean that the output of the quantitative function may only approximate actual numbers of grains for quantities above that which can be directly quantified via the PI (parallel individuation) cognitive system (Section 4.3).

---

[15] In a more sophisticated model, reflected in the probability value should be that the evidence for $s_{\mathrm{making\ dinner}}$ is indirect (making $s_{\mathrm{making\ dinner}} : \neg \mathrm{rice}$ less certain). A promising route would be to adopt something akin to Lassiter's representation of indirect evidence in terms of Bayesian networks (Lassiter 2016).

[16] We assume, following Cooper *et al.* (2015), that negation is classical. Instances of $[x : Stuff]$ have been suppressed for brevity.

However, across contexts in which there are much larger quantities of grains present, the judgement set may be far more consistent. For example, a learner will rarely experience a whole packet of rice not being judged as rice, i.e., not falling under the predicate *rice*, and so is far more confident about classifying larger amounts of rice as *rice*. In short, in this way we capture the observation by Chierchia (2010) that when it comes to classifying with granular nouns like *rice*, quantity matters. Independently of context, one may not be safe to classify ten grains as *rice*, but one could, with high confidence, classify a packet of rice as *rice*.

This means that, although an individuation function for *rice* that identifies single grains does succeed in identifying disjoint (potentially countable) entities, it is not wholly reliable when applied across contexts to establish, with a high degree of certainty, when to apply the predicate *rice*. A more reliable schema could be found by opting for an individuation schema that picks out larger collections of rice grains. Such a move could end up failing to properly individuate disjoint entities suitable for counting, however (since larger collections overlap). In Section 5, we will show how this tension can be formally captured within probM-TTR.

5 THE LEARNING PRESSURES OF RELIABILITY AND INDIVIDUATION

Given the insights of formal (mereological) theories (Section 3), we propose that in addition to identifying a reliable criterion for applying a predicate, learners also seek to identify an individuation schema for a predicate. This means that pressures on nominal predicate learning will be at least twofold:

(i) RELIABILITY: to establish with a high degree of certainty when to apply a predicate.

(ii) INDIVIDUATION: to establish (if possible) an individuation schema for a predicate.

In some cases, these two pressures will operate in unison, for example, for *cat*, accurately judging a situation to contain one or more cat-individuals is a very good ground to judge those entities as falling under the number neutral predicate *cat*. However, as we shall argue, this is not always the case for other predicates. For example, individual rice grains are the clearly individuable units for counting rice, but the presence of a single grain is not a reliable criterion for applying *rice* since there are many contexts in which a single grain is not a sufficient quantity to count as *rice*. Furthermore, we argue in Section 7 that tensions between these two pressures generate exactly the cases where we find cross- and intralinguistic mass/count variation.

5.1   *Formalising the requirement of reliability*

Reliability is a pressure on a learner to find a set of properties that reliably predict when to apply a predicate. We have proposed that these properties include both qualitative and quantitative criteria. Reliability itself is therefore a balance between using a P_{Ind} predicate, the upward closure of which ($*P_{Ind}$) includes too much in P; and using a P_{Ind} predicate, the upward closure of which ($*P_{Ind}$) includes too little in P. Of course, the ideal balance means using a P_{Ind} predicate that neither includes too much nor too little in P. In other words, the most reliable individuating predicate will be one that maximises the conditional probabilities in (34) and (35).[17]

(34) $Max_j(p(s : \left[\ s_P\ :\ P(x)\ \right] \mid s : \left[\ s_{P\text{-}ind}\ :\ *P_{Ind_j}(x)\ \right]))$

(35) $Max_j(p(s : \left[\ s_{P\text{-}ind}\ :\ *P_{Ind_j}(x)\ \right] \mid s : \left[\ s_P\ :\ P(x)\ \right]))$

Maximising the probability in (34) means that being a P-individual or a sum of P-individuals is a very strong indicator of being a P. This militates against the over-inclusivity of P_{Ind_j}. Maximising the probability in (35) means that being a P is a very strong indicator of being a P-individual or a sum of P-individuals. This militates against the under-inclusivity of P_{Ind_j}. Balancing these two (optimally maximising both probabilities) should result in as close an approximation of P and $*P_{Ind}$ as possible. In the trivial case, this would just be to use P as P_{Ind}. However, in most cases, doing this would fail to individuate any entities at all.

To make this clearer, take the three simple cases which are graphically represented in Figure 4. (i) This represents the case where the application conditions for the predicate are perfectly matched to the application conditions for the upward closure of the P_{Ind} predicate,

---

[17] The specifications of $x : Stuff$ here and further below are omitted for brevity.

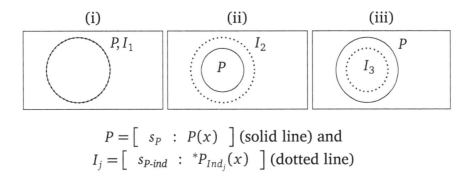

$$P = \begin{bmatrix} s_P & : & P(x) \end{bmatrix} \text{(solid line) and}$$
$$I_j = \begin{bmatrix} s_{P\text{-}ind} & : & {}^*P_{Ind_j}(x) \end{bmatrix} \text{(dotted line)}$$

Figure 4: Maximising both conditional probabilities vs. maximising one.

therefore both conditional probabilities (34) and (35) are maximised. (ii) This represents the case where there are some things which are P individuals or sums thereof that are not correctly judged as P. This means the the probability in (35) is maximised, but the probability in (34) is not. (iii) This represents the case where there are some things which are correctly judged as P which are not P individuals or sums thereof. This means that the probability in (34) is maximised, but the probability in (35) is not.

5.2 *Formalising the requirement of individuation*

The pressure that can push in the opposite direction to reliability is *individuation*. This pressure can be derived from a more general pressure towards informativeness (Piantadosi *et al.* 2011). The main idea in the context of countability is that disjoint individuation schemas/predicates P_{Ind} have minimum entropy with respect to determining counting results compared with predicates that are not disjoint. The reason for this, building on Landman's (2011) insights, is that when we have an overlapping set of entities, there are multiple answers to the question 'how many?'. Uncertainty over how many things (relative to a predicate) there are equates to a higher level of entropy compared with a single answer.

In order to formally capture the pressure towards individuation, we will define a probabilistic notion of disjointness of a type, and then relate this to minimising entropy (with respect to the disjoint variants of a type). The (probabilistic) notion of disjointness which will be used below is a condition for the maximal individuation of P_{Ind} predicates. This follows the standard mereological notion of disjointness, but adds the condition that the only relevant entities are those that are of the relevant type with sufficient amounts of certainty. We formalise 'sufficient degree of certainty' using a probability threshold θ.

> A type T is mereologically pairwise disjoint relative to a probability threshold θ iff:
> $$\forall x, y[(p(x:T) \geq \theta \wedge p(y:T) \geq \theta) \rightarrow \neg \exists z[z \leq x \wedge z \leq y]]$$

In words, any two entities, taken pairwise, that are of a type with a probability above the threshold cannot share a part with one another.

Disjoint types have only one maximally disjoint subtype (akin to variants in Landman (2011)), namely the type itself. For types that are not disjoint, one can form, possibly multiple, maximally disjoint subtypes. For example, if $a, b, a \sqcup b : T$, then, relative to $a, b, a \sqcup b$, there are two maximally disjoint subtypes v_1 and v_2 such that $a, b : v_1$ and $a \sqcup b : v_2$, but where $a \sqcup b / v_1$ and $a, b / v_2$.

The pressure of individuation can be modelled as pushing towards the use of a disjoint P_{Ind} type. At a first pass, we could, therefore, suggest that the pressure of individuation is a requirement merely to minimise entropy as in (36).

(36) $$Min_j\left(-\sum_{v_i \in V} p(v_i|P_{Ind_j}) \times \log p(v_i|P_{Ind_j})\right)$$

Here, entropy values give the average amount of information needed to determine a specific counting result. For example, assuming an equal distribution over variants, and a base-2 logarithm, numbers of variants and entropy values would be as follows:[18]

Number of variants	1	2	4	8	16
Entropy	0	1	2	3	4

The effect is that minimising entropy pushes towards a disjoint P_{Ind} predicate because disjoint predicates have an entropy of 0.

However, the definition in (36) misses some details. As we have seen, there are nouns such as *fence, twig, line* which display context-sensitivity with respect to what counts as a single individual (focused on by Zucchi and White (1996, 2001) and Rothstein (2010)). If the

---

[18] For example, if there are four variants such that $p(v_1|P_{Ind_j}) = p(v_2|P_{Ind_j}) = p(v_3|P_{Ind_j}) = p(v_4|P_{Ind_j}) = 0.25$, then the surprisal for each variant equals $0.25 \times \log_2 0.25 = -0.5$ and entropy equals $-(-0.5 + -0.5 + -0.5 + -0.5) = 2$.

Rothstein-type analysis for such nouns is correct, then, at every (default) context, there will only be a disjoint set of fence entities, even if across contexts, these entities overlap. The denotations of prototypical count nouns, such as *cat* and *chair*, intuitively, have inherently individuated denotations, unlike the denotations of count nouns such as *fence* that require context to identify countable entities in their denotation. We should, therefore, include, in the calculation for minimising entropy, some cost C that increases entropy in relation to the number of admissible (disjoint) P_{Ind} predicates. This is given in (37).

(37) $$Min_j\left(-\left(\sum_{v_i \in V} p(v_i|P_{Ind_j}) \times \log p(v_i|P_{Ind_j})\right) + C\right)$$

To give an example, let us compare three cases. Context general P_{Ind} predicates are predicates that can be applied to correctly individuate *P*s across all contexts.

(i) A context general, disjoint P_{Ind} predicate. This will apply to nouns with individuation schemas that pick out naturally atomic, clearly disjoint objects. In this case, there is only one variant, P_{Ind} itself, so $\log p(v_i|P_{Ind_j}) = 0$, and there is only one P_{Ind} predicate, so $C = 0$. Applying (37) gives an entropy value of 0.

(ii) A context general, not-disjoint P_{Ind} predicate with, for instance, four variants. This will apply to nouns such as *furniture*, which, following the analysis in Landman (2011), have denotations in which what counts as one overlaps in the same context. If the four variants are equally probable, conditional on P_{Ind}, this would make $\sum_{v_i \in V} p(v_i|P_{Ind_j}) \times \log p(v_i|P_{Ind_j}) = 2$. There is only one P_{Ind} predicate, so $C = 0$. The total entropy value will thus be 2 (see footnote 18).

(iii) A collection of two disjoint P_{Ind} predicates that each only apply in specific contexts. This will apply to nouns, such as *fence* and *huonekalu* ('furniture', Finnish, count), where what counts as one varies from context to context. Each context-specific P_{Ind} predicate is disjoint and has only one variant (itself), so $\sum_{v_i \in V} p(v_i|P_{Ind_j}) \times \log p(v_i|P_{Ind_j}) = 0$ for each j. However, given that there are, in this simple example, two P_{Ind} predicates (one for some contexts, the other for the other contexts), one of which must be chosen in each context, there is some cost added. The final result will be the value of C.[19]

---

[19] Arguably, C should itself be sensitive to the probability that a context selects

On its own, individuation pushes towards finding a single disjoint P_{Ind} predicate and sticking with it across contexts. However, if individuation were the only factor, then any arbitrary disjoint P_{Ind} predicate would suffice as an individuation schema, since there would be no requirement for this schema to reliably identify Ps. Clearly, the upward closure of this predicate type should predict, with reasonable certainty, when to apply P. This is what the competing pressure of *reliability* ensures.

5.3   *Summary of reliability and individuation*

Considered independently, the pressures of *individuation* and *reliability* are each insufficient to capture a good criterion for applying a predicate P. Reliability alone would not ensure adequate informativeness for individuation (entropy would be high, on the assumption made here that disjoint individuation schemas/predicates P_{Ind} have minimum entropy compared to predicates that are not disjoint). Individuation on its own would not ensure adequate reliability (what counts as one P in some contexts is not a reliable indicator for what counts as one P in another, hence a single individuation schema will not reliably indicate what counts as P across contexts).

In Sections 6–7, we will see that some nouns allow a ready balance between these pressures. These nouns will turn out to be those that are fairly stably lexicalized as count cross-linguistically e.g. *cat* and *chair*. Other nouns will exemplify how these two pressures can be in direct conflict. Resolution of this conflict can only come by prioritising one pressure or the other. In these cases, the count/mass encoding of the noun will reflect which pressure is prioritised, and most importantly, as we argue, predicts the variation in mass/count encoding across different languages (e.g., the mass noun *furniture* and the Finnish count noun *huonekalu* ('furniture')) as well as within a particular language. In yet a third case, we will argue that individuation cannot really be satisfied. This case motivates the 'stubborn' encoding of nouns as mass, as we find with prototypical mass nouns, such as *mud* and *blood*.

---

a particular P_{Ind} predicate. For example, there should, reasonably, be a lower cost for a situation where the same individuation schema is selected 99 percent of the time, versus the situation in which two schemas are equally probable. We leave inclusion of such factors to further work.

6   THE SEMANTICS OF CONCRETE NOUNS IN PROBM–TTR

Some recent theories of the mass/count distinction propose to represent lexical entries of nouns as pairs where one projection of the pair determines the standard denotation of a noun and the other determines the counting base and/or individuation schema to apply to that noun (Rothstein 2010; Landman 2011, 2016; Sutton and Filip 2016a). In keeping with this general idea, we represent lexical entries of common nouns as a complex frame in which there are two record types.

One specifies the situation type for the predicate being learned, for instance, cat(x), which is a number neutral predicate a learner associates with situations in which competent speakers make judgements that something is a cat or that some things are cats. We label this s_{pred}. The learner simultaneously learns how such number neutral predicates correspond to the perceptual and functional properties of the objects they witness competent speakers referring to.

Representations of such perceptual and functional properties are encoded in the other part of the lexical entry which we label s_{c_base}. This specifies the counting base for this predicate and includes both the quantitative and qualitative criteria of application for the number neutral predicate in the sense of Krifka (1989). The disjointness of this type is what enters into calculations regarding individuation (Section 5.2). The upward closure of this type is what enters into the reliability calculations (Section 5.1). The motivation for this bipartite lexical structure is that a learner requires both kinds of information in order to learn how to use natural language predicates such as *cat*.

A schema for a noun entry is given in (38). In the frame-based representation offered by TTR, these two record types feature as parts of the same complex type and so can be abstracted over so as to receive the same values when applied to a record containing some physical entity (e.g. an entity such as felix labelled x in the record r in (38)).

$$
(38)\ \lambda r : [x : \textit{Stuff}].\ p\left(
\begin{bmatrix}
s_{pred} : & \begin{bmatrix} \text{Rec. type for predicate} \\ \text{(contains label } r.x) \end{bmatrix} \\
s_{c\_base} : & \begin{bmatrix} \text{Rec. type for counting base} \\ \text{(contains label } r.x) \end{bmatrix}
\end{bmatrix}
\right)
$$

We also adopt the basic structure for a common noun lexical entry in prob-TTR given by Cooper *et al.* (2015)[20] for which the result of applying a record of the requisite type is the probability of the relevant record type.

The simplest case is that of prototypical count nouns such as *woman, cat, chair, car*. They are associated with a record type that includes the relevant number neutral predicate, and a record type for the counting base which contains the relevant P_{Ind} predicate. For example, the entry for *cat* is given in (39), and the entry for *cats* is given in (40).

(39) $[\![\text{cat}]\!] = \lambda r : [x : \mathit{Stuff}].p(\begin{bmatrix} s_{pred} & : & [& s_{cat} : \text{cat}(r.x) &] \\ s_{c\_base} & : & [& s_{cat_{Ind}} : \text{cat}_{Ind}(r.x) &] \end{bmatrix})$

(40) $[\![\text{cats}]\!] = \lambda r : [x : \mathit{Stuff}].p(\begin{bmatrix} s_{pred} & : & [& s_{cat} : \text{cat}(r.x) &] \\ s_{c\_base} & : & [& s_{cat_{Ind*}} : {}^*\text{cat}_{Ind}(r.x) &] \end{bmatrix})$

This structure for the semantics of concrete nouns also encodes our conception of the semantic learning of these nouns as being guided by the establishment, if possible, of a counting base, namely the type labeled s_{c_base} which may then serve as reliable criteria for applying the type labelled s_{pred}. For cases such as *cat*, this is relatively straightforward, because being of the type of a cat individual is a reliable criterion for applying the number neutral predicate *cat* (39).

Reliability: On the assumption that a suitably accurate individuation schema for cats can be found, the upward closure of this predicate will be a highly reliable indicator of when to use the predicate *cat*. That is to say, there are very few instances of things having the requisite properties of being a cat individual or of a cat sum for which the judgement *cat(x)* would be inappropriate (recall that we assume that the predicate type *cat(x)* is number neutral). Likewise, there are relatively few mispredications (relatively few *cat* judgements made by competent speakers to refer to entities without the properties of being cat individuals (or sums thereof)). Hence, such a cat_{Ind} predicate would yield high conditional probabilities of the sort in (41) and (42).

(41) $p(r : [s_{cat} : \text{cat}(x)] \mid r : [s_{cat\text{-}ind} : {}^*\text{cat}_{Ind}(x)]) = \text{high}$

(42) $p(r : [s_{cat\text{-}ind} : {}^*\text{cat}_{Ind}(x)]) \mid r : [s_{cat} : \text{cat}(x)]) = \text{high}$

---

[20] Cooper *et al.* use pTTR.

Individuation: Furthermore, whatever schema yields the highest balance of these probabilities will be a predicate type that is disjoint (it will be the type for individual cats). This means that it will satisfy the entropy minimisation requirement as in (43).[21]

(43) $$-\sum_{v_i \in V} p(v_i|\text{cat}_{Ind}) \times \log p(v_i|\text{cat}_{Ind}) = 0$$

With reliability and individuation acting in unison, the lexical entry in (39) is predicted. It has a disjoint counting base, which constitutes a part of the lexical entry for a count noun. This account further predicts that lexicalisations for the *cat* predicate will be stably count.

However, there are nouns for which it is less straightforward to establish a counting base, because the learning pressures of reliability and individuation conflict. In these cases, we argue, there are two ways of conceptualising a referent, one in which individuation is paramount, in which case the result is a count noun, and another in which reliability is paramount, in which case the result is a mass noun. We connect the source of this conflict between reliability and individuation to the types of context sensitivity that play a key role in the theories of the mass/count distinction in Chierchia (2010), Rothstein (2010) and Landman (2011), which we discussed in Section 3. In the next section, we offer a probM-TTR proposal of how context sensitivity can impact the weighting of individuation and reliability in generating predictions about variation in mass/count lexicalization patterns.

7   MASS/COUNT VARIATION: THE EFFECTS OF CONTEXT SENSITIVITY ON INDIVIDUATION AND RELIABILITY

Contemporary mereological theories of the mass/count distinction converge on the idea that the concepts on which the distinction is based are context-sensitive in one way or another. However, the proposals differ with respect to the degree and nature of the relevant context-sensitivity. In particular, Rothstein (2010) and Landman (2011) emphasise disjointness and overlap, which we argue can be interpreted as generating a conflict between the learning pressures of

---

[21] We omit the cost C when $C = 0$.

reliability and individuation (or, alternately, as generating competing requirements on the nature of lexical predicate's meaning). Another source of conflict between the learning pressures of reliability
and individuation stems from what Chierchia (2010) calls 'vagueness'.
However, we suggest this would be more aptly considered a form of
context-sensitivity (in a sense we explain below).

Crucially, we argue that the way these conflicts are resolved
tracks differences in count/mass lexicalisation of nouns, and hence
the specific resolution strategies could serve as a motivation for the
lexicalisation of nouns as mass or count, both within a particular language and crosslinguistically.

Let us first consider the notion of disjointness. As in Landman
(2011), we assume that there is a grammatical counting function
which is sensitive to disjointness. In our account, the counting function
is of the type in (44) and applies to the record type in a lexical entry
labeled s_{c_base}, which captures the idea that what is counted are the entities of the type in the counting base. Hence, for a counting function
f_{count} and probability threshold θ, we propose a type restriction:

(44) $f_{count,\theta} : (RecType \wedge Disj_\theta \rightarrow \mathbb{R})$

This type restriction means that the counting function is only defined
for types that are disjoint relative to some probability threshold and
outputs a real number.

The notion of context used in Rothstein (2010) is that of a 'counting context'. Counting contexts are subsets of the domain, i.e., a set
of entities that count as atoms, as one, in a particular context, which
are then intersected with the root noun denotation of a noun to form
a disjoint set, in 'default' cases. As a formal device, this representation has the right motivation and effect for nouns such as *fence*. However, there are two weak points of Rothstein's account that we improve
upon. First, both counting contexts and individuation remain at a pre-
theoretical level in Rothstein's account. Second, Rothstein (2010) effectively subsumes prototypical count nouns like *cat* as a special case
of context-sensitive count nouns like *fence*, for which there just happens to be no variation in what counts as one across contexts. Intuitively, what is one cat is stable across all contexts, but what is one
fence varies with context. Our formalism improves on Rothstein's idea
of counting contexts by modelling them as contexts in which some in-

dividuation schema is used, where the different individuation schemas that are licensed in a given context are grounded in our account of semantic learning. As a result, we can explain and better motivate why there is only one licensed individuation schema for nouns such as *cat*, but multiple such schemas for nouns such as *fence*.

7.1   *Mass/count variation in collective artifacts*

The term 'collective artifacts' here refers to nouns which denote collections of entities like, for example, furniture and kitchenware. The main point of this section is to show that the way in which nouns for collective artifacts denote in context allows for two distinct ways of forming concepts. One is compatible with counting, and the other is not. Therefore, we should expect to find variation in mass/count encoding in this class. A good example is the mass noun *furniture* in English and the count noun *huonekalu-t$_{+C,PL}$* ('furniture') in Finnish. What ultimately motivates whether a noun, say, *furniture* is mass in English, and not count, may well be wholly conventional (guided by, for example, etymological factors). Here, we focus on the issue of variation in mass/count encoding, which is separate from the question why, say, *furniture* is mass in English, which we leave aside here.

When it comes to collective artifacts, we propose that it is reasonable to assume that what counts as one item of furniture will largely be derived from the function of the relevant item and to a lesser degree from its perceptual qualities. A vanity, formed of a mirror and a table, has a joint function *qua* item of furniture, so plausibly counts as a single item. However, the mirror and the dressing table each have its own function and each can stand and be used as an individual item of furniture in its own right. Likewise, we see similar patterns crosslinguistically, even when collective artifacts are lexicalized as count nouns. For example, what counts as one for the count noun *huonekalu* ('furniture', Finnish) varies with context in the same way as for the English *furniture*.

The kind of contextual variation that we observe with respect to what counts as one for *furniture* or for *huonekalu* presents a learning challenge to our basic picture of learning an individuation schema for a given noun predicate. Recall that individuation schemas are modelled as the type for which a quantitative function outputs 1. They apply to functionally – and also perceptually – characterised situation types (of the qualitative criterion type) and are used to individuate the entities within a situation (record) relative to a predicate. A learning challenge arises because the same entity, the vanity, plausibly counts as one item of furniture in one schema and as two items of furniture in another. But that means that no single function should be able to output both of these results for a situation (record) containing a vanity. Put simply, witnessing the same kind of item being treated as one thing in one situation, and two (or more) things in other situations, is evidence that there is more than one felicitous individuation schema for *furniture*.

In other words, we have a case such as the one outlined in Section 5, in which a learner has evidence for multiple context-specific individuation schemas. This generates a conflict between the two learning pressures of individuation and reliability. Take *furniture*, for instance. Opting for a single individuation schema would keep stable what is individuated as one item of furniture in every situation, but it is not a reliable way of individuating, since one single schema will wrongly individuate in some situations. For example, a schema that individuates a table and a mirror as two entities will be incorrect in circumstances where they should count as one item of furniture, a vanity.

Faced with this challenge, a learner has two strategies available: namely, either to learn to apply a different schema depending on the situation, or to form a single complex join type based on all licensed schemas. For example, if P_{Ind_i} is a licensed individuation schema, a more generally applicable type would be the join type formed of all such schemas. This is shown in (45).

(45) $P_{Ind_{join}} = P_{Ind_1} \vee P_{Ind_2} \vee ... \vee P_{Ind_n}$

The kind of context sensitivity that affects what counts as one for collective artifacts gives rise to two alternative ways of encoding the semantics of a *furniture*-like noun. We now detail these with respect to the formal characterisations of reliability and individuation.

First, one can opt for a complex join schema, and so have a reliable indicator of when to apply the noun predicate in most (possibly all) contexts. This is indicated by the high conditional probabilities in (46) and (47). Given an individuating predicate that is the join of all contextually specific ones, the upward closure of this predicate will closely track how one should apply the predicate *furn*.

(46) $p(r : \left[s_{furn} : \text{furn}(x)\right] | r : \left[s_{furn\text{-}ind} : {}^{*}\text{furn}_{Ind_{join}}(x)\right]) = \text{high}$

(47) $p(r : \left[s_{furn\text{-}ind} : {}^{*}\text{furn}_{Ind_{join}}(x)\right] | r : \left[s_{furn} : \text{furn}(x)\right]) = \text{high}$

Obviously, an individuating predicate that is the join of all contextually specific ones cannot individuate or yield a disjoint type which can support determinate counting results in a specific situation, due to overlaps of the individuals picked by different individuation schemas of that join individuating predicate. This captures Landman's (2011) intuition that overlapping entities can "simultaneously in the same context" count as one. As shown in (48), the fact that there are a number of different ways to resolve overlap in respect to what counts as one item of furniture leads to a comparatively high level of entropy.

(48) $-\sum_{v_i \in V} p(v_i | \text{furn}_{Ind_{join}}) \times \log p(v_i | \text{furn}_{Ind_{join}}) = \text{high}$

Second, one can make the selection of one's individuation schema context sensitive, i.e. apply individuation schemas that may vary from situation to situation. However, as shown in (49) and (50), this has a negative effect on reliability. Although the probability of *furn* is high given the upward closure of any specific individuating predicate $\text{furn}_{Ind_{c_i}}$, the inverse conditional probability is lower than in the complex join individuation schema, because most particular schemas will exclude those bits of furniture that are parts of that which count as one under a different individuation schema. For example, if an agent has an individuation schema that classifies a vanity (table and mirror) as one item of furniture, then this will exclude its parts from counting as one. However, this means that the probability of applying this particular schema given a *furn* judgement will be lower than for the context general join-type case, since the context specific schema (for vanity) will not be reliable for situations in which the table and mirror should count as two items of furniture. This lowers the conditional probability in (50).

(49) $p(r : \left[s_{furn} : \text{furn}(x)\right] \mid r : \left[s_{furn\text{-}ind} : {}^{*}\text{furn}_{Ind_{c_i}}(x)\right]) = \text{high}$

(50) $p(r : \left[s_{furn\text{-}ind} : {}^{*}\text{furn}_{Ind_{c_i}}(x)\right]) \mid r : \left[s_{furn} : \text{furn}(x)\right]) = \text{lowish}$

However, the entropy value is arguably lower than in the single join schema case. That is, in the case of a single join schema, every specific schema will yield an entropy value of 0, since each one is a disjoint predicate, but since there are many such schemas, the task of determining the right one in context incurs a cost C (see case (iii) in Section 5.2). This is shown in (51). Provided that the cost value is lower than the entropy value for the join type in (48), the specific case will fare better at minimising entropy (maximising individuation).

(51) $-\left(\sum_{v_j \in V} \sum_{c_i \in C} p(v_j|\text{furn}_{Ind_{c_i}}) \times \log p(v_j|\text{furn}_{Ind_{c_i}})\right) + C = C$

In summary, if one tries to maximise reliability, the context general join-type individuation schema wins out over adopting a number of context specific ones. However, if one minimises entropy, selecting a context specific schema wins out over the context general join-type individuation schema.

This creates a tension. One simple outcome is merely to prioritise either reliability (and thereby encode a context general join-type individuation schema), or prioritise individuation (and thereby encode a context specific schema). Choosing the former strategy results in a counting base that is not disjoint. This means, as per our Landman-inspired account of the mass-count distinction, that the resulting lexical entry is one for a mass noun. Choosing the latter strategy results in a counting base that is disjoint. This means that the resulting lexical entry is one for a count noun, as in the case of the Finnish singular count noun *huonekalu*. The results of these two strategies are given in (52) and (53).

(52) $[\![\text{furniture}]\!]^{c_i} = \lambda r : [x : Stuff].p\left(\begin{bmatrix} s_{pred} & :[s_{furn} : \text{furn}(r.x)] \\ s_{c\_base} & :[s_{furn_{Ind}} : \text{furn}_{Ind_{join}}(r.x)] \end{bmatrix}\right)$

(53) $[\![\text{huonekalu}]\!]^{c_i} = \lambda r:[x : Stuff].p\left(\begin{bmatrix} s_{pred} & :[s_{furn} : \text{furn}(r.x)] \\ s_{c\_base} & :[s_{furn_{Ind}} : \text{furn}_{Ind_{c_i}}(r.x)] \end{bmatrix}\right)$

The lexical entry for *furniture* in (52) has a generalized schema as the base, but this will not yield a noun suitable for counting, since $\text{furn}_{Ind_{join}}$ will not be a disjoint type (both the vanity and the mirror and table that comprise the vanity will be of this type). However, the lexical entry for *huonekalu* in (53) will yield a count noun, since every single individuation schema $\text{furn}_{Ind_{c_i}}$ will be disjoint.

7.2   *Mass/count variation in non-bounded objects*

The explanation we have just used to motivate the variation in the mass/count encoding of collective artifacts across different languages (e.g., *furniture* (mass) versus *huonekalu* (count) 'furniture', Finnish) can also be applied to motivate the intralinguistic variation exhibited by pairs such as *fence* (count) and *fencing* (mass), which constitute a well-defined semantic subclass we dub here 'non-bounded objects.' The entry for *fence* is given in (54) and the entry for *fencing* is given in (55).

(54) $[\![\text{fence}]\!]^{c_i} = \lambda r : [x : Stuff].p(\begin{bmatrix} s_{pred} & :[s_{fence} : \text{fence}(r.x)] \\ s_{c\_base} & :[s_{fence_{Ind}} : \text{fence}_{Ind_{c_i}}(r.x)] \end{bmatrix})$

(55) $[\![\text{fencing}]\!]^{c_i} = \lambda r:[x : Stuff].p(\begin{bmatrix} s_{pred} & :[s_{fence} : \text{fence}(r.x)] \\ s_{c\_base} & :[s_{fence_{Ind}} : \text{fence}_{Ind_{join}}(r.x)] \end{bmatrix})$

Across situations, *fence* is interpreted relative to a context specific individuation schema $fence_{Ind_{c_i}}$ where c_i is selected depending on the situation. From this it follows that individuation is maximised, but not reliability. In a given context, $fence_{Ind_{c_i}}$ is disjoint, and so defined for counting, which leads to the desirable prediction that the exact result of counting the same stretch of fencing may result in different answers across situations.

In contrast, *fencing* applies the same individuation schema across situations, namely, one that is defined in terms of a join individuation schema type $fence_{Ind_{join}}$, which consists of a number of individuation schemas. But this means that it is not disjoint. Take, for example, Rothstein's square field example, where the sum of four fence sides is of type $fence_{Ind_{join}}$, but so too are the four fence-sides taken individually, whereby the former overlaps with the latter. But this means that the question 'How many fences are there?' has two different possible answers: 'one' or 'four'. In this sense, non-disjoint types are not countable, and so *fencing* is mass (Landman 2011).

7.3   *Mass/count variation in granulars*

In Section 5, we outlined how, for small quantities of rice, an agent may be left with a high degree of uncertainty whether or not to judge it as satisfying the predicate *rice*. If, as observed by Chierchia (2010), quantity of grains is a major factor affecting the applicability of a predicate like *rice* to a collection of entities, then we should also expect the amount of uncertainty along an axis of quantity to be relatively smooth (graded).

For nouns that are context sensitive in this way, a learning challenge arises. We argued, in Section 5, that semantic learning for concrete nouns is largely governed by two pressures. One is to ascertain a consistent and reliable criterion for the application of a noun; the other is to establish what, if anything, the individuable units in the noun's denotation are, which is a prerequisite for counting. In simple cases, identifying the individuable units in a noun's denotation is to identify what the minimal entities are to license applying a predicate. This is the case for prototypical count nouns such as *cat*. If one has either a single cat, or a sum of single cats, one can correctly use the noun *cat* of them.

It is precisely the context sensitivity of granular nouns, such as *rice* and *lentils*, which provides a compelling argument in support of reliability and individuation as two pressures on semantic learning implicated in the acquisition of the mass/count distinction, because learning of granulars pushes reliability and individuation in opposite directions. The denotations of granulars contain perceptually individuable units (e.g., single rice grains, or single lentils). However, having either a single grain of rice or a single lentil does not always license that the noun *rice* or *lentil(s)* can be felicitously applied to them. This is because there are many contexts in which single grains of rice or single lentils, or even small quantities of rice grains or lentils are insufficient in quantity to count as *rice* or *lentil(s)*. Hence, individuating in terms of grains loses reliability.

One way to increase reliability is to make the quantitative function one that identifies aggregates of entities with the requisite properties such as colour, shape, etc., especially if the sizes of these aggregates are those most predictive of the appropriate conditions for using the relevant predicate. The most diagnostic sizes of aggregates will be those that are frequently encountered and have a high correlation with correct application of the relevant predicate. For example, if, say, spoonfuls, bowlfuls and packets of lentils are the most frequently encountered aggregates of lentils and almost always get judged to be lentils by competent speakers, then if an aggregate of lentils is a spoonful, a bowlful or a packet of lentils in size, then one has very good reason to apply *lentils* to that aggregate. Furthermore, if someone has used the term *lentils* one has good reason to expect it to refer to such a frequently encountered aggregate size. Doing this would satisfy the pressure to establish a reliable criterion; however, it would do so at the expense of satisfying the individuation pressure.

We label the individuating predicate that is based on such single-grain properties *lentil$_{Ind\_gr}$*. This schema will not provide good results for one aspect of reliability such as the conditional probability in (56), because small quantities of lentils are not good predictors for when to make a *lentil* judgement. In many contexts, larger quantities are required to count as *lentils*. With respect to the inverse conditional probability (57), it fares better, since the upward closure of the predicate which picks out single lentils will match the conditions for applying *lentil* in all but the cases where sub-grain parts of lentils count as *lentils*.

(56) $p(r : [s_{\text{lentil}} : \text{lentil}(x)] \,|\, r : [s_{\text{lentil-ind}} : {}^{*}\text{lentil}_{Ind\_gr}(x)]) = \text{lowish}$

(57) $p(r : [s_{\text{lentil-ind}} : {}^{*}\text{lentil}_{Ind\_gr}(x)] \,|\, r : [s_{\text{lentil}} : \text{lentil}(x)]) = \text{highish}$

The individuating predicate lentil$_{Ind\_gr}$ maximises individuation, however. It applies to single lentils, which are disjoint. This means that there is only one variant, the predicate itself, hence entropy is 0.

(58) $-\sum_{v_i \in V} p(v_i | \text{lentil}_{Ind\_gr}) \times \log p(v_i | \text{lentil}_{Ind\_gr}) = 0$

So, adopting lentil$_{Ind\_gr}$ maximises individuation, but does so at the expense of reliability.

The alternative strategy is to choose a schema that is more reliable, namely in terms of aggregates (which were formally characterised in Sections 4.2-4.2). Instead of individuating only in terms of single grains, one could instead use a schema that identifies the sizes of aggregates of grains that are most diagnostic of when to apply the predicate *lentil* (a join type of the most diagnostic lentil aggregate sizes). Call this lentil$_{join\_agg}$. As formalised in (60), the lentil$_{join\_agg}$ predicate may also miss out on some cases where very small collections of lentils count as lentils (which indicates that our representation is missing some element of further context-sensitivity for granulars). However, it will do better with respect to predicting when to apply *lentil*, given the schema as shown in (59). This is because the cases where there are insufficient amounts of lentils to make a *lentil* judgement will also be cases where it is insufficient to make a *lentil*$_{join\_agg}$ judgement.

(59) $p(r : [s_{\text{lentil}} : \text{lentil}(x)] | r : [s_{lentil\text{-}ind} : {}^*\text{lentil}_{join\_agg}(x)]) = \text{high}$

(60) $p(r : [s_{lentil\text{-}ind} : {}^*\text{lentil}_{join\_agg}(x)] | r : [s_{lentil} : \text{lentil}(x)] = \text{highish}$

However, the aggregating strategy fares badly with respect to individuation. A join individuating predicate that identifies aggregates of some minimum sizes is not disjoint because e.g. spoonful sized aggregates form proper parts of e.g. bowlful sized aggregates. Such join types have multiple maximally disjoint variants. Therefore, each context specific schema yields a higher entropy value than in the *lentil*$_{Ind\_gr}$ case:

(61) $-\sum_{v_i \in V} p(v_i | \text{lentil}_{join\_agg}) \times \log p(v_i | \text{lentil}_{join\_agg}) = \text{high}$

Neither of the two alternatives for individuation schemas can satisfy both pressures of individuation and reliability. *Lentil*$_{Ind\_gr}$ minimises entropy, thereby maximising individuation, but does not maximise reliability. *Lentil*$_{join\_agg}$ maximises reliability, but does not maximise individuation. As in the *furniture* and *fence* cases, this tension can result in two kinds of lexical entries involving the same number-neutral type *lentil*. Equation (62) uses *lentil*$_{Ind\_gr}$, has a disjoint counting base, and so is the entry for a count noun such as the English *lentil*. Equation (63) uses *lentil*$_{join\_agg}$, does not have a disjoint counting base, and so is the entry for a mass noun such as the Czech *čočka* ('lentil').

(62) $[[\text{lentil}]] = \lambda r : [x : Stuff].p(\begin{bmatrix} s_{pred} & :[s_{lentil} : \text{lentil}(r.x)] \\ s_{c\_base} & :[s_{lentil\text{-}ind} : \text{lentil}_{Ind\_gr}(r.x)] \end{bmatrix})$

(63) $[[\text{čočka}]] = \lambda r : [x : Stuff].p(\begin{bmatrix} s_{pred} & :[s_{lentil} : \text{lentil}(r.x)] \\ s_{c\_base} & :[s_{lentil\text{-}ind} : \text{lentil}_{join\_agg}(r.x)] \end{bmatrix})$

7.4   *Mass/count stability in substances, liquids and gasses*

When it comes to mass nouns like *mud*, *blood*, and *air*, similarly to granulars, the quantity of a substance has an impact on the applicability of the noun in a way that varies with context. For example, a speck of mud on one's shoes could count as *mud* in a scientific clean room context, but not in a context where one is entering a garden shed. The principal difference between substances and granulars is in the perceptual properties of their references. Whereas in the granular case, there are clearly individuable entities which could be judged to be of some P_{Ind} type (e.g. *lentil_{Ind_gr}*), substances lack any such thing.

This means that, of the strategies so far considered, there is only one type individuation schema one might try to use, namely an amassment, the substance noun counterpart to an aggregating schema, that individuates in terms of a join of amassments of stuff with mud properties which are, jointly, the best indicators of when to apply mud. In a similar vein to the granulars case we have considered, the amassment schemas would fare well with respect to reliability ((64) and (65)).

(64) $p(r : [s_{mud} : \mathrm{mud}(x)] \,|\, r : [s_{mud\text{-}ind} : {}^*\mathrm{mud}_{join\_amass}(x)]) = \mathrm{high}$

(65) $p(r : [s_{mud\text{-}ind} : {}^*\mathrm{mud}_{join\_amass}(x)] \,|\, r : [s_{mud} : \mathrm{mud}(x)]) = \mathrm{highish}$

Individuation is militated against with such a schema, however, since there is a high number of admissible (disjoint) variants and presumably none of them will be particularly weighted over the others:

(66) $-\sum_{v_i \in V} p(v_i | \mathrm{mud}_{join\_amass}) \times \log p(v_i | \mathrm{mud}_{join\_amass}) = \mathrm{high}$

On the face of it, it may look as though this strategy is the only viable one. It maximises reliability, but does so at the expense of individuation. This leads us to expect most languages to develop a lexical entry for mud with an overlapping counting base, thus lexicalized with a mass noun. This is the case in English as in (67).

(67) $[\![\mathrm{mud}]\!]^{c_i} = \lambda r{:}[x : Stuff].p\left(\begin{bmatrix} s_{pred} & :[s_{mud} : \mathrm{mud}(r.x)] \\ s_{c\_base} & :[s_{mud\text{-}ind} : \mathrm{mud}_{join\_amass}(r.x)] \end{bmatrix} \right)$

Our account, therefore predicts relative stability in the mass lexicalization of substance, liquid and gas denoting nouns crosslinguistically.

However, we might ask if there is any way one could boost individuation, even for noun concepts which denote substances such as mud and blood. A clue for what kind of strategy might do this comes from languages like Yudja as reported in Lima (2014, 2016, a.o.). In Yudja, different sizes/portions of substances such as blood can be directly counted provided that they are contextually disjoint. Lima's (2014) analysis of Yudja relies on mereotopological concepts from Grimm (2012), and specifically on the concept of Maximal Self Connectedness (MSC) which is the property of countable entities. Informally, "an entity is self-connected means that whenever we partition this entity into two parts, these two parts are connected to each other." (Lima 2014, p. 140)

We formalise this in terms of *bounded amassments* (Section 4.2), namely, identifying, at a perceptual level, distinct bounded regions formed from stuff with the requisite properties. For example, an individuation schema such as $blood_{bounded}$ applies to stuff with blood properties that also forms a bounded region; namely, a disjoint part of space containing blood. As such, the $blood_{bounded}$ predicate will individuate as there will not be multiple variants (e.g. a drop of blood will not be formed of disjoint bounded drops of blood). Namely, we have zero entropy as shown in (68).

(68) $$-(\sum_{v_j \in V} p(v_j|\text{blood}_{bounded}) \times \log p(v_j|\text{blood}_{bounded})) = 0$$

However, although being a bounded region of e.g. blood may be a reliable indicator for applying *blood* (69), being blood may not be a reliable indicator for being a bounded region of blood or a sum thereof, since blood (and other substances) do not always come in bounded portions. This translates into a lowering of the conditional probability in (70).

(69) $p(r : [s_{blood} : \text{blood}(x)] | r : [s_{blood\text{-}ind} : {}^*\text{blood}_{bounded}(x)]) = \text{high}$

(70) $p(r : [s_{blood\text{-}ind} : {}^*\text{blood}_{bounded}(x)] | r : [s_{blood} : \text{blood}(x)] = \text{not high}$

Yudja does not have a rich lexicalized measurement system (aside from loan words (Lima p.c.)). The result is that the only way to quantify stuff (be it intuitively individuated or not) is by direct counting.[22] Languages with such relatively rare characteristics could therefore be ones which adopt a strategy of individuating any bounded, disjoint amounts of stuff with the relevant perceptual (or functional) properties (e.g. colour, consistency, etc.). This strategy, applied across the

---

[22] We are grateful to S. Rothstein for raising the possibility of this connection.

board to substance denoting nouns, could result in there being no genuine mass nouns in such languages, as is reported to be the case in Yudja (Lima 2014).

Substance denoting noun entries would, therefore, look like that for *apeta* ('blood', Yudja), as in (71), and would be count.

(71) $[\![\text{apeta}]\!]^{c_i} = \lambda r : [x : Stuff].p(\begin{bmatrix} s_{pred} & :[s_{blood} : \text{blood}(r.x)] \\ s_{c\_base} & :[s_{blood-ind} : \text{blood}_{bounded}(r.x)] \end{bmatrix})$

8   CONCLUSION AND SUMMARY

The formalism we have developed as a mereological enrichment of prob-TTR can be justified independently of issues surrounding the mass/count distinction. With respect to probabilistic semantics, there is increasing recognition that semantic, pragmatic, and knowledge representations, in order to be cognitively plausible, should be able to reflect gradience in judgements, and be consistent with a tractable account of semantic learning. Mereology is widely used in semantics for modelling plurality, tense, and aspect as well as the mass/count distinction. Using these formal tools, we tried to flesh out the intuition of Krifka (1989) that applying nouns involves both qualitative and quantitative criteria. We sketched how some properties, such as the size and boundedness of an aggregate of rice grains, could be modelled in a manner inspired by work on linking TTR representations to perceptual inputs, and how spatial perception is one factor in guiding the quantitative process of individuating entities. We have also shown how probM-TTR naturally accommodates cutting edge ideas on the semantics of the mass/count distinction, and, significantly, we are able to offer a unified explanation of why some classes of nouns display a wide amount of cross and intralinguistic mass/count variation while others do not; namely, as the result of balancing the pressures of individuation and reliability in semantic learning. Sometimes these pressures align (*prototypical objects*), sometimes they do not (*collective artifacts, non-bounded objects*, and *granulars*) and sometimes individuation cannot easily be prioritised at all (*substances*).

This yields four semantic classes of nouns which pattern differently with respect to the distribution their nouns have over the two grammatical properties MASS and COUNT. These are summarised in Table 1 and elaborated on below.

Table 1: Summary of noun classes and their properties

Noun class	Properties of counting base	Mass/count variation
Prototypical objects	Disjoint, single individuation schema across contexts	Rare
Collective artifacts & non-bounded objects	Multiple, disjoint, context specific schemas OR a single multiplicity of overlapping schemas	Common
Granulars	Disjoint schema picking out single grains, OR overlapping schema amassing aggregates of grains (e.g., spoonfuls, bowlfuls)	Common
Substances	Usually, an overlapping schema that groups frequently encountered amassments of stuff. Sometimes a schema that identifies contextually provided bounded amassments	Rare

Prototypical objects: The types that pick out the individuable entities in the denotations of prototypical object nouns are also highly consistent indicators of when to apply the nouns. The pressures of individuation and reliability work in the same direction, i.e., they converge on the count encoding. We, therefore, have no reason to expect much variation from the count encoding, cross- and intralinguistically.

Collective artifacts and non-bounded objects: The context-sensitivity of nouns in these classes affects the reliability with which any single individual predicate type applies. For example, across contexts, a sum of fence pieces can count as one fence, or two fences; and a pestle and mortar can count as one item of kitchenware or two items of kitchenware. This means that any particular individuation schema will unreliably determine the extension. To prioritise individuation, multiple individuation schemas, each indexed to a context, can be used. This yields count nouns such as *fence*, and *Küchengeräte* ('kitchenware' German). Alternatively, to prioritise reliability, all individuation schemas can be merged together. This yields a non-disjoint schema, and so motivates the encoding of nouns, such as *fencing* and *kitchenware*, as mass nouns.

Granulars: Context-sensitivity with granular noun denotations has an effect on what quantities of the relevant stuff are needed to qualify for that stuff to fall under a given noun denotation. Granular nouns tend to be easily perceptually individuable (in terms of salient individual grains), but given that single grains are not always enough to qualify as falling under a given noun denotation across all contexts, the type for single grains, that prioritises individuation, is inconsistent as a basis for applying a noun. Prioritising individuation yields a count noun encoding, which is commonly presupposed by pluralisation, e.g. *lentils, oats, kaurahiutale-et* ('oatmeal', Finnish). On the other hand, prioritising reliability yields a non-disjoint individuation schema, and so leads to a mass noun encoding, as in *oatmeal, kaura* ('oats', Finnish), *čočka* ('lentils', Czech).

Substances: Context-sensitivity also has an effect on amounts of quantities (e.g., of substances, liquids, and gases) reaching a certain threshold to qualify as falling under a given noun (e.g., *mud, blood,* and *air*). However, the perceptual qualities of the denotations of these nouns does not easily enable the prioritisation of individuation that could be achieved for count granular nouns. If individuation cannot easily be prioritised, then we should expect to find more cases where reliability will be. Therefore, we expect a heavy tendency towards mass encoding for these nouns.

REFERENCES

J. L. AUSTIN (1950/1979), Truth, in J. O. URMSON and G. J. WARNOCK, editors, *Philosophical Papers, Third Edition*, pp. 117–133, Oxford University Press, Oxford, Originally in: *Symposium: Truth, Proceedings of the Aristotelian Society*, Vol. 24 (1950).

Jon BARWISE and John ETCHEMENDY (1987), *The Liar: An Essay on Truth and Circularity*, Oxford University Press USA.

Gennaro CHIERCHIA (2010), Mass Nouns, Vagueness and Semantic Variation, *Synthese*, 174:99–149.

Robin COOPER (2012), Type Theory and Semantics in Flux, in R. KEMPSON, T. FERNANDO, and N. ASHER, editors, *Philosophy of Linguistics, Handbook of the Philosophy of Science*, pp. 271–323, Elsevier.

Robin COOPER, Simon DOBNIK, Shalom LAPPIN, and Staffan LARSSON (2014), A Probabilistic Rich Type Theory for Semantic Interpretation, *Proceedings of the EACL 2014 Workshop on Type Theory and Natural Language Semantics*.

Robin COOPER, Simon DOBNIK, Staffan LARSSON, and Shalom LAPPIN (2015), Probabilistic Type Theory and Natural Language Semantics, *LILT*, 10(4).

Simon DOBNIK, Robin COOPER, and Staffan LARSSON (2012), Modelling language, action, and perception in type theory with records, in *Constraint Solving and Language Processing*, pp. 70–91, Springer Berlin Heidelberg.

Jan van EIJCK and Shalom LAPPIN (2012), Probabilistic Semantics for Natural Language, in P. CHRISTOFF, N. GIERASIMSZUK, A. MARCOCI, and S. SMETS, editors, *Logic and Interactive Rationality Volume 2*, pp. 17–35, University of Amsterdam: ILLC.

Hana FILIP and Peter SUTTON (2017), Singular Count NPs in Measure Constructions, manuscript, to be presented at SALT 2017.

Charles J. FILLMORE (1975), An Alternative to Checklist Theories of Meaning, *Proceedings of the First Annual Meeting of the Berkeley Linguistics Society*, 1:123–131.

Charles J. FILLMORE (1976), Frame semantics and the nature of language, *Annals of the New York Academy of Sciences*, 280(1):20–32, ISSN 1749-6632.

Scott GRIMM (2012), *Number and Individuation*, PhD Dissertation, Stanford University.

Daniel C. HYDE and Elizabeth S. SPELKE (2011), Neural signatures of number processing in human infants: evidence for two core systems underlying numerical cognition, *Developmental Science*, 14(2):360–371, ISSN 1467-7687, doi:10.1111/j.1467-7687.2010.00987.x, http://dx.doi.org/10.1111/j.1467-7687.2010.00987.x.

Ray JACKENDOFF (1991), Parts and Boundaries, *Cognition*, 41:9–45.

A. KOLMOGOROV (1950), *Foundations of probability*, Chelsea Publishing, New York.

Manfred KRIFKA (1989), Nominal Reference, Temporal Constitution and Quantification in Event Semantics, in Renate Bartsch and J. F. A. K. van Benthem and P. van Emde BOAS, editor, *Semantics and Contextual Expression*, pp. 75–115, Foris Publications.

Fred LANDMAN (2011), Count Nouns – Mass Nouns – Neat Nouns – Mess Nouns, *The Baltic International Yearbook of Cognition*, 6:1–67.

Fred LANDMAN (2016), Iceberg Semantics for Count Nouns and Mass Nouns: The evidence from portions, *The Baltic International Yearbook of Cognition Logic and Communication*, 11:1–48.

Daniel LASSITER (2016), Must, knowledge, and (in)directness, *Natural Language Semantics*, 24(2):117–163, ISSN 1572-865X, doi:10.1007/s11050-016-9121-8, http://dx.doi.org/10.1007/s11050-016-9121-8.

Suzi LIMA (2014), All notional mass nouns are count nouns in Yudja, *Proceedings of SALT*, 24:534–554.

Suzi LIMA (2016), Container constructions in Yudja: locatives, individuation and measure, *The Baltic International Yearbook of Cognition Logic and Communication*, 11:1–40.

Godehard LINK (1983), The Logical Analysis of Plurals and Mass Terms: A Lattice-Theoretic Approach, in P. PORTNER and B. H. PARTEE, editors, *Formal Semantics - the Essential Readings*, pp. 127–147, Blackwell.

S. PIANTADOSI, H. TILY, and E. GIBSON (2011), The communicative function of ambiguity in language, *PNAS*, 108(9):3526–3529.

Roberta PIRES DE OLIVEIRA and Susan ROTHSTEIN (2011), Bare singular noun phrases are mass in Brazilian Portugese, *Lingua*, 121:2153–2175.

James PUSTEJOVSKY (1995), *The Generative Lexicon*, MIT Press.

Susan ROTHSTEIN (2010), Counting and the Mass/Count Distinction, *Journal of Semantics*, 27(3):343–397, doi:10.1093/jos/ffq007.

Peter R. SUTTON and Hana FILIP (2016a), Mass/Count Variation, a Mereological, Two-Dimensional Semantics, *The Baltic International Yearbook of Cognition Logic and Communication*, 11:1–45.

Peter R. SUTTON and Hana FILIP (2016b), A probabilistic, mereological account of the mass/count distinction, *LNCS 10148, Proceedings of TbiLLC 2015*, p. To appear.

Leonard TALMY (2000), *Toward a Cognitive Semantics – Vol. 1*, The MIT Press.

Sandro ZUCCHI and Michael WHITE (1996), Twigs, Sequences and the Temporal Constitution of Predicates, in Teresa GALLOWAY and Justin SPENCE, editors, *Proceedings of SALT 6*, pp. 223–270, Linguistic Society of America.

Sandro ZUCCHI and Michael WHITE (2001), Twigs, Sequences and the Temporal Constitution of Predicates, *Linguistics and Philosophy*, 24(2):223–270.

3

Type Theories and Lexical Networks: using Serious Games as the basis for Multi–Sorted Typed Systems

Stergios Chatzikyriakidis[1], Mathieu Lafourcade[2], Lionel Ramadier[3], and Manel Zarrouk[4]

[1] Centre for Linguistic Theory and Studies in Probability (CLASP), Department of Philosophy, Linguistics and Theory of Science, University of Gothenburg; Open University of Cyprus

[2] LIRMM, University of Montpellier

[3] Radiology Dept. CHU Montpellier

[4] National University of Ireland, Galway

Keywords: Lexical Networks, JeuxDeMots, Type Theory, Type Ontologies, Formal Semantics, Natural Language Inference

ABSTRACT

In this paper, we show how a rich lexico-semantic network which has been built using serious games, JeuxDeMots, can help us in grounding our semantic ontologies in doing formal semantics using rich or modern type theories (type theories within the tradition of Martin Löf). We discuss the issue of base types, adjectival and verbal types, hyperonymy/hyponymy relations as well as more advanced issues like homophony and polysemy. We show how one can take advantage of this wealth of lexical semantics in a formal compositional semantics framework. We argue that this is a way to sidestep the problem of deciding what the type ontology should look like once a move to a many sorted type system has been made. Furthermore, we show how this kind of information can be extracted from a lexico-semantic network like JeuxDeMots and inserted into a proof-assistant like Coq in order to perform reasoning tasks.

---

*The first author supported by a grant from the Swedish Research Council for the establishment of the Centre for Linguistic Theory and Studies in Probability (CLASP) at the University of Gothenburg.

1   INTRODUCTION

Modern Type Theories (MTTs), i.e. Type Theories within the tradition of Martin-Löf (1975); Martin-Löf (1984), have become a major
alternative to Montague Semantics (MS) in the last twenty years.
A number of influential approaches using MTTs have been proposed
throughout this period (Ranta 1994; Luo 2011; Retoré 2014; Cooper
et al. 2014), showing that the rich typing system offered by these
approaches (type many-sortedness, dependent types, type universes
among other things) has considerable advantages over simple typed
systems predominantly used in mainstream formal semantics. A further important aspect for considering the use of MTTs over traditional Montagovian frameworks concerns the proof-theoretic nature
of the former but not of the latter.[1] This latter fact makes MTTs
a suited formal semantics language to perform reasoning tasks, as
these are exemplified for example in work on inference using proof-
assistant technology (Chatzikyriakidis and Luo 2014b,a; Bernardy
and Chatzikyriakidis 2017). However, this expressiveness of typing
comes with a cost. For example, how does one decide on the base
types to be represented? On the one hand, we do have a way to get
a more fine-grained type system unlike the monolithic domain of entities found in MS, but on the other hand, constructing such a type
ontology is not at all a straightforward and easy task. Different approaches and assumptions have been put forward w.r.t this issue. For
example Luo (2011, 2012); Chatzikyriakidis and Luo (2017b) proposed to treat CNs as types, in effect arguing that every CN is a type
(roughly a one to one correspondence between common nouns and
types). Approaches like Retoré (2014) on the other hand, take a more
moderate view and build their typing ontology according to classifier
systems, i.e. the intuitions for deciding which types are to be represented or not are taken from classifier systems found in a number of
natural languages. On the other hand, work in lexical-semantic networks have provided us with structured lexicons specifying elaborate

---

[1] At least in the way it is employed in the Montagovian setting, simple type
theory can be viewed as model theoretic. However, there is interesting work on
the proof theory of simple type theory. The higher order theorem prover LEO-
II Benzmüller *et al.* (2007) is an example of such work. We are grateful to an
anonymous reviewer for pointing this out to us.

lexical and semantic relations. A classic such case is e.g. WordNet Fellbaum (1998). A very promising line of research in lexico-semantic network construction concerns networks which are built collabora-tively by using Games with a Purpose (GWAPs). This is the case of the Lexical Network JeuxDeMots (JDM) (Lafourcade 2007b). JDM is con-structed through many GWAPs along with a contributive tool (Diko) which allows players/users to contribute directly and to browse the knowledge base.

Given this background, what we want to propose in this paper is the grounding of our semantic ontologies, as well as any other infor-mation needed in order to perform reasoning tasks using MTT seman-tics, in JDM. In order to do this, we present some first thoughts on how such an endeavour can be accomplished by looking at the way a translation procedure from JDM to MTTs can be performed. Issues to be discussed include the domain of base types, instances of these types, adjectival and verbal types, hyponymy/hypernomy relations, as well as more advanced issues like homophony and polysemy. We then show how one can exploit this translation procedure by extracting this infor-mation from JDM in order to feed a reasoning device that implements an MTT. We show some easy cases of inference that are taken care of via a combination of the lexical semantics information extracted from JDM and the proof theoretic power of MTTs (performed by the proof-assistant Coq) and further show how JDM can actually help us in order to reason with cases where reasoning with implicit premises is at play. The structure of the paper is as follows: in Section 2, the JDM project is described as well as the produced lexical network. In Section 3, we describe two main endogenous inference mechanisms (deductive and inductive scheme), followed by a discussion on the annotation of re-lations between terms. Then, in Section 4, we discuss the building of type ontologies using information from JDM and propose a number of translation procedures between JDM and an MTT. The section also includes a brief intro to MTT semantics, highlighting aspects of the theory that will play a role in this paper the most. Lastly, in Section 5 we look at the possibility of performing natural language inference tasks using MTT semantics powered by information drawn from JDM. We present a number of inference cases that rely mostly on lexical-semantic information taken by JDM and the proof-theoretic power of MTT semantics using the proof-assistant Coq.

2   BUILDING A LEXICAL NETWORK

JeuxDeMots[2], a project launched in September 2007, aims to build a large lexico-semantic network (Lafourcade 2007a). The network is composed of terms (nodes or vertices) and typed relations (links between nodes). It contains terms and possible refinements in the same spirit as WordNet synsets (Miller 1995), although being organized as decision trees. There are more than 80 different relation types which occurrences are directed, weighted, and possibly annotated (Lafourcade *et al.* 2015).

2.1   *GWAPs*

The game JeuxDeMots is a two player GWAP (Game With A Purpose, see von Ahn and Dabbish 2008), where people are supposed to *earn and collect* words. The main mechanism whereby this goal is achieved is the provision of lexical and semantic associations to terms proposed by the system.

When a Player (let's call him/her A) starts a game, a term T, along with some instructions concerning the type of lexical relation (e.g. synonym, antonym, domain, etc.), is displayed. The term T could have been chosen from the database by the system or offered to be played by other players. Player A has a limited amount of time (around 60 seconds) to enter terms which, to his/her mind, are relevant w.r.t. both the term T and the lexical relation. The maximum number of terms a player can enter is limited, thus encouraging the player to think carefully about his/her choices. A screenshot of the user interface is shown in Figure 1.

The very same term T, along with the same set of instructions, will be later given to another player, Player B, for whom the process is identical. In order to make the game more entertaining, the two players score points for words they both choose. Score calculation is explained in Lafourcade (2007a) and was designed to increase both precision and recall in the construction of the database. The more 'original' a proposition given by both players is, the more it is rewarded. Figure 2 shows an end of game with collected rewards. Answers given by both players are displayed and those common to both players, as well as their scores, are highlighted.

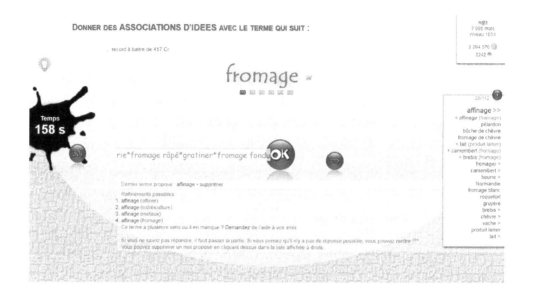

Figure 1: Screenshot of an ongoing game with the target verb *fromage* (cheese). Several propositions have been given by the user and are listed on the right hand side

Figure 2: Screenshot of the game result with the target noun *fromage*. Proposals of both players are displayed, along with points won by both

For a target term T, common answers from both players are inserted into the database. Answers given by only one of the two players are not, thus reducing noise and the chance of database corruption. The semantic network is, therefore, constructed by connecting terms by typed and weighted relations, validated by pairs of players. These relations are labeled according to the instructions given to the players and weighted according to the number of pairs of players who choose them. Initially, prior to putting the game online, the database was populated with nodes. However if a pair of players suggests a non-existing term, the new node is added to the database.

In the interest of quality and consistency, it was decided that the validation process would involve anonymous players playing together. A relation is considered valid if and only if it is given by at least one pair of players. This validation process is similar to that presented by von Ahn and Dabbish (2004) for the indexing of images, by Lieberman *et al.* (2007) and von Ahn *et al.* (2006) to collect common sense knowledge, and Siorpaes and Hepp (2008) for knowledge extraction. As far as we know, this technique has never been used for building semantic networks. Similar Web-based systems already exist in NLP, such as Open Mind Word Expert (Mihalcea and Chklovski 2003), which aims to create large sense-tagged corpora with the help of Web users, and SemKey Marchetti *et al.* (2007), which makes use of WordNet and Wikipedia to disambiguate lexical forms referring to concepts, thus identifying semantic keywords.

For the design of JeuxDeMots, we could have chosen to take into account all of the players' answers according to their frequency from the very outset. The database would have grown much quicker this way, but to the detriment of quality. The rationale behind this choice was to limit the impact of fanciful answers or errors due to misinterpreted instructions or terms. The integration of rarer terms and expressions is slower; nevertheless, these terms are added to the database eventually, once the more common solutions have been exhausted, thanks to the process of creating *taboo* terms. Once a relation with term T has been proposed by a large number of pairs of players, it becomes taboo. During a game, taboo terms are displayed along with term T, discouraging (but not forbidding) players from entering them. In this way, players are encouraged to make other, more original choices. Therefore, more infrequent terms eventually find their way into the database, and the chances of error are reduced to a minimum.

Even if a relation becomes taboo, its weight can, and does, evolve. However, this tends to be done slowly as the relation is proposed to the players less often. It is important to allow relation weights to continue to evolve, as we can hardly consider such a relation as complete. Eventually, a given term can become taboo when involved in several different relation types. The fact that taboo relations continue to evolve is essential, otherwise the weights of two given relations could become equal and then information about the relative strength relations would be lost.

The approach presented here complements that developed by Zock and Bilac (2004) and Zock and Schwab (2008) who tried to create an index based on the notion of association to assist users in navigating the Web or elsewhere, or to help a person find a word on the tip of their tongue. Their approach is bottom-up, i.e. the terms are known (based on word proximity in corpora), but the nature of the link isn't. This has to be inferred, which is far from an easy task. In our case, we provide one of the two terms, term T as well as the relation type. It is the target terms which interest us. Our approach is top-down.

Some other games[3] complement the main game of JDM. Their purpose is to cross validate the information collected in the main game, or to accelerate the relation harvesting for some specific types of relations. For instance, there are games for collecting word polarity (positive, negative, and neutral), for sentiments associated with words, guessing games, sorting games, location preposition games, and so on.

Since September 2007, around 1.5 million matches have been played for JDM, a total of 25 000 hours of cumulative playing. More than 250 million matches have been played for the other games of the JDM platforms.[4]

2.2   *Direct crowdsourcing*

Playing games in order to fill the lexical network is a kind of indirect crowdsourcing, where people (players) do not negotiate their contribution beforehand. In some cases, direct crowdsourcing (with negotiation between contributors) is desirable. Indeed, some lexical relation might be complicated enough to be playable without some linguistic knowledge. This is for example the case for TELIC ROLE, which is the goal/purpose of an object (or action). For instance, a *butcher knife* has the telic role of *cutting meat*. It is to be differentiated from the INSTRUMENT of a predicate, which indicates what can be done with the object. A butcher knife could be used to *stab someone*, but this is not its telic role.

In some other cases (depending on each term), a given relation might not be productive enough to be playable. For example, the CAN PRODUCE relation for *cow* could reasonably be *milk*, but there are not many other answers.

All theses considerations lead to the need of a more direct crowdsourcing interface. The Diko[5] service allows to visualize and contribute to the JDM lexical network. A voting mechanism is at the core of the validation (or invalidation) of proposed relations between terms.

2.3   *Inside the JDM Lexical Network*

As mentioned above, the structure of the lexical network we are building relies on the notions of nodes and relations between nodes, as it was initially introduced in the end of 1960s by Collins and Quillian (1969), developed in Sowa and Zachman (1992), used in the small worlds by Gaume *et al.* (2007), and more recently clarified by Polguère (2014). Every node of the network is composed of a label (which is a term or an expression, or potentially any kind of string) grouping together all of its possible meanings.

The relations between nodes are typed. Each type corresponding to specific semantics that could be more or less precise. Some of these relations correspond to lexical functions, some of which have been made explicit by Mel'cuk and Zholkovsky (1988) and Polguère (2003). We would have liked our network to contain all the lexical functions defined by Mel'cuk, but, considering the principle of our software, JDM, this is not viable. Indeed, some of these lexical functions are too specialized and typically aim at some generative procedure (instead of automatic text analysis and understanding), as in our case. For example, we can consider the distinction between the Conversive, Antonym, and Contrastive functions, a distinction that could be made through annotations for a quite generic antonym relation. Mel'cuk also considers function refinements, with lexical functions characterized as "wider" or "narrower". Given that JDM is intended for users who are "simple Internet users" and not necessarily experts in linguistics, such functions could be wrongly interpreted. Furthermore, some of these functions are clearly too poorly lexicalized, that is, very few terms feature occurrences of such relations. This is, for example, the case of the functions of 'Metaphor' or 'Functioning with difficulty'.

JDM has a predefined list of around 80 relation types, and players cannot define new types by themselves. These types of relations fall into several categories:

• Lexical relations: synonymy, antonymy, expression, lexical family. These types of relations are about vocabulary and lexicalization.

• Ontological relations: generic (hyperonymy), specific (hyponymy), part of (meronymy), whole of (holonymy), mater/substance, instances (named entities), typical location, characteristics and relevant properties.

• Associative relations: free associations, associated feelings, meanings, similar objects, more and less intense (Magn and anti-Magn). These relations are rather about subjective and global knowledge; some of them can be considered phrasal associations.

• Predicative relations: typical agent, typical patient, typical instrument, location where the action takes place, typical manner, typical cause, typical consequence etc. These relations are about types of relations associated with a verb (or action noun) as well as the values of its arguments (in a very wide sense).

Some relation types are specific to some noun classes. For example, for a noun referring to an intellectual piece of work (book, novel, movie, piece of art, etc.), the relation of *author* is defined. In case of a medical entity, targets and symptoms are defined.

Some outgoing relations for the French word *fromage* are shown below:

fromage → r_associated 800 → lait
fromage → r_associated 692 → camembert
fromage → r_associated 671 → chèvre

fromage → r_associated 580 → vache
fromage → r_associated 571 → gruyère
fromage → r_associated 460 → brebis
fromage → r_associated 419 → roquefort
fromage → r_isa 310 → produit laitier
fromage → r_associated 257 → produit laitier
fromage → r_associated 221 → brie
fromage → r_hypo 214 → gruyère
fromage → r_meaning 205 → produit laitier
fromage → r_hypo 204 → brie
fromage → r_associated 201 → dessert
fromage → r_associated 201 → fromage blanc
fromage → r_locution 199 → fromage de brebis
fromage → r_patient-1 199 → manger
fromage → r_locution 195 → fromage de tête
fromage → r_hypo 189 → fromage blanc
fromage → r_isa 189 → aliment
fromage → r_raff_sem 183 → fromage > produit laitier
fromage → r_isa 182 → ingrédient
fromage → r_lieu 182 → pizza
fromage → r_carac 180 → puant
fromage → r_sentiment 177 → envie
fromage → r_consequence 173 → puer du bec
fromage → r_holo 171 → pizza
fromage → r_associated 168 → laitage
fromage → r_hypo 167 → fromage de vache
fromage → r_hypo 163 → fromage double crème
fromage → r_hypo 163 → fromage à pâte pressée cuite
fromage → r_part_of 163 → lipide
fromage → r_part_of 161 → croûte
fromage → r_lieu :160 → plateau à fromage
fromage → r_carac 160 → odorant
fromage → r_associated#0:154 → raclette
fromage → r_locution :154 → dommage fromage
fromage → r_associated 149 → cancoillotte
fromage → r_locution 148 → faire tout un fromage
fromage → r_locution :148 → fromage analogue
fromage → r_locution :148 → fromage de synthèse

fromage → r_hypo 148 → fromage à pâte dure
fromage → r_similar 148 → substitut de fromage
fromage → r_hypo#8:147 → emmental
...

2.4   *Refinements*

Word senses (or usages) of a given term T are represented as standard nodes $T > glose_1$, $T > glose_2$, ..., $T > glose_n$ which are linked with RE-FINE(ment) relations. Glosses are terms that help the reader to identify the proper meanings of the term T. For example, consider the French term *frégate (Eng. frigate)*:

- *frégate*→REFINE→*frégate > navire*
  - *frégate > navire* →REFINE→ *frégate > navire > ancient*
  - *frégate > navire* →REFINE→ *frégate > navire > modern*
- *frégate*→REFINE→*frégate > bird*

A frigate can be a ship or a bird (both English and French have the same ambiguity for this word), and as a ship it can either be an ancient ship (with sails) or a modern one (with missiles and such). As can be seen in the above example, word refinements are organized as a decision tree, which can have some advantages over a flat list of word meanings for lexical disambiguation.

A given word sense is treated as any standard term; it can be played regularly. The general polysemous term contains (in principle) the union set of all possible relations given by the senses. In practice, we proceed the other way around, trying to distribute relations from the appropriate term to the proper senses.

2.5   *Negative relations*

A given relation is weighted, and the weight could be negative. A negative weight is only the result of some contributive process (i.e. it is never an outcome of the games) where volunteers add information to the lexical network. The purpose of negative weights is to give some foundation to the inhibitory process that allows us to reject (instead of select) some given meaning during a Word Sense Disambiguation task.

- *frégate > navire* →REFINE→ *coque (Eng. hull)*
- *frégate > bird* →REFINE$_{<0}$→ *coque*

Consider the sentence (in English): *The frigate had her hull breached.* Obviously, the negative relations immediately forbid the frigate from being a bird in this sentence. Hence, negative relations are of primary interest for representing contrastive phenomena among the various senses of a given term.

2.6   *Aggregate nodes*

The JDM lexical network also contains aggregate nodes that are inferred from the set of relations produced by players and contributors. An aggregate (node) is a node that encompasses either:

- a predicate (a verb) + one argument, like for example:
  lion [AGENT] *eat,*
  eat [PATIENT] *salad.*

- a noun + one feature, like for example:
  cat [CARAC] *black,*
  cat [LOCATION] *sofa,*
  rabbit [MADE-OF] *chocolate.*

Aggregates can be combined recursively, for example (parentheses are given for for the purpose of readability):

A :: (*cat [CARAC] black*) [AGENT] *eat*
B :: (*cat [CARAC] black*) [AGENT] (*eat [PATIENT] mouse*)

The motive of such aggregate nodes is to associate information (through relations) with some contextualized items:

- *A* →PATIENT→ *bird*
- *B* →LOCATION→ *garden*

The choice of aggregate node depends on the weight of the relations in the lexical network. An automated process will randomly select some relations and propose them as the aggregate to the players. Those which are selected for playing are dubbed as interesting and reified (instantiated as node) in the lexical network. For example, the relation:

   soldier →AGENT→ *kill*
   it could lead to the aggregated node:
   soldier [AGENT] *kill*

can be proposed to player with various relation types to fill, as PA-
TIENT, LOCATION, MANNER, INSTRUMENT, etc.

2.7   *Some figures*

By February 2017, the JDM lexical network contained roughly 67 million relations between more than 1 million nodes. Around 24 000
terms are refined into 65 000 word senses (word usages). More than
800 000 relations are negative and can be used as inhibitory items. The
generic 'associated ideas' relations represent around 25% of the relation total. Annotations (see below) represent around 4.5% of the total. Informational relations (like part-of-speech, some conceptual values like HUMAN, ALIVE, PLACE, SUBSTANCE, ARTIFACT, etc.) stand
for 20%.

3   INFERRING AND ANNOTATING RELATION

Inference is the process of proposing new relations on the basis of the
actual contents of the network. Simple procedures tend to provide correct but mostly irrelevant results. In Sajous *et al.* (2013) an endogenous
enrichment of Wiktionary is done with the use of a crowdsourcing
tool. A similar approach of using crowdsourcing has been considering by (Zeichner *et al.* (2012)) for evaluating inference rules that are
discovered from texts.

In what follows, we describe two endogenous inference mechanisms which assist the annotation spreading, although other schemas
are running in the inference engine, producing new relations and deriving benefit from the produced annotations (Zarrouk 2015).

3.1   *Inference*

In order to increase the number of relations inside the JDM network,
an inference engine proposes relations to be validated by other human
contributors (or experts in the case of specialized knowledge). The
core ideas about inferences in our system are the following:

• as far as the engine is concerned, inferring is deriving candidate
  conclusions (in the form of relations between terms) from previously known ones (existing relations);

• candidate inferences may be logically blocked regarding the presence or absence of some other relations;

- candidate inferences can be filtered out on the basis of a strength evaluation.

3.1.1   Deductive scheme

The first type of inference we are describing is the deduction or top-down scheme, which is based on the transitivity of the ontological relation *is-a* (hypernym). If a term A is a kind of B and B holds a relation R with C, then we can expect that A holds the same relation with C. The scheme can be formally written as follows:

(1) $A \xrightarrow{is-a} B \ \wedge \ B \xrightarrow{R} C \ \Rightarrow \ A \xrightarrow{R} C$

If we consider a term T with a set of weighted hypernyms, for each hypernym, the inference engine deduces a set of inferences. Those inference sets are not disjoint in the general case, and the weight of a proposed inference in several sets is the incremental geometric mean of each occurrence.

Of course, the scheme above is far too naive, especially considering the resource we are using. Indeed, B may be, possibly, a polysemous term and ways to block inferences that are certainly wrong can be devised. If there are two different meanings of term B that hold between the first and the second relation (Figure 3), then the inference is most likely wrong.

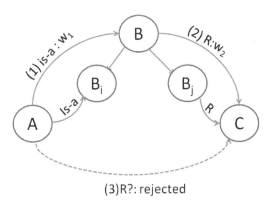

(3)R?: rejected

Figure 3: Triangular inference scheme with logical blocking based on the polysemy of B

Moreover, if one of the premises is tagged as *true but irrelevant*, then the inference is blocked. It is possible to assess a confidence level for each produced inference in a way that dubious inferences can be filtered out. The weight *w* of an inferred relation is the geometric mean of the weight of premises. If the second premise has a negative value,

the weight is not a number and the proposal is discarded. As the geometric mean is less tolerant of small values than the arithmetic mean,
inferences which are not based on two valid relations (premises) are
unlikely to go through.

3.1.2   Induction scheme

As for the deductive inference, induction exploits the transitivity of
the relation *is-a*. If a term B is a hypernym of A and A holds a relation
R with C, then we might expect that B could hold the same type of
relation with C.

(2) $A \xrightarrow{is-a} B \ \wedge \ A \xrightarrow{R} C \ \Rightarrow \ B \xrightarrow{R} C$

   This schema is a generalization inference. The global processing is
similar to the one applied to the deduction scheme and similarly some
logical and statistical filtering may be undertaken. The term joining
the two premises is possibly polysemous. If the term A presents two
distinct meanings which hold respectively of the premises (Figure 4),
then the inference done from that term may be probably wrong.

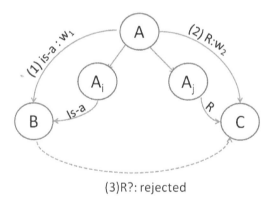

(3)R?: rejected

Figure 4: Induction scheme. Central Term A may be polysemous with meanings
holding premises, thus inducing a probably wrong relation

3.2   *Relation annotations*

JDM is a combined lexical semantic network (i.e one containing both
general knowledge but also specialist domain knowledge). Besides
being typed, relations are weighted and directed. In general, and especially in cases of specialized knowledge, the correlation between the
weight of the relation and its importance is not strict. This is why it
seems interesting to introduce annotations for some relations as these
can be of great help in such areas as medicine, for instance.

In information retrieval, this annotation can be helpful to the users. For instance, in the field of medicine, practitioners may want to know if the characteristic of a given pathology is rare or frequent. For example, the relation between *measles* and *children* is *frequent* and as such will be available in the network.

3.3   *Annotation values*

These annotations will have a filter function in the inference scheme. The types of annotations are of various kinds (mostly frequency and relevance information). The different main annotation labels are:

- frequency annotations: very rare, rare, possible, frequent, always true;
- usage annotations: often believed true, language misuse;
- quantifier: any number like 1, 2, 4, etc. or many, few;
- qualitative: pertinent, irrelevant, inferable, potential, preferred.

Concerning language misuse, a doctor can use the term flu (illness) instead of virus of influenza: it is a misuse of language as the doctor makes use of a "language shortcut". The annotation often believed true is applied to a wrong relation. This is very often considered true, for instance, *spider* (is-a/often believed true) *insect*. This kind of annotation could be used to block the inference scheme. Qualitative annotation relates to the inferable status of a relation, especially concerning inference. The pertinent annotation refers to a proper ontological level for a given relation. For instance: *living being* (charac/pertinent) *alive* or *living being* (can/pertinent) *die*. Another case concerns synonyms: in this case, it may be relevant to choose a preferred synonym, as in the case of hepatocellular *carcinoma* (preferred), *HCC, malignant hepatoma*.

The annotation **inferable** is used when a relation is inferable (or has been inferred) from an already existing relation. For example: *cat* (charac/inferable) alive because *cat* (is-a) *living being*.

The annotation **potential** may be used for terms above the pertinent ones in the ontological hierarchy, for example: *bird* (has-part/always true) *wings* and *animal* (has-part/potential) *wings*.

Finally, the annotation **irrelevant** is used for a valid relation that is considered as too far below the pertinent level, for example, *animal* (has-part/irrelevant) *atoms*.

The annotation **quantifier** represents the number of parts of an object. Each human has two lungs so the quantifier relation there is 2. This kind of annotation is not necessarily a numeral, but can be more or less a subjective value, e.g. *few, many*, etc.

The annotation **frequency** can be of five different types: *always true, frequent, possible, rare and exceptional*. There are also two qualitative types (*pertinent and irrelevant*).

The first annotations have been introduced manually, but with the help of the inference scheme, they will spread through the network. We assign empirical values to each annotation's label: 4 to always true, 3 to frequent, 2 to possible, 1 to rare and 0 to the rest of the annotations. These allow us to select annotations to facilitate or block an inference scheme.

The annotation **possible** is a special case. Depending of the configuration of the system, it may block (stricter approach) or not block (lenient approach) the inference mechanism. If a system is lenient, we may obtain many inference proposals that might be wrong (high recall, low precision). On the other hand, if a system is strict, we reduce the risk of wrong proposals, but at the cost of missing adequate ones (low recall, high precision).

4   FROM JDM TO MTTS

In this section, we show how we can exploit the richness of the lexico-semantic information found in JDM, in order to decide on the typing ontology and assign types to objects in a compositional semantics framework that is richly typed. But before we get into this discussion, a very brief intro to MTT semantics.

4.1   *A gentle and brief intro to MTT semantics*

We use the term Modern Type Theory (MTT) to refer to a variant of a class of type theories as studied by Martin-Löf (1975); Martin-Löf (1984) and others, which have dependent types, inductive types and other powerful and expressive typing constructions. In this paper, we are going to employ one of these variants, namely the Unified Theory of dependent Types (UTT) complemented with the coercive subtyping mechanism (Luo 1994, 1999; Luo *et al.* 2012). Given the different typing constructions found in MTTs, various interpretations of linguistic semantics might be different than what we usually find in traditional Montagovian formal semantics based on simple type theory.

4.1.1   Common nouns as types and subtyping

A key difference between MTT-semantics and Montague semantics (MS) lies in the interpretation of common nouns (CNs). In Montague (1974), the underlying logic, i.e. Church's simple type theory (Church 1940), is 'single-sorted' in the sense that there is only one type, e, of all entities. The other types such as the type of truth values, i.e. t, and the function types generated from types e and t do not stand for types of entities. Thus, no fine-grained distinctions between the elements of type e exist, and as such all individuals are interpreted using the same type. For example, *John* and *Mary* have the same type in simple type theory, i.e. the type e of individuals. An MTT, on the other hand, can be regarded as a 'many-sorted' logical system in that it contains many types. In this respect, MTTs can make fine-grained distinctions between individuals and use those different types to interpret subclasses of individuals. For example, one can have *John* : *man* and *Mary* : *woman*, where *man* and *woman* are different types. Another very basic difference between MS and MTTs is that common nouns in MTTs (CNs) are interpreted as *types* (Ranta 1994) rather than sets or predicates (i.e., objects of type $e \rightarrow t$) as in MS. The CNs *man, human, table* and *book* are interpreted as types *man, human, table* and *book*, respectively. Then, individuals are interpreted as being of one of the types used to interpret CNs.

This many-sortedness has the welcome result that a number of semantically infelicitous sentences, which are however syntactically well-formed, like e.g. *the ham sandwich walks* can be explained easily. This is because a verb like *walks* will be specified as being of type *Animal* $\rightarrow$ *Prop* while the type for *ham sandwich* will be *food* or *sandwich*:[6]

---

[6] This is of course based on the assumption that the definite NP is of a lower type and not a Generalized Quantifier. Furthermore, the idea that common nouns should be interpreted as types rather than predicates has been argued in Luo (2012) on philosophical grounds as well. There, Luo argues that the observation found in Geach (1962) according to which common nouns, in contrast to other linguistic categories, have criteria of identity that enable them to be compared, counted or quantified, has an interesting link with the constructive notion of

(3) *the ham sandwich* : *food*

(4) *walk* : *human → Prop*

Interpreting CNs as types rather than predicates has also a significant methodological implication: compatibility with subtyping. For instance, one may introduce various subtyping relations by postulating a collection of subtypes (physical objects, informational objects, eventualities, etc.) of the type *Entity* (Asher 2012). It is a well-known fact that if CNs are interpreted as predicates as in the traditional Montagovian setting, introducing such subtyping relations would cause problems given that the contravariance of function types would predict that if $A < B$, then $B \rightarrow Prop < A \rightarrow Prop$ would be the case. Substituting A with type *man* and B with type *human*, we come to understand why interpreting CNs as predicates is not a good idea if we want to add a coercive subtyping mechanism.

The subtyping mechanism used in the MTT endorsed in this paper is that of coercive subtyping (Luo 1999; Luo *et al.* 2012). Coercive subtyping can be seen as an abbreviation mechanism: A is a (proper) subtype of B ($A < B$) if there is a unique implicit coercion c from type A to type B and, if so, an object a of type A can be used in any context $\mathfrak{C}_B[\_]$ that expects an object of type B: $\mathfrak{C}_B[a]$ to be legal (well-typed) and equal to $\mathfrak{C}_B[c(a)]$.

To give an example: assume that both *man* and *human* are base types. One may then introduce the following as a basic subtyping relation:

(5) *man < human*

4.1.2   Σ-types, Π-types and universes

In this subsection, the dependent types Σ and Π. as well as universes are briefly introduced.

Dependent Σ-types. One of the basic features of MTTs is the use of Dependent Types. A dependent type is a family of types that depend

---

set/type: in constructive mathematics, sets (types) are not constructed only by specifying their objects but they additionally involve an equality relation. The argument is then that the interpretation of CNs as types in MTTs is explained and justified to a certain extent. Extensions and further theoretical advances using the CNs as types approach can be found in Chatzikyriakidis and Luo (2017b).

on some values. The constructor/operator Σ is a generalization of the Cartesian product of two sets that allows the second set to depend on the values of the first. For instance, if *human* is a type and *male : human* $\rightarrow$ *Prop*, then the Σ-type $\Sigma h : human.\ male(h)$ is intuitively the type of humans who are male.

More formally, if A is a type and B is an A-indexed family of types, then $\Sigma(A, B)$, or sometimes written as $\Sigma x{:}A.B(x)$, is a type, consisting of pairs (a, b) such that a is of type A and b is of type $B(a)$. When $B(x)$ is a constant type (i.e., always the same type no matter what x is), the Σ-type degenerates into the product type $A \times B$ of non-dependent pairs. Σ-types (and product types) are associated projection operations π_1 and π_2 so that $\pi_1(a, b) = a$ and $\pi_2(a, b) = b$, for every (a, b) of type $\Sigma(A, B)$ or $A \times B$.

The linguistic relevance of Σ-types can be directly appreciated once we understand that in their dependent case Σ-types can be used to interpret linguistic phenomena of central importance, like adjectival modification (see for example Ranta 1994). To give an example, *handsome man* is interpreted as Σ-type (6), the type of handsome men (or more precisely, of those men together with proofs that they are handsome):

(6) $\Sigma m : man.\ handsome(m)$

where *handsome*(m) is a family of propositions/types that depends on the man m.

Dependent Π-types. The other basic constructor for dependent types is Π. Π-types can be seen as a generalization of the normal function space where the second type is a family of types that might be dependent on the values of the first. A Π-type degenerates to the function type $A \rightarrow B$ in the non-dependent case. In more detail, when A is a type and P is a predicate over A, $\Pi x{:}A.P(x)$ is the dependent function type that, in the embedded logic, stands for the universally quantified proposition $\forall x{:}A.P(x)$. For example, the following sentence (7) is interpreted as (8):

(7) Every man walks.

(8) $\Pi x : man.walk(x)$

Π-types are very useful in formulating the typings for a number of linguistic categories like VP adverbs or quantifiers. The idea is that adverbs and quantifiers range over the universe of (the interpretations of) CNs and as such we need a way to represent this fact. In this case, Π-types can be used, universally quantifying over the universe CN. Example (9) is the type for VP adverbs[7] while (10) is the type for quantifiers:

(9) $\Pi A : \text{CN}. \ (A \to Prop) \to (A \to Prop)$

(10) $\Pi A : \text{CN}. \ (A \to Prop) \to Prop$

Further explanations of the above types are given after we have introduced the concept of type universe below.

Type Universes. An advanced feature of MTTs, which will be shown to be very relevant in interpreting NL semantics in general, is that of universes. Informally, a universe is a collection of (the names of) types put into a type (Martin-Löf 1984).[8] For example, one may want to collect all the names of the types that interpret common nouns into a universe CN : **Type**. The idea is that for each type A that interprets a common noun, there is a name $\overline{A}$ in CN. For example,

$$\overline{[\![man]\!]} : \text{CN} \quad \text{and} \quad T_{\text{CN}}(\overline{[\![man]\!]}) = [\![man]\!].$$

In practice, we do not distinguish a type in CN and its name by omitting the overlines and the operator T_{CN} by simply writing, for instance, $[\![man]\!]$: CN.

Having introduced the universe CN, it is now possible to explain (9) and (10). The type in (10) says that for all elements A of type CN, we get a function type $(A \to Prop) \to Prop$. The idea is that the element A is now the type used. To illustrate how this works let us imagine the case of the quantifier *some* which has the typing in (10). The first argument we need has to be of type CN. Thus *some human* is

---

[7] This was proposed for the first time in Luo (2011).

[8] There is quite a long discussion on what properties these universes should have. In particular, the debate is largely concentrated on whether a universe should be predicative or impredicative. A strongly impredicative universe U of all types (with $U : U$ and Π-types) has been shown by Girard (1971) to be paradoxical, and as such logically inconsistent. The theory UTT we use here has only one impredicative universe $Prop$ (representing the world of logical formulas) together with infinitely many predicative universes which as such avoids Girard's paradox (Luo 1994).

of type $(human \rightarrow Prop) \rightarrow Prop$ given that the A here is $human : \text{CN}$ (A becomes the type $human$ in $(human \rightarrow Prop) \rightarrow Prop$). Then given a predicate like $walk : human \rightarrow Prop$, we can apply $some\ human$ to get $some\ human : Prop$.

4.2   *Getting MTT typings from JDM*

In this section, we will show how we can define a translation procedure between JDM and MTTs, in order to base our typing judgments and other related lexico-semantic information in JDM. We show some basic examples in which this can be done.

4.2.1   Base types and instances of base types

MTTs, as already said, are many-sorted systems in that they involve a multitude of types rather than just one monolithic type e domain of entities. In the accounts proposed by Luo (2011, 2012), every common noun is associated with a base type. What this idea amounts to, among other things, is that in this approach, CNs are base types and as such, are clearly separated in terms of their formal status with either adjectives or intransitive verbs. The type of CNs, like *Man, Human* and *Animal* is CN, the universe of common nouns.

The idea is then to extract these base types from common nouns in JDM (terms in JDM). POS tagging of JDM will provide information about which words are the common nouns. What we further have to do in getting the base types, is to exclude instances of terms (for example *John* as an instance of *Man*) in order to distinguish between instances of terms and the terms themselves (CNs).[9] This can be done by excluding named entities (NEs). The second part of the conjunction takes care of that by not allowing A to be an instance, i.e. an NE:[10]

(11) $\forall A.POS(N,A) \wedge \neg(Ins(A)) \Rightarrow A{:}\text{CN}.$

---

[9] This does not mean that we are not interested in instances. On the contrary. What we are saying here is that this rule distinguishes between CNs and instances of these CNs (the difference between a type like *Man* and an instance of this type, e.g. *John*). There will be a separate rule to derive instances.

[10] Note that modified CNs are also going to be of type CN. To give an example, consider the analysis of adjectival modification. In MTTs, this would be a Σ type, where the first component would be an element A of type CN and the second projection a predicate over A. The first projection is defined as a coercion, and thus the modified CN can be used as being of type CN. For more information on this, please refer to (Chatzikyriakidis and Luo 2013, 2017a) for more information.

Hyponym and hypernym (noted as *isa* in JDM) relations naturally correspond to subtypes and supertypes. We only use the subtype relation in order to provide a translation procedure:

(12) $\forall A, B.Hyp(A, B) \Rightarrow A < B{:}\textsc{cn}.$

(13) $\forall A, B.Hyper(A, B) \Rightarrow B < A{:}\textsc{cn}.$

This basically means that as soon as you have, let us say, a hyponym relation, e.g. $Hyp(A, B)$, this will be translated into a type-theoretic judgment of the following form:

(14) $A < B{:}\textsc{cn}$

If we want to be more meticulous, we first have to judge A and B as being of type $\textsc{cn}$ and then we can further add the subtype relation. Moving on to synonyms, these can be defined using equality:[11]

(15) $\forall A, B.Syn(A, B) \Rightarrow A = B{:}\textsc{cn}.$

Synonymicity is not only relevant for CNs but for other linguistic categories. We can encode this intuition as follows:

(16) $\forall A, B.Syn(A, B) \Rightarrow A = B{:}C(CLType)$

The above rule can declare synonymous words that have the same type via the equality relation. The type itself belongs in the universe *LType*. *LType* can be seen as a universe of linguistic types. The main intuition is that it includes the types instantiated in linguistic semantics (CN, adjectival and verbal types, types for quantifiers etc.). The interested reader is directed to Chatzikyriakidis and Luo (2012) for more details as well as some of the introduction rules for *LType*).

For instances of terms, such as proper names, we define the following:[12]

(17) $\forall A.\exists B.Ins(A, B) \Rightarrow A{:}B$

This means that if A is an instance of B, then A is of type B. For example, if *Einstein* is an instance of *person*, then what we get is

---

[11] Of course, this will treat A and B as perfect synonyms. We make this simple-minded assumption in this paper, even though perfect synonyms do not really exist in natural language.

[12] Note that here we overload the notation and sometimes treat *Ins* as an one place predicate and sometimes like a two place predicate.

Einstein:person with *person*:CN. In more detail, the procedure is as follows: given an instance *A* of a term *B*, first you declare *B*:CN and then judge the instance *A* to be of that type, i.e. *B*. This is the easy straightforward case and assumes that every instance will be an instance of one term. However, things are more complicated in practice. Given that JDM is a very elaborate lexical network, proper names will be instances of many terms (and thus, in MTT terms, types). To give an example: in the case of a proper name like *Einstein*, what we get is a number of terms from JDM that Einstein is an instance of: *physicist, scientist, human individual*. The question is which one do we choose. This is not an easy question to answer. One option would be to go for the term that is the most specific. But how do we define this? One way to do this, and given the discussion on relations of hyponymy, is to define it by saying that the term chosen should not have any subtypes in the given entry. For example *individual* will have subtypes (*scientist*, and also *physicist*) *scientist* (*physicist*). In this case, we are left with *physicist*. This is one way to do it. Note that given subtyping, we do get that *Einstein* is also an instance of the supertypes. This is a viable solution provided that all the terms are somehow connected in terms of subtyping. But there might be discontinuous relations. For example, imagine the case of the term *man*. Let us assume that *Einstein* is an instance of this term (surprisingly the term does not arise in JDM). Now, *physicist* and *scientist* are not subtypes of *man*. In this case, it seems that one has to make a decision about the type of *Einstein* based on those two types. It seems to us that in principle one should be able to make use of both types depending on the context. How one disambiguates is another issue however. Another way to do this is to assume that such instances are complex types, and treat them as disjoint union types in type-theoretical terms. Doing so will mean that *Einstein* will be of the following complex type *physicistman*:

(18) *physicistman = physicist + man*

(19) *Einstein:physicist + man*

Now, in this situation one can have such a complex case without actually resorting to context. The correct type will be disambiguated according to what is needed. In case a term of type *man* is needed like in *Einstein was a bachelor*, then the type *man* is going to be used. In cases like *Einstein was a well-known physicist*, the type *physicist* is to be

used. Note that this relies on the assumption that a subtyping mechanism is at play which will provide us with the following subtyping
relations:

(20) *physicistman* < *man*

(21) *physicistman* < *physicist*

In this context, a more general way of translating these cases into
MTTs would be as follows:

$$\forall A, D. \exists B, C. Ins(A, B) \Rightarrow \begin{cases} A{:}B & \text{iff } Ins(A, D) \wedge B < D \\ A{:}B + C, & \text{iff } Ins(A, C) \wedge Ins(A, D) \rightarrow \neg\,(B < D \vee C < D) \end{cases}$$

The first case is trivial. The second case says that each A that is
an instance of type B has the type $B + C$, in case it is also an instance
of C and for every other type D that A is an instance of, it is not the
case that either B or C are subtypes of D.

4.2.2   Predicates and world knowledge information

The next question is, how can one extract information on the type of
predicates, like for example verbs. JDM provides loads of information
with every word, for example characteristics, synonyms, antonyms,
collocations. For verbs, *agent, patient* and thematic relations in general
are defined. This is particularly helpful for a rich type theory like the
one used here, since predicates also make use of type many-sortedness.
Thus, *walk* will be defined as being a function from type *animal* to
propositions, *black* from type *object* to propositions and so on:

(22) *walk:animal* → *Prop*

(23) *black:object* → *Prop*

The information in JDM is enough to provide MTT typings for
predicates as well. In JDM, as already said, one can look at semantic relations like *action,patient*, dubbed as predicative relations in the
classification given in the previous section, and various other such relations. For example, *man* appears as the agent of a number of verbs
that express actions, e.g. *question*. But, the most helpful relation is the
inverse agent/theme/patient relation, $agent^{-1}$. This relation returns a
list of terms (and instances of terms) that can function as the agent
for the action denoted by the verb. For example, the verb *question* will

involve among others *teacher, mother, child, daugther, person, human*. How can we make sense in order to provide typings in MTTs? There is a straightforward way to do this. What we need is to find the most general term, i.e. the term of which all the other terms are hyponyms. Instances of terms are not needed in this process.[13]

(24) $\forall A, B. \exists C. Ag(A, B) \wedge (Hyp(A, C) \vee (A = C)) \Rightarrow B{:}C \rightarrow Prop$

However, things may be less straightforward than that simply because there exists no term in the $agent^{-1}$ relation that is a supertype of all the others. In this case, we see two plausible options: a) introduce a supertype or b) split the refinements into different classes. For example in case we have refinements *human, man, pilot, vehicle, car, bike*, we can split this into class A = *pilot, man* < *human* and class B = *bike, car* < *vehicle* and propose an overloaded polysemous type for the verb in question, with two different typings, *human* → *Prop* and *vehicle* → *Prop*. As far as the supertype is concerned, the suggestion is that we go for a default supertype, which will be the supertype of all types. For example in the work of Chatzikyriakidis and Luo (2014a), this type is *object*. We can think of such a type, no matter whether we agree that this should be type *object* or not (denoted as *Toptype* below). Then, with these considerations in mind, we may want to update the previous correspondence:

$$\forall A, B. Ag(A, B) \Rightarrow \begin{cases} \text{B:C} \rightarrow Prop \text{ iff } \exists \text{ C.}((Hyp(\text{A,C}) \wedge Ag(\text{C,B})) \vee (\text{A} = \text{C})) \\ \text{B:D} \rightarrow Prop \text{ iff } \neg \exists C.(Hyp(\text{A}, C) \wedge D = TopType) \end{cases}$$

The first condition says that if A is the agent of predicate B (expressed by an adjective here), then in case there is a type C that is also the agent of B, it is a supertype of A as well as a supertype of all other types that are agents of B,[14] or if C is actually A, then the type for the adjective will just be a predicate over C. In case there is no hypernym of A, we choose as our type a predicate over the Toptype (the type of which all other types are subtypes).

---

[13] The formula reads as follows: for all A and B, where A is an agent of B (so B is a predicate), if there exists a C such than all A are either hyponyms of C or are equal to C, the predicate $C \rightarrow Prop$ is returned.

[14] This last bit is not actually encoded in the rule for formatting reasons. The following condition is implicit: $\forall$ E.Ag(E,B)→Hyp(E,C).

Moving on to adjectives, similar processes can be defined. However, this time we look at another relation, called *carac* (characteristic) that denotes a characteristic of a term. For example, for *grand*, we find the characteristics *chose* and *homme*, 'object' and 'man' respectively among others. There are two ways to assign types for adjectives here: a) propose a type using the same reasoning for predicates above or b) propose a polymorphic type extending over a universe which includes the most general type found satisfying the characteristic in question (e.g. blackness, bigness, etc.), along with its subtypes:[15]

(25) $\forall A, B.\exists C.Car(A,B) \wedge (Hyp(A,C) \vee (A=C)) \Rightarrow C \rightarrow Prop$

(26) $\forall A, B.\exists C.Car(A,B) \wedge (Hyp(A,C) \vee (A=C)) \Rightarrow \Pi U{:}\text{CN}_C.U \rightarrow Prop$

Using a polymorphic universe in terms of inference will suffice in order to take care of the class of adjectives known as subsective (e.g. *skilful*), while for intersective adjectives (e.g. *black*) a non-polymorphic type is needed. This, along with the use of Σ types for modified, by adjectives, CNs (e.g. *black man, skillful surgeon* etc.) will suffice to take care of the basic inferential properties of the two classes of adjectives Chatzikyriakidis and Luo (2013, 2017a) for more details on this analysis). However, as in the case of verbs, more should be said in order to take care of the complications already discussed for verbs previously. Taking these issues into consideration, the updated rule is as follows:

$$\forall A, B.Car(A,B) \Rightarrow \begin{cases} B{:}C \rightarrow Prop & \text{iff } \exists\ C.((Hyp(A,C) \wedge Ag(C,B)) \vee (A=C)) \\ B{:}D \rightarrow Prop & \text{iff } \neg\exists C.(Hyp(A,C) \wedge D = TopType) \end{cases}$$

$$\forall A, B.Car(A,B) \Rightarrow \begin{cases} B{:}\Pi U{:}CN_C\ U \rightarrow Prop & \text{iff } \exists\ C.((Hyp(A,C) \wedge Ag(C,B)) \vee (A=C)) \\ B{:}\Pi U{:}CN_D\ U \rightarrow Prop & \text{iff } \neg\exists C.(Hyp(A,C) \wedge D = TopType) \end{cases}$$

The above two rules are for intersective and subsective adjectives. Hyponymy relations between adjectives can be encoded as meaning postulates.

(27) $\forall A, B.POS(adj,A) \wedge POS(Adj,B) \wedge Hyp(A,B) \Rightarrow \forall x{:}C.A(x) \rightarrow B(x)$
    where $A, B{:}C \rightarrow Prop$

---

[15] For example the universe $U{:}\text{CN}_C$ will contain the type C along with its subtypes.

Due to the abundance of information that JDM has to offer, one can further encode different sorts of information in the form of axioms or definitions. For example the *has_part* relation, in effect a mereological relation, can be translated as a *part of* relation with *part_of:object* → *object* → *Prop* and follow a translation procedure along standard assumptions for mereology for formal semantics[16]. There are many more interesting relations in JDM, like for example the collocation relation, (*locution* in JDM) or the magnifying and its inverse anti-magnifying relation, *magn* and *anti-magn* respectively. Now, there is no clear way of what we can do with these relations. One can of course just encode a similar relation in the type-theoretic language used, but the question is what do we gain in terms of reasoning for example, by doing so. For instance, looking at the entry for *homme* 'man', we see a number of collocations like *homme grande* and *homme libre*. The collocations that involve adjectival modification most of the times give rise to subsective inferences. For example a great man is a man and a free man is also a man. It would be tempting in this respect to treat these cases as subtypes of the term. In this case, we allow some non-compositionality and treat collocations as involving one word. Of course, this will not give us the correct results in all cases. For example, think of the term *objet* 'object'. Among the collocations in the category discussed, e.g. *object du désir* or *objet de curiosité*, there are also collocations like *programmation orientée objet* 'object oriented programming' that will give us the wrong results if we go the subtyping route. One can however decide on whether to take such a stance based on the amount of collocations that can be correctly captured in going the subtype route in relation to those that are not. This is a complex issue with which we will not deal in this paper.

4.2.3   Polysemy

The next issue we want to look at is polysemy, more specifically the translation process in case of polysemous terms. First of all, we have to note here that JDM does not distinguish between homophony and polysemy in the sense these are usualy understood in the literature on formal semantics (e.g. *bank* as homophonous and *book* as polysemous). For JDM, there is only one term to refer to both homophony

---

[16] For an overview see Champollion and Krifka (2016).

and polysemy, and this is polysemy. This is what we are going to use here as well, a single notion for all cases where different meanings associated with a given word are found. For JDM, there is this first level where words with more than one meaning (irrespective of whether the meanings are related or not) are dubbed as polysemous, and then additional levels of refinement are provided. In MTTs, as in formal semantics in general, there are different treatments with respect to cases of homophony and cases of polysemy. For example, in Luo (2011), homophony is treated via local coercions (local subtyping relations), while logical polysemy (cases like *book*) via introducing dot-types, types that encode two senses that do not share any components (Luo 2010). It is a difficult task to be able to translate from a polysemous term identified in JDM to the correct mapping in MTTs. However, there are some preliminary thoughts on how this can be achieved. First of all, let us look at some cases of polysemy identified in JDM that would not be considered such cases in mainstream formal semantics. For example the term *individual* is marked as polysemous in JDM. The reason for this is that JDM goes into more detail than what most formal semantics theories do. For example, JDM distinguishes different meanings of *individual* with respect to its domain of appearance, e.g. a different notion of individual is found in the domain of statistics, a different one in the domain of biology, and so on. This level of fine-grainedness is usually not found in formal semantics. However, there is no reason why we should not go into this level of detail in MTTs. In order to encode domains, we use type theoretic contexts as these have been used by Ranta (1994); Chatzikyriakidis and Luo (2014c), among others. The idea is that a relation can appear in different domains. If this is the case, then different relations might be at play depending on the domain. For example, different refinements of a term might be possible in a domain A than in a domain B.[17]

(28) $\forall A, C . Domain(C) \wedge POS(N, A) \; in \; C \wedge \neg(Ins(A)) \Rightarrow A{:}\text{CN} \; in \; \Gamma_C$

---

[17] An anonymous reviewer asks how does the equation help us in using this information. The idea is that as soon as the conditions are satisfied, i.e. there is a relevant domain for a given type declaration, then this declaration is made inside the relevant type theoretic context, e.g. the context of zoology, philosophy, etc. In the case of Coq, this can be done by introducing local sections.

The above example identifies a noun, which is not an instance, in a domain C and declares this to be of type CN in context Γ_C. All this information such as POS, domain and instance status is part of the JDM network. To give an example, take the term French term *fracture* (fracture) in JDM. This is associated with a number of different domains, let us mention two here, *géologie* and *médicine*. This will basically add the term *fracture* into two different contexts where the relations between *fracture* and other terms in the given context might differ in the different contexts. For example, one might have a term B being a subtype of *fracture* in one domain but not in the other:

What about other cases of polysemy like *book* or *bank*? One way to look at the translation process in these cases is the following: in case a term is dubbed polysemous in JDM, we look at the semantic refinements and introduce all these refinements as subtypes of the initial term:

(29) $\forall A, C.POS(N,A) \wedge \neg(Ins(A)) \wedge Ref(A, C) \Rightarrow A < C:$CN

Now in order to decide whether we are going to use local coercions or dot-types we proceed as follows: the types that participate in dot-types are limited and enumerable:[18] some of these include *phy, info, event, inst* among others. We can thus create such a set of refinements that can be senses of a dot-type. Call this set *dot refinements, DR*. Now, in case the refinements happen to be members of this set then we can form a dot-type out of the individual refinements:

(30) $\forall A, B, C.POS(N,A) \wedge Ref(A(B, C)) \in DR \Rightarrow A:$CN $< B \bullet C$

Other cases of polysemy that should be taken into consideration involve cases where the two meanings are associated with different types (e.g. cases like *run*). In this case, we have at least two verbal meanings with a different verbal arity as well as a different CN argument. An easy way to do this is to just overload the types to take care of situations like these. For example, in Luo (2011), the polysemy of

---

[18] An anonymous reviewer asks how these types are chosen. This is not an easy question. For the needs of this paper, and given that dot-types have specific properties compared to other polysemous terms, the types comprising the dot-types are limited. We enumerate these types based on existing theoretical work on co-predication by Pustejovsky (1995) and Asher (2008), among others.

run is assumed to be captured using a Unit type which allows us to overload the type with the two different typings:

(31) $run_1 : human \rightarrow Prop$

(32) $run_2 : human \rightarrow institution \rightarrow Prop$

With this last note, we will move on to look how information from JDM can be used in order to perform reasoning tasks. What we are going to do is to look at simple cases of lexical semantics information extraction from JeuxdeMots, their direct translation to MTT semantics feeding the proof-assistant Coq. Reasoning is then performed using the assistant.

5   JDM, MTTS AND REASONING USING PROOF–ASSISTANTS

Coq is an interactive theorem prover (proof-assistant). The idea behind it and proof-assistants in general is simple and can be roughly summarized as follows: one uses Coq in order to check whether propositions based on statements previously pre-defined or user defined (definitions, parameters, variables) can be proven or not. Coq is a dependently typed proof-assistant implementing the calculus of Inductive Constructions (CiC, see Coq 2007). This means that the language used for expressing these various propositions is an MTT. To give a very short example of how Coq operates, let us say we want to prove the following propositional tautology in Coq:

(33) $((P \vee Q) \wedge (P \rightarrow R) \wedge (Q \rightarrow R)) \rightarrow R$

Given Coq's typed nature we have to introduce the variables P, Q, R as being of type *Prop* $(P, Q, R:Prop)$. To get Coq into proof mode, we have to use the command *Theorem*, followed by the name we give to this theorem, followed by the theorem we want to prove:

(34) *Theorem A:* $((P \vee Q) \wedge (P \rightarrow R) \wedge (Q \rightarrow R)) \rightarrow R$

This will put Coq into proof mode:

```
Theorem A:((P\/Q)/\(P -> R)/\(Q->R))->R.
1 subgoal
============================
(P\/Q)/\(P -> R)/\(Q -> R)->R
```

Now, we have to guide the prover to a proof using its pre-defined proof tactics (or we can define our own). For the case under consideration, we first introduce the antecedent as an assumption using *intro*:[19]

```
A < intro.
1 subgoal
H :(P \/ Q)/\(P -> R)/\(Q -> R)
============================
R
```

We split the hypothesis into individual hypothesis using *destruct*:[20]

```
destruct H. destruct H0.
1 subgoal
H : P \/ Q
H0 : P -> R
H1 : Q -> R

============================
R
```

Now, we can apply the elimination rule for disjunction which will basically result in two subgoals:

```
elim H.
2 subgoals
H : P \/ Q
H0 : P -> R
H1 : Q -> R

============================
P -> R
subgoal 2 is:
Q -> R
```

The two subgoals are already in the hypotheses. We can use the *assumption* tactic that matches the goal in case an identical premise exists, and the proof is completed:

---

[19] This tactic moves the antecedent of the goal into the proof context as a hypothesis.

[20] After destructing H, we get $H0$ as $H0:(P \to R) \land (Q \land R)$.

```
assumption. assumption.
1 subgoal
H : P \/ Q
H0 : P -> R
H1 : Q -> R
============================
Q -> R
Proof completed.
```

Now, as we have already said, Coq implements an MTT. In this respect, Coq 'speaks' an MTT so to say. It is also a powerful reasoner, i.e. it can perform elaborate reasoning tasks. These two facts open up the possibility of using Coq for reasoning with NL using MTT semantics. Indeed, earlier work has shown that Coq can be used to perform very elaborate reasoning tasks with very high precision (Mineshima *et al.*; Bernardy and Chatzikyriakidis 2017). To give an example, consider the case of the existential quantifier *some*. Quantifiers in MTTs are given the following type, where A extends over the CN (this is reminiscent of the type used for VP adverbs):

(35) $\Pi A : \text{CN}. (A \to Prop) \to (A \to Prop)$

We provide a definition based on this type, giving rather standard semantics for the existential quantifier (in Coq notation):

```
Definition some:=fun(A:CN)(P:A->Prop)=>exists x:A,P x.
```

This says that given an A of type CN and a predicate over A, there is an $x{:}A$ such that P holds of x. Imagine, now, that we want to see the consequences of this definition. For example we may want to check whether *John walks* implies that *some man walks* or that *some man walks* implies that *some human walks*. We define, following our theoretical assumptions about CNs, *man* and *human* to be of type CN and declare the subtyping relation *man < human*. The subtyping relations in Coq are declared by first introducing them as axioms and then coercing them:

```
Parameter man human: CN
Axiom mh: man -> human. Coercion mh: man >-> human.
```

This is all we need to get the above inferences. These assumptions suffice to prove these inferences in Coq. We formulate the theorem and put Coq into proof mode:

```
Theorem EX: walk John-> (some man) walk.
```

Unfold the definition for *some* and use *intro*

```
EX < intro.
1 subgoal
H : walk John
============================
exists x : man, walk x
```

Using the *exists* tactic to substitute x for $John$. Using *assumption* the theorem is proven. Now, what we want to show is that we can actually use JDM to extract lexical and typing information, translate this information into MTT semantics in the form of Coq code and then perform reasoning tasks. Let us look at the following example:

(36) John Fitzgerald Kennedy ate some gruyère

Suppose, now, that we further want to check whether the following is true:

(37) John Fitzgerald Kennedy ate some gruyère ⇒ John Fitzgerald Kennedy ate some cheese

Let us see whether we can extract this information from JDM. We use the JDM XML version, and further use simple Python code to extract the relevant information and turn it into Coq code. We first extract all the synonyms and subtypes of cheese and translate them to MTT semantics (in Coq code). The result is more than 200 subtypes for cheese (*fromage* in French), among them the type for *gruyère*. What the code does is that it first declares all subtypes to be of type CN and then further declares them to be subtypes of the CN in question (cheese in our case. The result is something like this (we use the first 5 subtypes to illustrate this):

```
Parameter gruyere:CN.
Parameter brie:CN.
Parameter kiri:CN.
```

```
Parameter camembert:CN.
Axiom  Gruyere:gruyere -> fromage.
Coercion Gruyere:gruyere>-> fromage.
Axiom Brie:brie->fromage.Coercion Brie:brie>->fromage.
Axiom Kiri:kiri->fromage.Coercion Kiri:kiri>->fromage.
Axiom Camembert:camembert->fromage.
Coercion Camembert:camembert>-> fromage.
```

The next step is to extract information about *John Fitzgerald Kennedy*. The only thing needed here is to extract the information for the instances of the type *man* (*homme* in French). Simple coding in Python can extract all the subtypes for *man* as well as its instances, declaring them as being of type *man*. What we get in doing so is the following (we only show the information relevant to our example):

```
Parameter man: CN.
Parameter John Fitzgerald Kennedy: man.
```

The next step is extracting the information for the verb *eat* (*manger* in French). Here we use a more simple and less elegant way of extracting the function types than we have described in the previous section. We first chose 6 very basic types, *woman, man, human, animal, food, object*. If any of these types is present as an agent argument (starting hierarchically from type *object* and all the way down to the other types), it is added as an argument to the function type. Thus, in case of a predicate which has an object agent, the type *object* → *Prop* is returned. The other types, even if present, are neglected. If *object* is not present, the next type is checked and so on. Doing so, we end up with the type *Animal* → *food* → *Prop* for *eat*. *Cheese* is of course a subtype of *food* (we get this from the hyponyms of *food*), and *human* of *animal*. So, the only thing left is a definition of the quantifier. Quantifiers and related elements can perhaps be assumed to belong to a closed set of words that can be given their semantics manually. This is what we do here by manually providing a definition for *some*. With this in place, what we get is the following information for Coq (only the relevant code to the example is shown):

```
Definition CN:= Set.
Definition some:= fun(A:CN)(P:A->Prop)=>exists x:A,P x.
Parameters man woman human animal food object: CN.
```

```
Axiom   Man:man->human. Coercion Man:man>->human.
Axiom   Human: human->animal.Coercion Human:human>->animal.
Axiom   Animal: animal->object.
Coercion Animal: animal>->object.
Axiom   Food: food->object.Coercion food:food>->object.
Axiom   Woman: woman->human. Coercion Woman:woman>->human.
Parameter gruyere: CN.
Axiom   Gruyere: gruyere->fromage.
Coercion Gruyere:gruyere>-> fromage.
Parameter John_Fitzgerald_Kennedy: human.
```

This is in fact enough to work through the inference we are interested in. Of course, this is not a very elaborate example, but it is a nice way to exemplify how information from a lexical network can be used in a compositional semantics framework to perform reasoning tasks. Note, that a number of other inferences also follow from the previous example:

(38) John Kennedy ate some gruyère ⇒ some man ate some gruyère.

(39) John Kennedy ate some gruyère ⇒ John Kennedy ate some food.

Let us look at another example:

(40) The frigate had its hull breached.

In this example, what we need to predict is that the *bird* sense cannot be used. On the contrary, we should predict that the *ship* sense is required. First of all, the way this is achieved in JDM is via using negative weights as we have mentioned in chapter 2. We will now see that compositional semantics can further help us in this task. We start with the assumption that frigate is not yet refined or can be either a *bird* or a *ship*. The next thing we have is an NP with a possessive pronoun. Following Ranta (1994), we assume a pronominalization and a genitive rule. The two rules are shown below (adapted from Ranta (1994):[21]

$$
\frac{A{:}\mathrm{CN} \quad a{:}A}{\begin{cases} \mathrm{PRON}(A,a){:}A \\ \mathrm{PRON}(A,a) = a{:}A \end{cases}}
\qquad
\frac{A{:}\mathrm{CN} \quad B{:}\mathrm{CN} \quad C(x{:}A,y{:}B) \quad a{:}A b{:}B \quad c{:}C(a,b)}{\begin{cases} \mathrm{Gen}(A,B(x,y),C(x,y),a,b,c){:}B \\ \mathrm{Gen}(A,B(x,y),C(x,y),a,b,c=b){:}B \end{cases}}
$$

[21] Ranta (1994) uses type *Set* instead of CN that we are using.

The result of sugaring in English will be *A's B*. The pronominal-ization rule will depend on the type that *A* will take. For example *Pron(man, a)* will return *he*, *Pron(woman, a)* *she* and *Pron(object, a)* *it*. Returning to our example, the possessive *its* is a combination of the two rules we have presented, i.e. *Pron* and *Gen*. As we have said, the semantics for pronouns will depend on the value for CN. This is also the case obviously for *its*. Let us assume that *A* takes the value *frigate*. This will give us:

(41) *Gen(frigate, hull(x, y), C(x, y), Pron(frigate, a), b hull, c):hull.*

The *C* relation is an underspecified relation, since it can take different values, given the semantic polysemy of the genitive. Assuming that the relation involved in our example is one of meronymy, what we get is an elaboration of $C(a, b)$ to *has_part(a, b)*. Now, notice that JDM provides meronymy relation refinement between two objects, of which one is a ship and the other a hull, but not between a bird and a hull. Specifically, supplies us with the following information (translated into MTT semantics):

(42) $\forall a$*:ship.*$\exists b$*:hull.has_part(a)(b)*

But not:

(43) $\forall a$*:bird.*$\exists b$*:hull. has_part(a)(b)*

Parsing *The frigate had its hull breached*, what we get is the following (simplified):

(44) *breached(the(ship, a))(Gen(ship, hull(x, y), has_part(x, y),*
       Pron(ship, a), b:hull, c))

Now, we can assume that the negative weight amounts to the negation of the has_part relation:

(45) $\forall a$*:bird*$\neg$*(*$\exists b$*:hull.(has_part(a)(b)))*

If now, we substitute with bird and given the information associated with hull as a refinement of bird, what we will get is a contradiction:

(46) *breached(the(ship, a))(Gen(bird, hull(x, y), has_part(x, y),*
       Pron(ship, a), b:hull, c)) $\land$ $\forall a$*:bird.*$\neg$*(*$\exists b$*:hull.(has_part(a)(b)))*

If we have a system that can spot contradictions between information derived from lexical semantics (in our case the negative weight translating into a meaning postulate) and information derived for semantic compositionality, we might use this in order to disambiguate word senses as well. For example, one can define a ranking algorithm that will rank the senses of a given word in a sentence depending on whether they give rise to contradictions between lexical semantics information and information derived for semantic compositionality. In this manner, one can seek to define a combined strategy to disambiguate using insights from both the lexical network itself as well as the formal system in which this information is encoded.

5.1   *Reasoning with missing premises: enthymematic reasoning*

It is a well-known fact that natural language inference (NLI) is not only about logical inference. Better put, logical inference is only part of NLI. Other kinds of non-logical inferencing is going in NLI, e.g. implicatures, presuppositions, or enthymematic reasoning to name a few. The latter form of reasoning is particularly important for the scope of this article, since enthymematic reasoning is basically deriving conclusions from missing premises or implicit premises. Consider the following classic case of an enthymeme:

(47) Socrates is human, therefore he is mortal

In this example, there is an implicit premise at play, namely that all humans are mortal. This is not given however. It is somehow presupposed as part of the general world knowledge. What would be interesting to see is to check whether such implicit arguments can be retrieved via the richness of a network like JDM. Indeed, this can be done. In particular, the entry for *mortal* in JDM, specifies *human* as one of its hyponyms. So, extracting lexical relations for *human* will also extract the synonym relation. Thus, it is easy to get the inference we are interested in. The same kind of information that can lead to retrieving the implicit argument in further examples like the ones shown below can be found using the richness of a network like JDM:[22]

(48) He coughs. He is ill.

---

[22] We are rather simplifying here, given that in JDM there is more than one relation between *human* and *mortal*. One finds the hyponym relation, the synonym relation as well as the characteristic relation (mortality as a characteristic

(49) She has a child, thus she has given birth.

Of course, it would be naive to think that enthymematic inference can be dealt with in full via using only information present in a lexical network, no matter how rich that network is. We are not suggesting anything like this. The interested reader that wants to have a deeper look at the issue of enthymemes and reasoning with them in a type-theoretic framework is directed to Breitholtz (2014). For the needs of this paper, it is enough to mention that at least some cases of enthymemes can be captured via a combination of lexical semantics information taken from a rich lexical network like JDM and their feeding to a richly typed logical system like the one we are endorsing in this paper.

6   CONCLUSION

In this paper we have looked at the way one can use information from a rich GWAP lexical network in order to construct typing ontologies for NL in rich type theories. Rich or modern type theories offer us elaborate typing structures and type many-sortedness, where the monolithic domain of individuals is substituted by a multitude of types. The problem that is created however, given this context, concerns which types need to be represented and which not, as well as the criteria that one uses in order to reach to such a decision. In this paper, we have proposed that one does not have to take such a decision but rather leave this information flow from a lexical network, in our case a rich GWAP network, JDM. We have proposed an initial way of doing this, namely extracting information from JDM w.r.t. to base types for common nouns as well as the types for other categories like verbs and adjectives. We have also proposed to use MTTs for several other types of information obtained from such a rich network. Lastly, we have initiated a discussion on how one can further use this

---

of humans). From a logical point of view, it cannot be the case that two terms are both synonyms and hyponyms. Furthermore, as one of the reviewer's notes, the synonym relation in JDM seems to be assymetrical, otherwise one would expect things like *pandas are human* to be inferred. This raises a more general issue, i.e. handling potentially contradictory information in the network. This is something that we will definitely explore in the future.

richness of information, especially common knowledge information, in order to deal with aspects of inference. On the one hand you have a wealth of lexical-semantic relations and on the other, a very rich and expressive compositional framework with powerful reasoning mechanisms. The result one would aim at, given this situation, is a combination of these two aspects in order to perform reasoning tasks with NLI. We have discussed some simple reasoning examples using the Coq proof-assistant, a proof-assistant that implements an MTT. Information is extracted from JDM and then translated into Coq code (thus into an MTT variant). The results are promising, showing a potential to deal with important aspects of NL reasoning. Furthermore, some easy cases of reasoning under implicit premises, i.e. enthymematic inference, were also shown to be captured via retrieving the implicit premises as lexical information associated with words appearing in the explicit premises. It is our hope that this work will initiate a more active discussion on the need for more fine grained frameworks for formal semantics as well as an active dialogue between people working on lexical networks and type theoretical (or logical in general) semantics from both a theoretical and an implementational point of view.

REFERENCES

Nicholas ASHER (2008), A type driven theory of predication with complex types, *Fundamenta Informaticae*, 84(2):151–183.

Nicholas ASHER (2012), *Lexical Meaning in Context: a Web of Words*, Cambridge University Press.

Christoph BENZMÜLLER, Frank THEISS, and Arnaud FIETZKE (2007), The LEO-II Project, in *Automated Reasoning Workshop*.

Jean-Philippe BERNARDY and Stergios CHATZIKYRIAKIDIS (2017), A Type-Theoretical system for the FraCaS test suite: Grammatical Framework meets Coq, ms, University of Gothenburg.
`http://www.stergioschatzikyriakidis.com/uploads/1/0/3/6/`
`10363759/iwcs_bercha.pdf`.

Ellen BREITHOLTZ (2014), *Enthymemes in Dialogue: A micro-rhetorical approach*, Ph.D. thesis, University of Gothenburg.

Lucas CHAMPOLLION and Manfred KRIFKA (2016), Mereology, in Paul DEKKER and Maria ALONI, editors, *Cambridge Handbook of Semantics*, pp. 369–388, Cambridge University Press.

Stergios CHATZIKYRIAKIDIS and Zhaohui LUO (2012), An Account of Natural Language Coordination in Type Theory with Coercive Subtyping, in Y. PARMENTIER and D. DUCHIER, editors, *proceedings of Constraint Solving and Language Processing (CSLP12). LNCS 8114*, pp. 31–51, Orleans.

Stergios CHATZIKYRIAKIDIS and Zhaohui LUO (2013), Adjectives in a modern type-theoretical setting, in G. MORRILL and J.M NEDERHOF, editors, *Proceedings of Formal Grammar 2013. LNCS 8036*, pp. 159–174.

Stergios CHATZIKYRIAKIDIS and Zhaohui LUO (2014a), Natural Language Inference in Coq, *Journal of Logic, Language and Information.*, 23(4):441–480.

Stergios CHATZIKYRIAKIDIS and Zhaohui LUO (2014b), Natural Language Reasoning Using proof-assistant technology: Rich Typing and beyond, in *Proceedings of the EACL 2014 Workshop on Type Theory and Natural Language Semantics (TTNLS)*, pp. 37–45.

Stergios CHATZIKYRIAKIDIS and Zhaohui LUO (2014c), Using Signatures in Type Theory to Represent Situations, *Logic and Engineering of Natural Language Semantics 11. Tokyo.*

Stergios CHATZIKYRIAKIDIS and Zhaohui LUO (2017a), Adjectival and Adverbial Modification: The View from Modern Type Theories, *Journal of Logic, Language and Information*, 26(1):45–88.

Stergios CHATZIKYRIAKIDIS and Zhaohui LUO (2017b), *On the Interpretation of Common Nouns: Types Versus Predicates*, pp. 43–70, Springer International Publishing.

Alonzo CHURCH (1940), A Formulation of the Simple Theory of Types, *J. Symbolic Logic*, 5(1).

Allan M COLLINS and M Ross QUILLIAN (1969), Retrieval time from semantic memory, *Journal of verbal learning and verbal behavior*, 8(2):240–247.

Robin COOPER, Simon DOBNIK, Shalom LAPPIN, and Staffan LARSSON (2014), A probabilistic rich type theory for semantic interpretation, in *Proceedings of the EACL 2014 Workshop on Type Theory and Natural Language Semantics (TTNLS)*, pp. 72–79.

Coq 2007 (2007), *The Coq Proof Assistant Reference Manual (Version 8.1)*, INRIA, The Coq Development Team.

Christiane FELLBAUM (1998), *WordNet: An Electronic Lexical Database*, MIT press.

Bruno GAUME, Karine DUVIGNAU, and Martine VANHOVE (2007), Semantic associations and confluences in paradigmatic networks, in Martine VANHOVE, editor, *Typologie des rapprochements sémantiques*, p. (on line), John Benjamins Publishing Company.

Peter GEACH (1962), *Reference and Generality: An examination of some Medieval and Modern Theories*, Cornell University Press.

Jean-Yves GIRARD (1971), Une extension de l'interpretation fonctionelle de Gödel à l'analyse et son application à l'élimination des coupures dans et la thèorie des types, *in proceedings of the 2nd Scandinavian Logic Symposium.* North-Holland, Amsterdam, pp. 63–92.

Mathieu LAFOURCADE (2007a), Making people play for Lexical Acquisition., in *SNLP 2007, 7th Symposium on Natural Language Processing. Pattaya, Thailande, 13-15 December 2007.*

Mathieu LAFOURCADE (2007b), Making people play for Lexical Acquisition with the JeuxDeMots prototype, in *SNLP'07: 7th international symposium on natural language processing,* p. 7.

Mathieu LAFOURCADE, Alain JOUBERT, and Nathalie. LE BRUN (2015), *Games with a Purpose (GWAPS),* Focus Series in Cognitive Science and Knowledge Management, Wiley, ISBN 9781848218031.

Henry LIEBERMAN, Dustin SMITH, and Alea TEETERS (2007), Common Consensus: a web-based game for collecting commonsense goals., in *Workshop on Common Sense for Intelligent Interfaces, ACM Conferences for Intelligent User Interfaces (IUI 2007), Honolulu.*

Zhaohui LUO (1994), *Computation and Reasoning: A Type Theory for Computer Science,* Oxford University Press.

Zhaohui LUO (1999), Coercive subtyping, *Journal of Logic and Computation,* 9(1):105–130.

Zhaohui LUO (2010), Type-Theoretical Semantics with Coercive Subtyping, *Semantics and Linguistic Theory 20 (SALT20), Vancouver.*

Zhaohui LUO (2011), Contextual analysis of word meanings in type-theoretical semantics, *Logical Aspects of Computational Linguistics (LACL'2011). LNAI 6736.*

Zhaohui LUO (2012), Common Nouns as Types, in *LACL'2012, LNCS 7351.*

Zhaohui LUO, Sergei SOLOVIEV, and Tao XUE (2012), Coercive subtyping: theory and implementation, *Information and Computation,* 223:18–42.

Andrea MARCHETTI, Maurizio TESCONI, Francesco RONZANO, Marco ROSELLA, and Salvatore MINUTOLI (2007), SemKey: A Semantic Collaborative Tagging System, in *Tagging and Metadata for Social Information Organization Workshop, WWW07.*

Per MARTIN-LÖF (1975), An Intuitionistic Theory of Types: predicative part, in H.ROSE and J.C.SHEPHERDSON, editors, *Logic Colloquium'73.*

Per MARTIN-LÖF (1984), *Intuitionistic Type Theory,* Bibliopolis.

Igor MEL'CUK and Andrei ZHOLKOVSKY (1988), The Explanatory Combinatorial Dictionary, in Martha Walton EVENS, editor, *Relational Models of the Lexicon: Representing Knowledge in Semantic Networks,* pp. 41–74, Cambridge University Press, Cambridge.

Rada MIHALCEA and Timothy CHKLOVSKI (2003), Building sense tagged corpora with volunteer contributions over the Web, in *RANLP*, volume 260 of *Current Issues in Linguistic Theory (CILT)*, pp. 357–366, John Benjamins, Amsterdam/Philadelphia.

George A. MILLER (1995), WordNet: A Lexical Database for English, *Commun. ACM*, 38(11):39–41.

Koji MINESHIMA, Yusuke MIYAO, and Daisuke BEKKI (), Higher-order logical inference with compositional semantics, in *Proceedings of EMNLP15*, pp. 2055–2061.

Richard MONTAGUE (1974), *Formal Philosophy*, Yale University Press, collected papers edited by R. Thomason.

Alain POLGUÈRE (2003), Collocations et fonctions lexicales : pour un modèle d'apprentissage., *Revue Française de Linguistique Appliquée*, E(1):117—133.

Alain POLGUÈRE (2014), From Writing Dictionaries to Weaving Lexical Networks, *International Journal of Lexicography*, 27(4):396—418.

James PUSTEJOVSKY (1995), *The Generative Lexicon*, MIT.

Aarne RANTA (1994), *Type-Theoretical Grammar*, Oxford University Press.

Christian RETORÉ (2014), The Montagovian Generative Lexicon Lambda Ty: a Type Theoretical Framework for Natural Language Semantics, in Ralph MATTHES and Aleksy SCHUBERT, editors, *19th International Conference on Types for Proofs and Programs (TYPES 2013)*, volume 26 of *Leibniz International Proceedings in Informatics (LIPIcs)*, pp. 202–229, Schloss Dagstuhl–Leibniz-Zentrum fuer Informatik, Dagstuhl, Germany, ISBN 978-3-939897-72-9, ISSN 1868-8969, doi:http://dx.doi.org/10.4230/LIPIcs.TYPES.2013.202, http://drops.dagstuhl.de/opus/volltexte/2014/4633.

Franck SAJOUS, Emmanuel NAVARRO, Bruno GAUME, Laurent PRÉVOT, and Yannick CHUDY (2013), Semi-automatic enrichment of crowdsourced synonymy networks: the WISIGOTH system applied to Wiktionary, *Language Resources and Evaluation*, 47(1):63–96.

Katharina SIORPAES and Martin HEPP (2008), Games with a Purpose for the Semantic Web, 23:50–60, ISSN 1541-1672, doi:10.1109/MIS.2008.45, http://ieeexplore.ieee.org/xpl/freeabs_all.jsp?arnumber=4525142.

John SOWA and John ZACHMAN (1992), Extending and Formalizing the Framework for Information Systems Architecture, *IBM Systems Journal*, 31(3):590–616.

Luis VON AHN and Laura DABBISH (2004), Labeling Images with a Computer Game, in *Proceedings of the SIGCHI Conference on Human Factors in Computing Systems*, CHI '04, pp. 319–326, ACM, New York, NY, USA.

Luis VON AHN and Laura DABBISH (2008), Designing games with a purpose, *Commun. ACM*, 51(8):58–67.

Luis VON AHN, Mihir KEDIA, and Manuel BLUM (2006), Verbosity: a game for collecting common-sense facts, in *CHI*, pp. 75–78, ACM.

Manel ZARROUK (2015), *Endogeneous Consolidation of Lexical Semantic Networks*, Theses, Université de Montpellier.

Naomi ZEICHNER, Jonathan BERANT, and Ido DAGAN (2012), Crowdsourcing inference-rule evaluation, in *Proceedings of the 50th Annual Meeting of the Association for Computational Linguistics: Short Papers-Volume 2*, pp. 156–160, Association for Computational Linguistics.

Michael ZOCK and Slaven BILAC (2004), Word lookup on the basis of associations: from an idea to a roadmap., in *Proceedings of the Workshop on Enhancing and Using Electronic Dictionaries, Association for Computational Linguistics.*, pp. 29–35.

Michael ZOCK and Didier SCHWAB (2008), Lexical Access Based on Underspecified Input, in *Proceedings of the Workshop on Cognitive Aspects of the Lexicon*, COGALEX '08, pp. 9–17, Association for Computational Linguistics, Stroudsburg, PA, USA.

4

Static and dynamic vector semantics for lambda calculus models of natural language

Mehrnoosh Sadrzadeh[1] *and Reinhard Muskens*[2]
[1] School of Electronic Engineering and Computer Science,
Queen Mary University of London.
[2] Department of Philosophy, Tilburg University

Keywords: simply typed lambda calculus, vector semantics, composition, context update potential, dynamic logic

ABSTRACT

Vector models of language are based on contextual aspects of language – distributions of words and how they co-occur in text. Truth conditional models focus on logical aspects of language and on how words combine to contribute to these aspects. In the truth conditional approach, there is a focus on the denotations of phrases. In vector models, the degree of co-occurrence of words in context determines how similar their meanings are. The two approaches have complementary virtues. In this paper we combine them and develop a vector semantics for language, based on the typed lambda calculus. We provide two types of vector semantics: a static one using techniques from the truth conditional tradition, and a dynamic one with a form of interpretation inspired by Heim's context change potentials. We show, with examples, how the dynamic model can be applied to entailment between a corpus and a sentence.

1   INTRODUCTION

Vector semantic models, otherwise known as distributional models, are based on the contextual aspects of language, i.e. the company each word keeps, and patterns of use in corpora of documents. Truth conditional models focus on the logical and denotational aspects of language. They typically describe how words can be represented by functions over sets, and how these functions can be composed. Vector semantics and truth conditional models are based on different philosophies: one takes the stance that language is contextual, the other asserts that it is logical. In recent years, there has been much effort to bring these two together. We have models based on a certain type of grammatical representation, e.g. the pregroup model (Coecke *et al.* 2010), the Lambek Calculus model (Coecke *et al.* 2013), and the combinatorial categorial models (Krishnamurthy and Mitchell 2013; Maillard *et al.* 2014). We also have more concrete models that draw inspiration from type theory, but whose major contribution lies in developing concrete ways of constructing linear and multi-linear algebraic counterparts for syntactic types, e.g. matrices and tensors (Grefenstette and Sadrzadeh 2015; Baroni *et al.* 2014), and relational clusters (Lewis and Steedman 2013).

What some of these approaches (Coecke *et al.* 2010; Krishnamurthy and Mitchell 2013; Maillard *et al.* 2014) lack more than others (Baroni *et al.* 2014; Lewis and Steedman 2013) is acknowledgement of the inherent gap between contextual and truth conditional semantics: they closely follow truth theoretic conditions to assign vector representations to (readings of) phrases and sentences.[1] Indeed, it is possible to develop a stand-alone compositional vector semantics along these lines, but this will result in a static semantics. From the perspective of the underlying theory, it will also be quite natural to have a vector semantics work in tandem with a dynamic theory, and let the two modules model different aspects of meaning. Distributional semantics is particularly apt at modelling associative aspects of meaning, while truth-conditional and dynamic forms of semantics are good at modelling the relation of language to reality, and also at modelling entailment. It is quite conceivable that a theory combining the two as separate modules will be simpler than trying to make one of the approaches do things it was never intended for.

In this paper, we first sketch how an approach to semantics, derived in many of its aspects from that pioneered by Montague (1974), can be used to assign vector meanings to linguistic phrases. The theory will be based on simply typed lambda calculus and, as a result, will

---

[1] Below, when we refer to phrases and sentences, strictly speaking, we mean *readings* of phrases and sentences.

be neutral with respect to the linguist's choice of syntax, in the sense that it can be combined with any existing syntax-semantics interface that assumes that the semantics is based on lambdas.[2] Our reason for using lambda calculus is that it directly relates our semantics to higher order logic, and makes standard ways of treating long-distance dependencies and coordination accessible to vector-based semantics. This approach results in a semantics similar to those of the static approaches listed above. The reason for providing it is to show that a lambda calculus model of language can be directly provided with a straightforward vector semantics. As will be seen, abstract lambda terms, which can be used as translations of linguistic expressions, have much in common with the Logical Forms of these expressions, and the lambda binders in them facilitate the treatment of long-distance dependencies. The use of lambda terms also makes standard ways of dealing with coordination accessible to distributional semantics. We provide extensive discussion of this process, and examples where the direct use of lambdas is an improvement on the above-listed static approaches.

The above semantics does not have an explicit notion of context, however. The second contribution of this paper is that, based on the same lambda calculus model of natural language, we develop a dynamic vector interpretation for this type theory, where denotations of sentences are "context change potentials", as introduced by Heim (1983). We show how to assign such a vector interpretation to words, and how these interpretations combine so that the vectors of the sentences containing them change the context, in a dynamic style similar to that proposed by Heim. As context can be interpreted in different ways, we work with two different notions of context in distributional semantics: co-occurrence matrices, and entity-relation graphs,

---

[2] Linguistic trees, for example, can be associated with the abstract lambda terms considered below via type-driven translation (Partee 1986; Klein and Sag 1985; Heim and Kratzer 1998). But other syntactic structures can be provided with them as well. In the framework of Lexical-Functional Grammar, abstract lambda terms can be assigned to f-structures with the help of linear logic acting as 'glue' (Dalrymple *et al.* 1993). In Combinatory Categorial Grammar, derivations can be associated with abstract lambda terms using combinators (Steedman 2000), while proofs in Lambek Categorial Grammar can be provided with them by the Curry-Howard morphism (van Benthem 1986).

encoded here in the form of cubes. Both of these are built from corpora of documents and record co-occurrence between words: in a simple neighbourhood window, in the case of co-occurrence matrices, and in a window structured by grammatical dependencies, in the case of an entity-relation cube. We believe our model is flexible enough for other distributional notions of contexts, such as networks of grammatical dependencies. We show how our approach relates to Heim's original notion of 'files' as contexts. Other dynamic approaches, such as update semantics (Veltman 1996) and continuation-based semantics (de Groote 2006), can also be used; we aim to do this in the future.

Compositional vector semantics is our goal, but the nature of this paper is theoretical. So we shall not propose – from the armchair so to speak – concrete representations of contexts and updates and a set of concrete vector composition operations for combining phrases, or concrete matrices or cubes that embody them. We thus leave exhaustive empirical evaluation of our model to future work, but show, by means of examples, how the notion of "admittance of sentences by contexts" from the context update logic of Heim (1983) and Karttunen (1974) can be applied to develop a relationship between matrix and cube contexts and sentences, and how this notion can be extended from a usual Boolean relation to one which has degrees, based on the notion of degrees of similarity between words. As this notion resembles that of "contextual entailment" between corpora and sentences, we review the current entailment datasets that are mainstream in distributional semantics and discuss how they can or cannot be applied to test this notion, but leave experimental evaluation to future work.

The lambda calculus approach we use is based on Lambda Grammars (Muskens 2001, 2003), which were independently introduced as Abstract Categorial Grammars (ACGs) in de Groote (2001). The theory developed here, however, can be based on any syntax-semantics interface that works with a lambda calculus semantics – our approach is agnostic as to the choice of a syntactic theory.

This paper is the journal version of our previous short paper (Muskens and Sadrzadeh 2016a) and extended abstract (Muskens and Sadrzadeh 2016b).

2   LAMBDA GRAMMARS

Lambda Grammars (Muskens 2001, 2003) were independently introduced as Abstract Categorial Grammars (ACGs, de Groote 2001). An ACG generates two languages, an *abstract* language and an *object* language. The abstract language will simply consist of all linear lambda terms (each lambda binder binds exactly one variable occurrence) over a given vocabulary typed with *abstract types*. The object language has its own vocabulary and its own types. We give some basic definitions here, assuming familiarity with the simply typed λ-calculus.

If $\mathscr{B}$ is some set of basic types, we write $TYP(\mathscr{B})$ for the smallest set containing $\mathscr{B}$ such that $(\alpha\beta) \in TYP(\mathscr{B})$ whenever $\alpha, \beta \in TYP(\mathscr{B})$. Let $\mathscr{B}_1$ and $\mathscr{B}_2$ be sets of basic types. A function η from $TYP(\mathscr{B}_1)$ to $TYP(\mathscr{B}_2)$ is said to be a *type homomorphism* if $\eta(\alpha\beta) = (\eta(\alpha)\eta(\beta))$, for all $\alpha, \beta \in TYP(\mathscr{B}_1)$. It is clear that a type homomorphism η with domain $TYP(\mathscr{B})$ is completely determined by the values of η for types $\alpha \in \mathscr{B}$.

Let us look at an example of a type homomorphism that can be used to provide a language fragment with a classical Montague-like meaning. Let $\mathscr{B}_1 = \{D, N, S\}$ (D stands for determiner phrases, N for nominal phrases, S for sentences), let $\mathscr{B}_2 = \{e, s, t\}$ (e is for entities, s for worlds, and t for truth-values), and let h_0 be defined by: $h_0(D) = e$, $h_0(N) = est$,[3] and $h_0(S) = st$. Then the types in the second column of Table 1 have images under h_0 as given in the fourth column. Additional information about the conventions used in Table 1 is given in a footnote.[4]

We now define the notion of *term homomorphism*. If C is some set of typed constants, we write $\Lambda(C)$ for the set of all lambda terms with constants only from C. The set of *linear* lambda terms over C is denoted by $\Lambda_0(C)$. Let C_1 be a set of constants typed by types from $TYP(\mathscr{B}_1)$ and let C_2 be a set of constants typed by types from $TYP(\mathscr{B}_2)$. A function $\vartheta : \Lambda(C_1) \to \Lambda(C_2)$ is a *term homomorphism based on* η if $\eta : TYP(\mathscr{B}_1) \to TYP(\mathscr{B}_2)$ is a type homomorphism and, whenever $M \in \Lambda(C_1)$:

---

[3] Association in types is to the right and outer parentheses are omitted; so *est* is short for $(e(st))$, arguably a good type for *predicates*.

[4] In Table 1, p is a variable of type st, while x is of type e. The variables w and w' are of type s, and P and P' are of type est. The constant K of type ess denotes the epistemic accessibility relation.

Table 1: An Abstract Categorial Grammar / Lambda Grammar connecting abstract terms with Montague-like meanings

constant c	type τ	$H_0(c)$	$h_0(\tau)$
woman	N	*woman*	est
man	N	*man*	est
tall	NN	*tall*	$(est)est$
smokes	DS	*smoke*	est
loves	DDS	*love*	$eest$
knows	SDS	$\lambda p\lambda x\lambda w.\forall w'(Kxww' \to pw')$	$(st)est$
every	$N(DS)S$	$\lambda P'\lambda P\lambda w.\forall x(P'xw \to Pxw)$	$(est)(est)st$
a	$N(DS)S$	$\lambda P'\lambda P\lambda w.\exists x(P'xw \wedge Pxw)$	$(est)(est)st$

- $\vartheta(M)$ is a term of type $\eta(\tau)$, if M is a constant of type τ;
- $\vartheta(M)$ is the n-th variable of type $\eta(\tau)$, if M is the n-th variable of type τ;
- $\vartheta(M) = (\vartheta(A)\vartheta(B))$, if $M \equiv (AB)$;
- $\vartheta(M) = \lambda y.\vartheta(A)$, where $y = \vartheta(x)$, if $M \equiv (\lambda x.A)$.

Note that this implies that $\vartheta(M)$ is a term of type $\eta(\tau)$, if M is of type τ.

Clearly, a term homomorphism ϑ with domain $\Lambda(C)$ is completely determined by the values $\vartheta(c)$ for $c \in C$. This continues to hold if we restrict the domain to the set of linear lambda terms $\Lambda_0(C)$. In order to show how this mechanism can be used, let us continue with the same example. Consider the (abstract) constants in the first column of Table 1, typed by the (abstract) types in the second column. We can now define a term homomorphism H_0 by sending the constants in the first column to their images in the third column, making sure that these have types as in the fourth column. Since H_0 is assumed to be a type homomorphism, *all* lambda terms over the constants in the first column will now automatically have images under H_0. For example, H_0 sends the abstract term:[5]

$$((a\ woman)\lambda\xi((every\ man)(loves\ \xi)))$$

---

[5] We use the standard notation of lambda terms. The application of M to N is written as (MN) (not as $M(N)$) and lambda abstractions are of the form $(\lambda X.A)$. The usual redundancy rules for parentheses apply, but will often not be used in abstract terms, in order to emphasise their closeness to linguistic expressions. In some cases, to improve clarity, we will bend the rules and write $M(N_1,\ldots,N_n)$ for $(MN_1\ldots N_n)$ or $A \wedge B$ for $\wedge AB$, for example.

(in which ξ is of type D), to a term $\beta\eta$-equivalent with:

$$\lambda w \exists y (woman\, y w \wedge \forall x (man\, xw \rightarrow love\, yxw)) \,.$$

This term denotes the set of worlds in which some specific woman is loved by all men.

This example sends abstract terms to translations that are close to those of Montague (1974). While such translations obviously will not serve as *vector* semantics, we will show in the next sections that it is possible to alter the object language while retaining the general translation mechanism. For more information about the procedure of obtaining an object language from an abstract language, see de Groote (2001) and Muskens (2003, 2010).

3   A STATIC VECTOR SEMANTICS

3.1   *Vector interpretations for the object language*

In order to provide an interpretation of our object language, the type theory used must be able to talk about vectors over some field, for which we choose the reals. We need a basic object type R such that, in all interpretations under consideration, the domain D_R of type R is equal to or 'close enough' to the set of reals $\mathbb{R}$, so that constants such as the following (of the types shown) have their usual interpretation:[6]

$$
\begin{array}{ccc}
0 & : & R \\
1 & : & R \\
+ & : & RRR \\
\cdot & : & RRR \\
< & : & RRt
\end{array}
$$

This can be done by imposing one of the sets of second-order axioms in Tarski (1965). Given these axioms, we have $D_R = \mathbb{R}$ in full models, whereas we have non-standard models under the Henkin interpretation (Henkin 1950).

Vectors can now be introduced as objects of type IR, where I is interpreted as some finite index set. Think of I as a set of words; if

---

[6] Constants such as $+$, $\cdot$, and $<$ will be written between their arguments.

Table 2: Vector types and their abbreviations

Type	Math Abbreviation	Letter Abbreviation	Description
IR	(I^1R)	V	Vector
IIR	I^2R	M	Matrix
$IIIR$	I^3R	C	Cube
$\vdots$	$\vdots$		

a word is associated with a vector $v : IR$, v assigns a real number to each word, which gives information about the company the word keeps. Since IR will be used often, we will abbreviate it as V. Similarly, IIR, abbreviated as M, can be associated with the type of *matrices*, and $IIIR$, abbreviated as C, with the type of *cubes*, and so on (see Table 2). In this paper, we work with a single index type, but one may also consider cases with several index types, so that phrases of distinct categories can live in their own space.

We need a toolkit of functions combining vectors, matrices, cubes, etc. In the following definitions, r is of type R; i, j, and k are of type I; v and u are of type V; m and c are of types M and C respectively; and indices are written as subscripts, so v_i is syntactic sugar for vi.

$$* := \lambda rvi.r \cdot v_i : RVV$$

$$\boxplus := \lambda vui.v_i + u_i : VVV$$

$$\odot := \lambda vui.v_i \cdot u_i : VVV$$

$$\times_1 := \lambda mvi. \sum_j m_{ij} \cdot v_j : MVV$$

$$\times_2 := \lambda cvij. \sum_k m_{ijk} \cdot v_k : CVM$$

$$\langle \cdot \mid \cdot \rangle := \lambda uv. \sum_i u_i + v_i : VVR$$

The reader will recognise $*$ as scalar product, $\boxplus$ as pointwise addition, $\odot$ as pointwise multiplication, $\times_1$ and $\times_2$ as matrix-vector and cube-vector multiplication, and $\langle \cdot \mid \cdot \rangle$ as the dot product. One can also consider further operations, such as various *rotation* operations with type $\rho : VVV$.

3.2   *Abstract types and type and term homomorphisms*

Let us assume again that our basic abstract types are D for determiner phrases, S for sentences, and N for nominal phrases. But this time our type and term homomorphisms will be chosen in a different way from that used in Section 2. A very simple type homomorphism h can be defined by:

$$h(D) = h(S) = h(N) = V \ .$$

So h assigns vectors to determiners, nominal phrases, and sentences. There are other possibilities for the range of h and, in the following section, we will sketch a more elaborate assignment in which a running context is used. The above simple h is chosen for the expository purposes of this section.

In Table 3, we again provide abstract constants in the first column and their abstract types in the second column; h assigns to these the object types in the fourth column. Here, Z is a variable of type VV, and v and u are of type V. As an example, consider the constant woman; it has the abstract type N, and a term homomorphic image woman, which is assigned the type V by h. We say that the translation of woman is of type V. Similarly, the translations of tall and smoke are of type VV, love and know are of type VVV, and those of every and a are of type VV. The term homomorphism H is defined by letting its value for any abstract constant in the first column be the corresponding object term in the third column. Using this table, we automatically obtain homomorphic images of any lambda term over the constants. But now our previous example term:[7]

$$((\text{a woman})\lambda\xi((\text{every man})(\text{loves } \xi)))$$

is sent to a term that is $\beta\eta$ equivalent with:

$$(\text{love} \times_2 (\text{a} \times_1 \text{woman})) \times_1 (\text{every} \times_1 \text{man}) \ .$$

In Table 3, nominal phrases like woman are represented by vectors, adjectives and intransitive verbs like tall and smoke by matrices, and transitive verbs (love) by cubes, as are constants like know. Generalised quantifiers are functions that take vectors to vectors. The composition operations used ($\times_1$ and $\times_2$) are cube-vector and matrix-vector instances of tensor contraction. There is still much debate as to

---

[7] The entry for man is no longer present in Table 3. But man can be treated in full analogy to woman. In further examples we will also use constants whose entries can easily be guessed.

Table 3: A fragment of static vector semantics. Abstract constants c are typed with abstract types τ and their term homomorphic images $H(c)$ typed by $h(\tau)$

c	τ	$H(c)$	$h(\tau)$
woman	N	woman	V
tall	NN	$\lambda v.(\text{tall} \times_1 v)$	VV
smokes	DS	$\lambda v.(\text{smoke} \times_1 v)$	VV
loves	DDS	$\lambda uv.(\text{love} \times_2 u) \times_1 v$	VVV
knows	SDS	$\lambda uv.(\text{know} \times_2 u) \times_1 v$	VVV
every	$N(DS)S$	$\lambda vZ.Z(\text{every} \times_1 v)$	$V(VV)V$
a	$N(DS)S$	$\lambda vZ.Z(\text{a} \times_1 v)$	$V(VV)V$

Table 4: Term homomorphic images $H(c)$ for pointwise addition and multiplication, and matrix multiplication as composition operations

Addition	Multiplication	Matrix Multiplication
$H(c)$	$H(c)$	$H(c)$
woman	woman	woman
$\lambda v.(\text{tall} \boxplus v)$	$\lambda v.(\text{tall} \odot v)$	$\lambda v.(\text{tall} \times_1 v)$
$\lambda v.(\text{smoke} \boxplus v)$	$\lambda v.(\text{smoke} \odot v)$	$\lambda v.(\text{smoke} \times_1 v)$
$\lambda uv.(\text{love} \boxplus u) \boxplus v$	$\lambda uv.(\text{love} \odot u) \odot v$	$\lambda uv.(\text{love} \times_2 u) \times_1 v$
$\lambda uv.(\text{know} \boxplus u) \boxplus v$	$\lambda uv.(\text{know} \odot u) \odot v$	$\lambda uv.(\text{know} \times_2 u) \times_1 v$
$\lambda vZ.Z(\text{every} \boxplus v)$	$\lambda vZ.Z(\text{every} \odot v)$	$\lambda vZ.Z(\text{every} \times_1 v)$
$\lambda vZ.Z(\text{a} \boxplus v)$	$\lambda vZ.Z(\text{a} \odot v)$	$\lambda vZ.Z(\text{a} \times_1 v)$

the best operations for composing vectors. Mitchell and Lapata (2010) consider pointwise addition and multiplication of vectors, while matrix multiplication is used in Baroni and Zamparelli (2010). Such operations are available to our theory. The table for these will have a different $H(c)$ column and will be the same in all other columns. The $H(c)$ columns for these models are given in Table 4.[8]

In this paper, we will not choose between these operations. Instead, we will explore how to combine such functions once an initial set has been established (and validated empirically). Functions in the initial set will typically combine vector meanings of adjacent phrases. Like Baroni *et al.* (2014), who provide an excellent introduction to and review of compositional vector semantics, our aim has been to pro-

---

[8] In Table 4, we use the same typographical conventions for variables as in Table 3, while, in its first two alternative columns, all constants written in sans serif are taken to be of type V. In its third column, the types of these constants (and in fact the whole column) are as in Table 3 again.

pose a general theory that also includes dependencies between non-adjacent phrases, e.g., in topicalisation or relative clause formation.

4   DYNAMIC VECTOR SEMANTICS
WITH CONTEXT CHANGE POTENTIALS

4.1   *Heim's files and distributional contexts*

Heim describes her contexts as files that have some kind of information written on (or in) them. Context changes are operations that update these files, e.g. by adding or deleting information from the files. Formally, a context is taken to be a set of sequence-world pairs in which the sequences come from some domain $\mathcal{D}_I$ of individuals, as follows:

$$ctx \subseteq \{(g,w) \mid g : \mathbb{N} \to \mathcal{D}_I, w \text{ a possible world}\}$$

We follow Heim (1983) here in letting the sequences in her sequence-world-pairs be infinite, although they are best thought of as finite.

Sentence meanings are *context change potentials* (CCPs) in Heim's work, functions from contexts to contexts – given any context, a sentence will transform it into a new context. In particular, a sentence S comes provided with a sequence of instructions that, given any context *ctx*, updates its information so that a new context results, denoted as:

$$ctx + S$$

The sequence of instructions that brings about this update is derived compositionally from the constituents of S.

In distributional semantics, contexts are words somehow related to each other via their patterns of use, e.g. by co-occurring in a neighbourhood word window of a fixed size, or via a dependency relation. In practice, one builds a context matrix M over $\mathbb{R}^2$, with rows and columns labelled by words from a vocabulary Σ, and with entries taking values from $\mathbb{R}$ (for a full description see Rubenstein and Goodenough 1965). Thus, M can be seen as the set of its vectors:

$$\{\overrightarrow{v} \mid \overrightarrow{v} : \Sigma \to \mathbb{R}\} \, ,$$

where each $\overrightarrow{v}$ is a row or column in M.

If we take Heim's domain of individuals $\mathscr{D}_I$ to be the vocabulary of a distributional model of meaning, that is $\mathscr{D}_I := \Sigma$, then a context matrix can be seen as a *quantized* version of a Heim context:

$$\{(\overrightarrow{g}, w) \mid \overrightarrow{g} : \Sigma \to \mathbb{R}, w \text{ a possible world}\} .$$

Thus a distributional context matrix is obtainable by endowing Heim's contexts with $\mathbb{R}$. In other words, we are assuming not only that a file has a set of individuals, but also that these individuals take some kind of values, e.g. from reals.

The role of possible worlds in distributional semantics is arguable, as vectors retrieved from a corpus are not naturally truth conditional. Keeping the possible worlds in the picture provides a mechanism to assign a proposition to a distributional vector by other means and can become very useful. We leave working with possible worlds to future studies and in this paper only work with sets of vectors as our contexts, as follows:

$$ctx \subseteq \{\overrightarrow{g} \mid \overrightarrow{g} : \Sigma \to \mathbb{R}, g \in M\} .$$

Distributional versions of CCPs can be defined based on Heim's intuitions and definitions. In what follows, we show how these instructions let contexts thread through vectorial semantics in a compositional manner.

4.2 *Dynamic type and term homomorphisms and their interpretations*

On the set of basic abstract types D, S, N, a *dynamic* type homomorphism ρ that takes into account the contexts of words is defined as follows:

$$\rho(N) = (VU)U, \quad \rho(D) = V, \quad \rho(S) = U .$$

Here, sentences are treated as *context change potentials*. They update contexts, and we therefore assign the type U (for 'update') to them. A context can be a matrix or a cube, so it can be of type I^2R or I^3R. A sentence can then be of type $(I^2R)(I^2R)$ or $(I^3R)(I^3R)$. We have previously abbreviated IR to V, I^2R to M, and I^3R to C. The sentence type then becomes MM or CC. The notation U can abbreviate either, depending on whether we choose to model contexts as cubes or as matrices. The concrete semantics obtained by each choice will be discussed in more detail in Section 5 and Section 6, respectively.

Update functions are presented in Table 5, where ρ is a type homomorphism, i.e. $\rho(AB) = \rho(A)\rho(B)$. Here, Z is a variable of type VU, Q is of type $(VU)U$, v of type V, c of type M, and p and q are of type U. The functions F, G, I, and J are explained in the following paragraphs. In the schematic entry for and, we write $\rho(\overline{\alpha})$ for $\rho(\alpha_1)\cdots\rho(\alpha_n)$, if $\overline{\alpha} = \alpha_1\cdots\alpha_n$. Simple words such as names, nouns, adjectives, and verbs are first assigned vectors, denoted by constants such as anna, woman, tall, and smoke (all of type V). These are then used by the typed lambda calculus given via $H(a)$, in the third column, to build certain functions, which will act as the meanings of these words in context. The object types assigned by ρ are as follows:

Type of nouns	:	$(VU)U$
Type of adjectives	:	$((VU)U)(VU)U$
Type of intransitive verbs	:	VU
Type of transitive verbs	:	VVU

The function Z updates the context of proper names and nouns based on their vectors e.g. anna and woman. These are essentially treated as vectors of type V, but, since they must be made capable of dynamic behaviour, they are 'lifted' to the higher type $(VU)U$.

The function F of an adjective takes a vector for the adjective, e.g. tall, a vector for its argument, e.g. v, and a vector for its context, e.g. c, then updates the context, e.g. as in $F(\text{tall}, v, c)$. The output of this function is then lifted to the higher type, i.e. $((VU)U)((VU)U)$, via the functions Z and Q, respectively.

Table 5: A fragment of dynamic vector semantics. Abstract constants a typed with abstract types τ and their term homomorphic images $H(a)$ typed by $\rho(\tau)$

a	τ	$H(a)$	$\rho(\tau)$
Anna	$(DS)S$	$\lambda Z.Z(\text{anna})$	$(VU)U$
woman	N	$\lambda Z.Z(\text{woman})$	$(VU)U$
tall	NN	$\lambda QZ.Q(\lambda vc.ZvF(\text{tall}, v, c))$	$((VU)U)(VU)U$
smokes	DS	$\lambda vc.G(\text{smoke}, v, c)$	VU
loves	DDS	$\lambda uvc.I(\text{love}, u, v, c)$	VVU
knows	SDS	$\lambda pvc.pJ(\text{know}, v, c)$	UVU
every	$N(DS)S$	$\lambda Q.Q$	$((VU)U)(VU)U$
who	$(DS)NN$	$\lambda Z'QZ.Q(\lambda vc.Zv(QZ'c))$	$(VU)((VU)U)(VU)U$
and	$(\overline{\alpha}S)(\overline{\alpha}S)(\overline{\alpha}S)$	$\lambda R'\lambda R\lambda\overline{X}\lambda c.R'\overline{X}(R\overline{X}c)$	$(\rho(\overline{\alpha})U)(\rho(\overline{\alpha})U)(\rho(\overline{\alpha})U)$

Functions G and I update contexts of verbs; they take a vector for the verb as well as a vector for each of its arguments, plus an input context, and then return a context as their output. So, the function G takes a vector for an intransitive verb, e.g. smoke, a vector v for its subject, plus a context c, and returns a modified context $G(\text{smoke}, v, c)$. The function I takes a vector for a transitive verb, a vector for its subject, a vector for its object, and a context, and returns a context.

The meanings of function words, such as conjunctions, relative pronouns, and quantifiers, will not (necessarily) be identified with vectors. The type of the quantifier *every* is $((VU)U)(VU)U$, where its noun argument has the required 'quantifier' type $(VU)U$. The lambda calculus entry for 'every', $\lambda Q.Q$, is the identity function; it takes a Q and then spits it out again. The alternative would be to have an entry similar to that of 'tall', but this would not make much sense. Content words, and not function words, seem to be important in a distributional setting.

The word *and* is treated as a generalised form of function composition. Its entry is schematic, as *and* does not only conjoin sentences, but also other phrases of any category. So the type of the abstract constant connected with the word is $(\overline{\alpha}S)(\overline{\alpha}S)(\overline{\alpha}S)$, in which $\overline{\alpha}$ can be any sequence of abstract types. Ignoring this generalisation for the moment, we obtain SSS as the abstract type for sentence conjunction, with a corresponding object type UUU, and meaning $\lambda pqc.p(qc)$, which is just function composition. This is defined such that the context updated by *and*'s left argument will be further updated by its right argument. So 'Sally smokes and John eats bananas' will, given an initial context c, first update c to $G(\text{Sally}, \text{smoke}, c)$, which is a context, and then update further with 'John eats bananas' to $I(\text{eat}, \text{John}, \text{bananas}, G(\text{smoke}, \text{Sally}, c))$. This treatment of *and* is easily extended to coordination in all categories. For example, the reader may check that and admires loves (which corresponds to *loves and admires*) has $\lambda uvc.I(\text{admire}, u, v, I(\text{love}, u, v, c))$ as its homomorphic image.

The update instructions pass through phrases and sentences compositionally. The sentence *every tall woman smokes*, for example, will be associated with the following lambda expression:

```
(((every (tall woman)) smokes))
```

This in its turn has a term homomorphic image that is β-equivalent with the following:

$$\lambda c.G(\text{smoke}, \text{woman}, F(\text{tall}, \text{woman}, c))$$

which describes a distributional context update for it. This term describes an initial update of the context c according to the rule for the constant `tall`, and then a second update according to the rule for the constant `smokes`. As a result of these, the value entries at the crossings of $\langle$tall, woman$\rangle$ and $\langle$woman, smokes$\rangle$ are increased. Much longer chains of context updates can be 'threaded' in this way.

In the following, we give some examples. In each case, sentence a is followed by an abstract term in b, thus capturing its syntactic structure. The update potential that follows in c is the homomorphic image of this abstract term.

(1) a. Sue loves and admires a stockbroker.

      b. `(a stockbroker)`$\lambda\xi$`.Sue(and admires loves `ξ`)`

      c. $\lambda c.I(\text{admire}, \text{stockbroker}, \text{sue}, I(\text{love}, \text{stockbroker}, \text{sue}, c))$

(2) a. Bill admires but Anna despises every cop.

      b. `(every cop)`
                      `(`$\lambda\xi$`.and(Anna(despise `ξ`))(Bill(admire `ξ`)))`

      c. $\lambda c.I(\text{despise}, \text{cop}, \text{anna}, I(\text{admire}, \text{cop}, \text{bill}, c))$

(3) a. The witch who Bill claims Anna saw disappeared.

      b. `the(who(`$\lambda\xi$`.Bill(claims(Anna(saw `ξ`)))))witch)`
                                     `disappears`

      c. $\lambda c.G(\text{disappear}, \text{witch}, I(\text{see}, \text{witch}, \text{anna}, J(\text{claim}, \text{bill}, c)))$

5   CO-OCCURENCE MATRIX CONTEXT AND ITS UPDATE

In this section, we assume that our contexts are the co-occurrence matrices of distributional semantics (Rubenstein and Goodenough 1965). Given a corpus of texts, a co-occurrence matrix has, for each of its entries, the degree of co-occurrence between that word and neighbouring words. The neighbourhood is usually a window of k words on either side of the word. The update type U associated with sentences will thus take the form $(I^2R)(I^2R)$, abbreviated to MM. That is, a sentence will take a co-occurrence matrix as input, update it with new entries, and return the updated matrix as output.

Since we are working with co-occurrence matrices, the updates simply increase the degrees of co-occurrence between the labelling words of the rows and columns of the matrix. In this paper, to keep things simple, we work on a co-occurrence matrix with raw co-occurrence numbers as entries. In this case, the update functions just add 1 to each entry at each update step. This may be extended to (or replaced with) logarithmic probabilistic entries, such as Pointwise Mutual Information (PMI) or its positive or smoothed version PPMI, PPMI_α, in which case the update functions have to recalculate these weighting schemes at each step (for an example, see Table 6). The cells whose entries are increased are chosen according to the grammatical roles of the labelling words. These are implemented in the functions F, G, I, J, which apply the updates to each word in the sentence. Updates are compositional, i.e. they can be applied compositionally to the words within a sentence. This is evident as the updates induced by words in a sentence are based on the grammatical roles of those words, which act as glue.

More formally, the object terms corresponding to a word a update a context matrix c with the information in a and the information in the vectors of arguments $u, v, \cdots$ of a. The result is a new context matrix c', with different entry values, depicted below:

$$
\begin{pmatrix}
m_{11} & \cdots & m_{1k} \\
m_{21} & \cdots & m_{2k} \\
\vdots & & \\
m_{n1} & \cdots & m_{nk}
\end{pmatrix}
+ \langle a, u, v, \cdots \rangle =
\begin{pmatrix}
m'_{11} & \cdots & m'_{1k} \\
m'_{21} & \cdots & m'_{2k} \\
\vdots & & \\
m'_{n1} & \cdots & m'_{nk}
\end{pmatrix}
$$

The m_{ij} and m'_{ij} entries are described as follows:

- The function $G(\text{smoke}, v, c)$ increases the entry value of m_{ij} in c by 1 in case i is the index of smoke and j is the index of its subject v. In all other cases $m'_{ij} = m_{ij}$.
- The function $I(\text{love}, u, v, c)$ increases the entry values of m_{ij}, m_{jk}, and m_{ik} in c by 1 in case i is the index of loves, j is the index of its subject u, and k the index of its object v. In all other cases $m'_{ij} = m_{ij}$.

- The function $F(\text{tall}, v, c)$ increases the entry value of m_{ij} in c by 1 in case i is the index of tall and j is the index of its modified noun v. In all other cases $m'_{ij} = m_{ij}$. The entry for *tall* in Table 1 uses this function, but allows for further update of context.

- The function $J(\text{know}, v, c)$ increases the entry value of m_{ij} in c by 1 in case i is the index of know and j is the index of its subject v. In all other cases $m'_{ij} = m_{ij}$. The updated matrix becomes the input for further update (by the context change potential of the sentence that is known).

As an example, consider the co-occurrence matrices depicted in Figure 1. The initial matrix is a snapshot just before a series of updates are applied. The rationale of this example is as follows: Anna is a woman and so this word is not frequently found in the context man; as a result, it has a low value of 100 at that entry; Anna loves cats (and has some herself), so the entry at the context cat is 700; she loves other things, such as smoking, and so there is a substantial

		1 man	2 cat	3 loves	4 fears	5 sleeps
1	Anna	100	700	800	500	400
2	woman	500	650	750	750	600
3	tall	300	50	500	400	400
4	smokes	400	50	600	600	200
5	loves	350	250	ϵ	600	500
6	knows	300	50	200	250	270

a series of updates by
$$\Longrightarrow$$
$F, G, I,$ and J

		1 man	2 cat	3 loves	4 fears	5 sleeps
1	Anna	100	700	800	500	400
2	woman	500	650	750	750	600
3	tall	650	50	500	400	400
4	smokes	700	50	600	600	200
5	loves	550	750	ϵ	600	500
6	knows	600	250	450	510	700

Figure 1: An example of updates by functions F, G, I, J on a co-occurrence matrix

entry at the context loves; and so on. The entries of the other words, i.e. tall, smokes, loves, knows, are also initialised to their distributional co-occurrence matrix vectors. When an entry c_{ij} corresponds to the same two words, e.g. when i and j are both love, as in the initial matrix in Figure 1, we use ϵ to indicate a predefined fixed value.

The intransitive verb smokes updates the initial matrix in Figure 1, via the function G at the entries c_{4j}. Here, in principle, j can be 1 and 2, as both man and cat, in their singular or plural forms, could have occurred as subjects of smokes in the corpus. Assuming that cats do not smoke and that a reasonable number of men do, a series of, for instance, 300 occurrences of smokes with the subject man, updates this entry and raises its value from 400 to 700. Similarly, the adjective tall updates the entries of the c_{3j} cells of the matrix via the function F, where j can in principle be 1 and 2, but since cats are not usually tall, it only updates c_{31}. Again, a series of, for example, 350 occurrences of the adjective tall as the modifier of man would raise this number from 300 to 650. The case for loves and function I is similar. For knows, men know cats love mice, and love to play and be stroked, etc.; they know that cats fear water and objects such as vacuum cleaners, and that they sleep a lot. As a result, the values of all of the entries in row 6, that is $c_{61}, c_{62}, c_{63}, c_{64}$ and c_{65}, will be updated by function J, for instance, to the values in the updated matrix.

6   ENTITY RELATION CUBE CONTEXT AND ITS UPDATE

A corpus of texts can be seen as a sequence of lexical items occurring in the vicinity of each other, and can thus be transformed into a co-occurrence matrix. It can also be seen as a sequence of entities

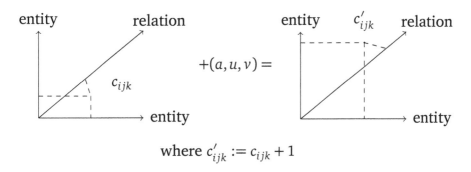

Figure 2: Updates of entries in an entity relation cube

related to each other via predicate-argument structures, which can therefore be transformed into an entity relation graph. This can be modelled in our setting by taking the contexts to be cubes, thus setting S to have the update type $U = (I^3R)(I^3R)$, abbreviated to CC. The entity relation graph approach needs a more costly preprocessing of the corpus, but it is useful for a systematic treatment of logical words such as negation and quantification, as well as coordination.

An entity relation graph can be derived from a variety of resources: a semantic network of concepts, a knowledge base such as WordNet or FrameNet. We work with entities and relations extracted from text. Creating such graphs from text corpora automatically has been the subject of much recent research (see, for example, Yao *et al.* 2012, and Riedel *et al.* 2010, for a direct approach; see also Kambhatla 2004, and Poon and Domingos 2009, for an approach based on semantic parsing). The elements of an entity relation graph are argument-relation-argument triples, sometimes referred to as *relation paths* (Yao *et al.* 2012). Similarly to Lewis and Steedman (2013), we position ourselves in a binary version of the world, where all relations are binary; we turn unary relations into binary ones using the is-a predicate.

Similar to the matrix case, the object terms corresponding to a constant a update a context cube c with the information in a and the information in the vectors of arguments of a. The result is a new context cube c', with entry values greater than or equal to the originals, as depicted in Figure 2.

The c_{ijk} and c'_{ijk} entries are similar to those in the matrix case, for example:

- The function $G(\text{smoke}, v, c)$ increases the entry value c_{ijk} of c in case i is the fixed index of is-a, j is the index of smoker, and k is the index of v, the subject of smoke. Other entry values remain unchanged.

- The function $F(\text{tall}, v, c)$ increases the entry value c_{ijk} of c in case i is the fixed index of is, j is the index of tall, and k is the index of v, the modified noun. Other entry values remain unchanged.

- The function denoted $I(\text{love}, u, v, c)$ increases the entry value c_{ijk} of c in case i is the index of love, j is the index of its subject u, and k is the index of its object v. Other entry values remain unchanged.

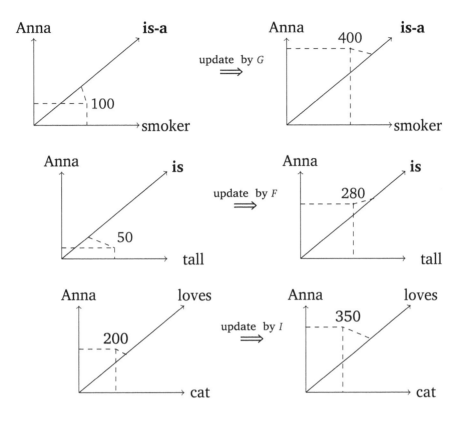

Figure 3: An example of updates by functions F, G, I on an entity-relation cube

As an example, consider the series of updates depicted in Figure 3. Relative pronouns such as *who* update the entry corresponding to the head of the relative clause and the rest of the clause. For example, in the clause 'the man who went home', we update c_{ijk} for i the index of 'man' as subject of the verb 'went' with index j and its object 'home' with index k (see also Section 4, example (3)). Propositional attitudes such as 'know' update the entry value of c_{ijk} for i the index of their subject, j the index of themselves, and k the index of their proposition. For instance, in the sentence 'John knows Mary slept', we update the entry value for 'John', 'know' and the proposition 'Mary slept'. The conjunctive *and* is modelled as before (in Section 4, compare examples (1) and (2)).

Negation can be modelled by providing an abstract term *not* of type SS with a term homomorphic image $\lambda pc.c \dot{-} pc$ of type UU, where $\dot{-}$ is pointwise subtraction of cubes (i.e. $\lambda cc'ijk.cijk - c'ijk$). The operation denoted by this term first updates the context with the non-negated sentence, after which the result is subtracted from the context again.

7   LOGIC FOR CONTEXT CHANGE POTENTIALS

The logic for sentences as context change potentials has the following syntax.

$$\phi ::= p \mid \neg\phi \mid \phi \wedge \psi$$

Disjunction and implication operations are defined using the De Morgan duality.

$$
\begin{aligned}
\phi \vee \psi &:= \quad \neg(\neg\phi \wedge \neg\psi) \\
\phi \rightarrow \psi &:= \quad \neg\phi \vee \psi
\end{aligned}
$$

This logic is the propositional fragment of the logic of context change potentials, presented in Muskens *et al.* (1997), based on the ideas of Heim (1983). Heim extends Karttunen's theory of presuppositions (Karttunen 1974) and defines the context change potential of a sentence as a function of the context change potentials of its parts, an idea that leads to the development of the above logic. The logic we consider here is the same logic but without the presupposition operation.

We refer to the language of this logic as $\mathscr{L}_{ccp}$. For a context c, a context change potential is defined as follows.

$$
\begin{aligned}
\|p\|(c) &:= \quad c + \|p\| \\
\|\neg\phi\|(c) &:= \quad c - \|\phi\|(c) \\
\|\phi \wedge \psi\| &:= \quad \|\psi\|(\|\phi\|(c))
\end{aligned}
$$

It is easy to verify that:

$$
\begin{aligned}
\|\phi \vee \psi\| &= \quad \|\psi\|(c) - \|\psi\|(\|\phi\|(c)) \\
\|\phi \rightarrow \psi\|(c) &= \quad c - (\|\phi\|(c) - \|\psi\|(\|\phi\|(c))) \,.
\end{aligned}
$$

Here, $\|\phi\|$ is the context change potential of ϕ and a function from contexts to contexts. Whereas, for Heim, both contexts and context change potentials of atomic sentences $\|p\|$ are sets of valuations, for us, contexts are co-occurrence matrices or entity relation cubes, and context change potentials of atomic sentences are vectors. Thus, where the context change potential operation (Heim 1983) simply takes the intersection of a context and a context change potential $c \cap \|p\|$, we perform an operation that acts on matrices/cubes rather than sets. We use the update operation of term homomorphisms, defined in the previous sections, and define a context change potential as follows.

Definition 1. *For S a sentence in $\mathcal{L}_{ccp}$, $\|S\|$ its context change potential, $H(S)$ the term homomorphic image of S, and c a co-occurrence matrix or an entity relation cube, we define:*

$$\|S\|(c) \quad := \quad c +' H(S)$$
$$c - H(S) \quad := \quad (c +' H(S))^{-1} \, ,$$

for $+'$ the update operation defined on term homomorphisms and $-'$ its inverse, defined as follows for matrices.

$$\begin{pmatrix} m_{11} & \cdots & m_{1k} \\ m_{21} & \cdots & m_{2k} \\ \vdots & & \\ m_{n1} & \cdots & m_{nk} \end{pmatrix} +' \langle a, u, v, \cdots \rangle = \begin{pmatrix} m'_{11} & \cdots & m'_{1k} \\ m'_{21} & \cdots & m'_{2k} \\ \vdots & & \\ m'_{n1} & \cdots & m'_{nk} \end{pmatrix}$$

$$\text{for} \quad m'_{ij} := \begin{cases} 1 & m_{ij} = 1 \\ 1 & m_{ij} = 0 \end{cases}$$

$$\begin{pmatrix} m_{11} & \cdots & m_{1k} \\ m_{21} & \cdots & m_{2k} \\ \vdots & & \\ m_{n1} & \cdots & m_{nk} \end{pmatrix} -' \langle a, u, v, \cdots \rangle = \begin{pmatrix} m'_{11} & \cdots & m'_{1k} \\ m'_{21} & \cdots & m'_{2k} \\ \vdots & & \\ m'_{n1} & \cdots & m'_{nk} \end{pmatrix}$$

$$\text{for} \quad m'_{ij} := \begin{cases} 0 & m_{ij} = 1 \\ 0 & m_{ij} = 0 \end{cases}$$

The definitions of $+'$ and $-'$ for cubes are similar.

The $+'$ operation updates the co-occurrence matrix in a binary fashion: if the entry m_{ij} of the matrix has already been updated and thus has value 1, then a succeeding update will not increase the value from 1 to 2 but will keep it as 1. Conversely, when the $-'$ operation acts on an entry m_{ij} which is already 0, it will not change its value, but if it acts on a non-zero m_{ij}, that is an m_{ij} which has value 1, it will decrease it to 0. The procedure is similar for cubes. The resulting matrices and cubes will have binary entries, that is, they will either be 1 or 0. A 1 indicates that at least one occurrence of the roles associated with the entries has previously been seen in the corpus; a 0 indicates that none has been seen or that a role and its negation have occurred.

Fixing a bijection between the elements $[1, n] \times [1, k]$ of our matrices and natural numbers $[1, n \times k]$ and between elements $[1, n] \times [1, k] \times [1, z]$ of the cubes and natural numbers $[1, n \times k \times z]$, one can show that $c +' H(S)$ is the table of a binary relation in the case of matrices, and of a ternary relation in the case of cubes. Those entries (i, j) of the matrices and (i, j, k) of the cubes that have a non-zero entry value are mapped to an element of the relation. An example of this isomorphism is shown below for a 2×2 matrix:

$$\begin{pmatrix} 1 & 0 \\ 1 & 1 \end{pmatrix} \mapsto \begin{array}{c|cc} & 1 & 2 \\ \hline 1 & 1 & 0 \\ 2 & 1 & 1 \end{array} \quad \{(1,1), (2,1), (2,2)\} \, .$$

These binary updates can be seen as providing a notion of 'contextual truth', that is, for example, a sentence S is true in a given a context c, whenever the update resulting from s is already included in the matrix or cube of its context, i.e. its update is one that does not change c.

As argued in Muskens *et al.* (1997), the semantics of this logic is dynamic, in the sense that the context change potential of a sequence of sentences is obtained by function composition, as follows:

$$\|S_1, \ldots, S_n\|(c) := \|S_1\| \circ \cdots \circ \|S_n\|(c) \, .$$

Using this dynamic semantics, it is straightforward to show that:

Proposition 1. *The context c corresponding to the sequence of sentences $S_1, \cdots, S_n$, is the zero vector updated by that sequence of sentences:*

$$c = \|S_1, \ldots, S_n\|(0) \, ,$$

where

$$\|S\|(c) \quad := \quad c + H(S)$$
$$c - H(S) \quad := \quad (c + H(S))^{-1} \, .$$

In the case of co-occurrence matrices, c is the co-occurrence matrix and 0 is the zero matrix. In the case of entity relation cubes, c is the entity relation cube and 0 is the zero cube. We are using the usual real number addition and subtraction on the m_{ij} and c_{ijk} entries of the matrices and cubes:

$$m'_{ij} := m_{ij} + 1 \qquad m'_{ij} := m_{ij} - 1$$
$$c'_{ijk} := c_{ijk} + 1 \qquad c'_{ijk} := c_{ijk} - 1 \, .$$

We will refer to a sequence of sentences as a *corpus*.

8   ADMITTANCE OF SENTENCES BY CONTEXTS

The notion of *admittance of a sentence by a context* was developed by Karttunen (1974) for presuppositions, and extended by Heim (1983) for context change potentials. We here define it as follows, for c a context and ϕ a proposition of $\mathscr{L}_{ccp}$.

$$\text{context } c \text{ admits proposition } \phi \iff \|\phi\|(c) = c$$

We use this notion and develop a similar notion between a corpus and a sentence.

Definition 2. *A corpus admits a sentence iff the context c (a co-occurrence matrix or entity relation cube) built from it admits it.*

Consider the following corpus:

Cats and dogs are animals that sleep. Cats chase cats and mice. Dogs chase all animals. Cats like mice, but mice fear cats, since cats eat mice. Cats smell mice and mice run from cats.

It admits the following sentences:

Cats are animals.
Dogs are animals.
Cats chase cats.
Cats chase mice.
Dogs chase cats and dogs.

Note that this notion of admittance caters for monotonicity of inference. For instance, in the above example, from the sentences "Cats [and dogs] are animals [that sleep]" and "Dogs chase all animals", we can infer that the context admits the sentence "Dogs chase cats".

On the other hand, c does not admit the negation of the above, for example it does not admit:

(*) Dogs do not chase cats.
(*) Dogs do not chase dogs.

It also does not admit the negations of derivations of the above or negations of sentences of the corpus, for example, it does not admit:

(*) Cats are not animals.
(*) Dogs do not sleep.

The corpus misses a sentence asserting that mice are also animals. Hence, c does not admit the sentence 'dogs chase mice'. Some other sentences that are not admitted by c are as follows:

(*) Cats like dogs.
(*) Cats eat dogs.
(*) Dogs run from cats.
(*) Dogs like mice.
(*) Mice fear dogs.
(*) Dogs eat mice.

One can argue that by binarizing the update operation and using $+'$ and $-'$ rather than the original $+$ and $-$, we are losing the full power of distributional semantics. It seems wasteful simply to record the presence or absence of co-occurrence, rather than build context matrices by counting co-occurrences. This can be overcome by working with a pair of contexts: a binarized one and a numerical one. The binarized context allows a notion of admittance to be defined as before, and the numerical one allows the use of numerical values, e.g. the degrees of similarity between words. The notion of word similarity used in distributional semantics is a direct consequence of the distributional hypothesis, where words that often occur in the same contexts have similar meanings (Firth 1957). Various formal notions have been used to measure the above degree of similarity; amongst the successful ones is the cosine of the angle between the vectors of the words. If the vectors are normalised to have length 1, which we shall assume, cosine becomes the same as the dot product of the vectors. One can then use these degrees of similarity to assign a numerical value to the admittance relation, e.g. as follows:

> A pair of binary and numerical co-occurrence matrices c and c' admit a sentence s' with degree d, if c admits s, and s' is obtained from s by replacing a word w of s with a word w' such that w' has the same grammatical role in s' as w in s and the degree of similarity between w and w' is d, computed from the numerical entries of c'.

Here, c admits s, and if there is a word in s that is similar to another word w', then if we replace w in s with w' (keeping the grammatical role that w had in s), the sentence resulting from this substitution,

Table 6: The normalised co-occurrence matrix built from the example corpus with the co-occurrence window taken to be occurrence within the same sentence

	1 animal	2 sleep	3 chase	4 like	5 fear	6 eat	7 smell	8 run
1- cats	$\frac{1}{8}$	$\frac{1}{8}$	$\frac{1}{8}$	$\frac{1}{8}$	$\frac{1}{8}$	$\frac{1}{8}$	$\frac{1}{8}$	$\frac{1}{8}$
2- mice	0	0	$\frac{1}{6}$	$\frac{1}{6}$	$\frac{1}{6}$	$\frac{1}{6}$	$\frac{1}{6}$	$\frac{1}{6}$
3- dogs	$\frac{1}{2}$	$\frac{1}{4}$	$\frac{1}{4}$	0	0	0	0	0

i.e. s', is also admitted by c, albeit with a degree equal to the degree of similarity between w and w'. This degree is computed using the numerical values recorded in c'. The above can be extended to the case where one replaces more than one word in s with words similar to them. Then the degree of entailment may be obtained by multiplying the degrees of similarity of the individually replaced words.

The normalised context matrix of our example corpus above is as in Table 6, where for simplicity the co-occurrence window is taken to be "occurrence within the same sentence".

From the context matrix, one obtains the following degrees of similarity.

$$\cos(\text{cats}, \text{mice}) = 6 \times \left(\frac{1}{6} \times \frac{1}{8} \right) = \frac{1}{8}$$

$$\cos(\text{cats}, \text{dogs}) = \left(\frac{1}{2} \right) \times 2 \times \left(\frac{1}{4} \times \frac{1}{8} \right) = \frac{1}{32}$$

$$\cos(\text{dogs}, \text{mice}) = \frac{1}{4} \times \frac{1}{6} = \frac{1}{24}$$

The corpus lacks an explicit sentence declaring that mice are also animals. Hence, from the sentences of the corpus, the negation of 'dogs chase mice' follows, which is a wrong entailment in the real world. This wrong can now be put right, since we can replace the word 'Cats' in the admitted sentence 'Cats are animals' with 'Mice'; as we have $\cos(\text{cats}, \text{mice}) = \frac{1}{8}$, thus obtaining the situation where c admits the following, both with degree $\frac{1}{8}$:

Mice are animals.
Dogs chase mice.

These were not possible before. We also obtain admittance of the following sentences, albeit with a lower degree of $\frac{1}{24}$:

(*) Cats like dogs.
(*) Cats eat dogs.
(*) Dogs run from cats.

Some other examples are as follows, with a still lower degree of $\frac{1}{32}$:

(*) Dogs like mice.
(*) Mice fear dogs.
(*) Dogs eat mice.

Some of the above are as likely as those that were derived with degree $\frac{1}{8}$. This is because the degrees come from co-occurrences in corpora, and our corpus is quite limited. One hopes that the bigger the corpus, the more reflective of the real world it will be. Another way of improving word-based entailments is by using linguistic resources such as WordNet, e.g. replacing words with their hypernyms.

8.1   *Evaluating on existing entailment datasets*

It remains to see if the notion of admittance of a sentence by a context can be applied to derive entailment relations between sentences. In future work, we will put this method to the test on inference datasets such as FraCaS (Cooper *et al.* 1996), SNLI (Bowman *et al.* 2015), the dataset in Zeichner *et al.* (2012), and the datasets in the RTE challenge. The FraCaS inferences are logical and the lambda calculus models of language should help in deriving them. As an example, consider the fracas-013 test case:

fracas-013   answer: yes
*P*1   Both leading tenors are excellent.
*P*2   Leading tenors who are excellent are indispensable.
Q   Are both leading tenors indispensable?
H   Both leading tenors are indispensable.

In our setting, using the updates resulting from P1 and P2, one can contextually derive H. In Zeichner *et al.* (2012), the similarity between words is also taken into account. An example is the following entailment between two sentences; this entailment was judged to be valid with confidence by human annotators:

Parents have great influence on the career development of their children.
Parents have a powerful influence on the career development of their children.

We can derive the above with a contextual entailment consisting of a cube updated by just the above two sentences, with the degree of similarity between 'powerful' and 'great', mined from the co-occurrence matrix of a large corpus.

Judgements on the SNLI dataset are more tricky, as they rely on external knowledge. For example, consider the entailment between the following phrases:

A soccer game with multiple males playing.
Some men are playing a sport.

or the contradiction between the following:

A black race car starts up in front of a crowd of people.
A man is driving down a lonely road.

Deciding these correctly is a challenge for our framework. The strength of our approach is in deciding whether a set of sentences follows from a given corpus of texts, rather than in judging entailment relations between a given pair or triple of sentences. Nevertheless, we shall try to experiment with all these datasets.

9   CONCLUSION AND FUTURE DIRECTIONS

We showed how a static interpretation of a lambda calculus model of natural language provides vector representations for phrases and sentences. Here, the type of the vector of a word depended on its abstract type, and could be an atomic vector, a matrix, or a cube, or a tensor of higher rank. Combinations of these vary, based on the tensor rank of the type of each word involved in the combination. For instance, one could take the matrix multiplication of the matrix of an intransitive verb with the vector of its subject, whereas for a transitive verb the sequence of operations was a contraction between the cube of the verb and the vector of its object, followed by a matrix multiplication between the resulting matrix and the vector of the subject. A toolkit of functions needed to perform these operations was defined. This toolkit can be restated for types of tensors of higher order, such as I^2R and I^3R, rather than the current *IR*, to provide a means of combining matrices, cubes, and their updates, if needed.

We extended the above setting by reasoning about the notion of context and its update, and developing a dynamic vector interpretation for the language of lambda terms. Truth conditional and vector models of language follow two very different philosophies. Vector models are based on contexts, truth models on denotations. Our first interpretation was static and based on truth conditions. Our second approach is based on a dynamic interpretation, where we followed the context update model of Heim (1983), and hence is deemed the more appropriate choice. We showed how Heim's files can be turned into vector contexts and how her context change potentials can be used to provide vector interpretations for phrases and sentences. We treated sentences as Heim's context change potentials and provided update instructions for words therein – including quantifiers, negation, and coordination words. We provided two concrete realisations of contexts, i.e. co-occurrence matrices and entity relation cubes, and in each case detailed how these context update instructions allow contexts to thread through vector semantics in a compositional manner. With an eye towards a large-scale empirical evaluation of the model, we defined a notion of 'contexts admitting sentences' and degrees thereof between contexts and sentences, and showed, by means of examples, how these notions can be used to judge whether a sentence is entailed by a cube context or by a pair of cube and matrix contexts. A large-scale empirical evaluation of the model is currently underway.

Our approach is applicable to the lambda terms obtained via other syntactic models, e.g. CCG, and Lambek grammars, and can also be modified to develop a vector semantics for LFG. We also aim to work with other update semantics, such as continuation-based approaches. One could also have a general formalisation wherein both the static approach of previous work and the dynamic one of this work cohabit. This can be achieved by working out a second pair of type-term homomorphisms that will also work with Heim's possible world part of the contexts. In this setting, the two concepts of meaning: truth theoretic and contextual, each with its own uses and possibilities, can work in tandem.

An intuitive connection to fuzzy logic is imaginable, wherein one interprets the logical words in more sophisticated ways: for instance, conjunction and disjunction take max and min of their entries, or add and subtract them. It may be worth investigating if such connections add to the applicability of the current model and, if so, make the connection formal.

ACKNOWLEDGEMENTS

We wish to thank the anonymous referees for their very valuable remarks. The anonymous referees of a short version of this paper, presented at LACL 2017, also gave excellent feedback. Carmela Chateau Smith's meticulous copy-editing considerably improved the readability of the paper and the grammaticality of its phrasing. All remaining errors are ours. The research for this paper was supported by the Royal Society International Exchange Award IE161631.

REFERENCES

Marco BARONI, Raffaella BERNARDI, and Roberto ZAMPARELLI (2014), Frege in space: A program for compositional distributional semantics, *Linguistic Issues in Language Technology*, 9:241–346.

Marco BARONI and Roberto ZAMPARELLI (2010), Nouns are vectors, adjectives are matrices: representing adjective-noun constructions in semantic space, in Hang LI and Lluís MÀRQUEZ, editors, *Proceedings of the 2010 Conference on Empirical Methods in Natural Language Processing*, EMNLP '10, pp. 1183–1193, Association for Computational Linguistics, Stroudsburg, PA, http://aclweb.org/anthology/D10-1115.

Johan VAN BENTHEM (1986), *Essays in Logical Semantics*, Studies in Linguistics and Philosophy 29, Reidel, Dordrecht.

Samuel BOWMAN, Gabor ANGELI, Christopher POTTS, and Christopher MANNING (2015), A large annotated corpus for learning natural language inference, in Lluís MÀRQUEZ, Chris CALLISON-BURCH, and Jian SU, editors, *Proceedings of the 2015 Conference on Empirical Methods in Natural Language Processing*, EMNLP '15, pp. 632–642, Association for Computational Linguistics, Stroudsburg, PA, http://aclweb.org/anthology/D15-1075.

Bob COECKE, Edward GREFENSTETTE, and Mehrnoosh SADRZADEH (2013), Lambek vs. Lambek: Functorial vector space semantics and string diagrams for Lambek calculus, *Annals of Pure and Applied Logic*, 164(11):1079–1100.

Bob COECKE, Mehrnoosh SADRZADEH, and Stephen CLARK (2010), Mathematical foundations for distributed compositional model of meaning, *Linguistic Analysis*, 36:345–384.

Robin COOPER, Dick CROUCH, Jan VAN EIJCK, Chris FOX, Johan
VAN GENABITH, Jan JASPARS, Hans KAMP, David MILWARD, Manfred
PINKAL, and Massimo POESIO (1996), *Using the framework*, Technical Report
LRE 62-051 D-16, The FraCaS Consortium.

Mary DALRYMPLE, John LAMPING, and Vijay SARASWAT (1993), LFG
semantics via constraints, in *Proceedings of the Sixth Conference on European
Chapter of the Association for Computational Linguistics*, EACL '93, pp. 97–105,
Association for Computational Linguistics, Stroudsburg, PA,
http://aclweb.org/anthology/E93-1013.

John Rupert FIRTH (1957), A synopsis of linguistic theory, 1930–1955, in
Studies in Linguistic Analysis, pp. 1–32, Blackwell, Oxford.

Edward GREFENSTETTE and Mehrnoosh SADRZADEH (2015), Concrete models
and empirical evaluations for the categorical compositional distributional
model of meaning, *Computational Linguistics*, 41:71–118.

Philippe DE GROOTE (2001), Towards abstract categorial grammars, in
*Proceedings of the 39th Annual Meeting of the Association for Computational
Linguistics and 10th Conference of the European Chapter of the Association for
Computational Linguistics*, ACL '01, pp. 252–259, Association for Computational
Linguistics, Stroudsburg, PA, http://aclweb.org/anthology/P01-1033.

Philippe DE GROOTE (2006), Towards a Montagovian account of dynamics,
Semantics and Linguistic Theory, 16:1–16.

Irene HEIM (1983), On the projection problem for presuppositions, in
Proceedings of the Second Annual West Coast Conference on Formal Linguistics,
pp. 114–125, reprinted in Portner and Partee (2002).

Irene HEIM and Angelika KRATZER (1998), *Semantics in Generative Grammar*,
Blackwell textbooks in linguistics, Blackwell, Oxford, ISBN 0-631-19712-5.

Leon HENKIN (1950), Completeness in the theory of types, *Journal of Symbolic
Logic*, 15:81–91.

Nanda KAMBHATLA (2004), Combining lexical, syntactic, and semantic
features with maximum entropy models for extracting relations, in *Proceedings
of the ACL 2004 on Interactive Poster and Demonstration Sessions*, ACLdemo '04,
Association for Computational Linguistics, Stroudsburg, PA,
http://aclweb.org/anthology/P04-3022.

Lauri KARTTUNEN (1974), Presupposition and linguistic context, *Theoretical
Linguistics*, 1(1–3):182–194.

Ewan KLEIN and Ivan SAG (1985), Type-driven translation, *Linguistics and
Philosophy*, 8(2):163–201.

Jayant KRISHNAMURTHY and Tom MITCHELL (2013), Vector space semantic
parsing: A framework for compositional vector space models, in *Proceedings of*

the 2013 ACL Workshop on Continuous Vector Space Models and their Compositionality, pp. 1–10, Association for Computational Linguistics, Stroudsburg, PA, http://aclweb.org/anthology/W13-3201.

Mike LEWIS and Mark STEEDMAN (2013), Combined distributional and logical semantics, *Transactions of the Association for Computational Linguistics*, 1:179–192, http://aclweb.org/anthology/Q13-1015.

Jean MAILLARD, Stephen CLARK, and Edward GREFENSTETTE (2014), A type-driven tensor-based semantics for CCG, in Robin COOPER, Simon DOBNIK, Shalom LAPPIN, and Staffan LARSSON, editors, *Proceedings of the EACL 2014 on Type Theory and Natural Language Semantics (TTNLS)*, pp. 46–54, Association for Computational Linguistics, Stroudsburg, PA, http://aclweb.org/anthology/W14-1406.

Jeff MITCHELL and Mirella LAPATA (2010), Composition in distributional models of semantics, *Cognitive Science*, 34(8):1388–1439.

Richard MONTAGUE (1974), The proper treatment of quantification in ordinary English, in Richmond THOMASON, editor, *Formal Philosophy. Selected Papers of Richard Montague*, pp. 247–270, Yale University Press, New Haven, CT.

Reinhard MUSKENS (2001), Categorial grammar and lexical-functional grammar, in Miriam BUTT and Tracy Holloway KING, editors, *Proceedings of the LFG01 Conference, University of Hong Kong*, pp. 259–279, CSLI, Stanford, CA, http://cslipublications.stanford.edu/LFG/6/lfg01.html.

Reinhard MUSKENS (2003), Language, lambdas, and logic, in Geert-Jan KRUIJFF and Richard OEHRLE, editors, *Resource-Sensitivity, Binding and Anaphora*, Studies in Linguistics and Philosophy, pp. 23–54, Kluwer, Dordrecht.

Reinhard MUSKENS (2010), New directions in type-theoretic grammars, *Journal of Logic, Language and Information*, 19(2):129–136.

Reinhard MUSKENS and Mehrnoosh SADRZADEH (2016a), Context update for lambdas and vectors, in Maxime AMBLARD, Philippe DE GROOTE, Sylvain POGODALLA, and Christian RETORÉ, editors, *Proceedings of the 9th International Conference on Logical Aspects of Computational Linguistics (LACL 2016)*, volume 10054 of *LNCS*, pp. 247–254, Springer-Verlag, Berlin, Heidelberg.

Reinhard MUSKENS and Mehrnoosh SADRZADEH (2016b), Lambdas and vectors, in *Workshop on Distributional Semantics and Linguistic Theory (DSALT), 28th European Summer School in Logic, Language and Information (ESSLLI)*, Free University of Bozen-Bolzano.

Reinhard MUSKENS, Johan VAN BENTHEM, and Albert VISSER (1997), Dynamics, in Johan VAN BENTHEM and Alice TER MEULEN, editors, *Handbook of Logic and Language*, pp. 587–648, Elsevier.

Barbara PARTEE (1986), Noun phrase interpretation and type-shifting principles, in Jeroen GROENENDIJK, Dick DE JONGH, and Martin STOKHOF, editors, *Studies in Discourse Representation and the Theory of Generalized Quantifiers*, pp. 115–143, Foris, Dordrecht.

Hoifung POON and Pedro DOMINGOS (2009), Unsupervised semantic parsing, in Philipp KOEHN and Rada MIHALCEA, editors, *Proceedings of the 2009 Conference on Empirical Methods in Natural Language Processing (EMNLP-9): Volume 1*, pp. 1–10, Association for Computational Linguistics, Stroudsburg, PA, ISBN 978-1-932432-59-6, http://aclweb.org/anthology/D09-1001.

Paul PORTNER and Barbara PARTEE (2002), *Formal Semantics: The Essential Readings*, Blackwell, Oxford.

Sebastian RIEDEL, Limin YAO, and Andrew MCCALLUM (2010), Modeling relations and their mentions without labeled text, in José Luis BALCÁZAR, Francesco BONCHI, Aristides GIONIS, and Michèle SEBAG, editors, *Proceedings of the 2010 European Conference on Machine Learning and Knowledge Discovery in Databases (ECML PKDD'10): Part III*, volume 6323 of *LNAI*, pp. 148–163, Springer-Verlag, Berlin, Heidelberg, ISBN 3-642-15938-9, 978-3-642-15938-1, http://dl.acm.org/citation.cfm?id=1889788.1889799.

Herbert RUBENSTEIN and John GOODENOUGH (1965), Contextual correlates of synonymy, *Communications of the ACM*, 8(10):627–633.

Mark STEEDMAN (2000), *The Syntactic Process*, MIT Press.

Alfred TARSKI (1965), *Introduction to Logic and to the Methodology of Deductive Sciences*, Oxford University Press, Oxford, 3rd edition.

Frank VELTMAN (1996), Defaults in update semantics, *Journal of Philosophical Logic*, 25(3):221–261.

Limin YAO, Sebastian RIEDEL, and Andrew MCCALLUM (2012), Unsupervised relation discovery with sense disambiguation, in Haizhou LI, Chin-Yew LIN, Miles OSBORNE, Gary Geunbae LEE, and Jong C. PARK, editors, *Proceedings of the 50th annual meeting of the Association for Computational Linguistics: long papers – Volume 1*, ACL '12, pp. 712–720, Association for Computational Linguistics, Stroudsburg, PA, http://aclweb.org/anthology/P12-1075.

Naomi ZEICHNER, Jonathan BERANT, and Ido DAGAN (2012), Crowdsourcing inference-rule evaluation, in Haizhou LI, Chin-Yew LIN, Miles OSBORNE, Gary Geunbae LEE, and Jong C. PARK, editors, *Proceedings of the 50th Annual Meeting of the Association for Computational Linguistics: Short Papers – Volume 2*, ACL '12, pp. 156–160, Association for Computational Linguistics, Stroudsburg, PA, http://aclweb.org/anthology/P12-2031.

5

Data–oriented parsing with discontinuous constituents and function tags

Andreas van Cranenburgh[1,2], Remko Scha[2], and Rens Bod[2]
[1] Huygens ING, Royal Netherlands Academy of Arts and Sciences
[2] Institute for Logic, Language and Computation, University of Amsterdam

Keywords: discontinuous constituents, statistical parsing, tree-substitution grammar

ABSTRACT

Statistical parsers are effective but are typically limited to producing projective dependencies or constituents. On the other hand, linguistically rich parsers recognize non-local relations and analyze both form and function phenomena but rely on extensive manual grammar engineering. We combine advantages of the two by building a statistical parser that produces richer analyses.

We investigate new techniques to implement treebank-based parsers that allow for discontinuous constituents. We present two systems. One system is based on a Linear Context-Free Rewriting System (LCFRS), while using a Probabilistic Discontinuous Tree-Substitution Grammar (PDTSG) to improve disambiguation performance. Another system encodes discontinuities in the labels of phrase-structure trees, allowing for efficient context-free grammar parsing.

The two systems demonstrate that tree fragments as used in tree-substitution grammar improve disambiguation performance while capturing non-local relations on an as-needed basis. Additionally, we present results for models that produce function tags, resulting in a more linguistically adequate model of the data. We report substantial accuracy improvements in discontinuous parsing for German, English, and Dutch, including results on spoken Dutch.

This article is a substantially revised and extended version of van Cranenburgh and Bod (2013). While finishing this article, we learned with great sadness of the passing of our co-author Remko Scha. We dedicate this article to his memory.

1   INTRODUCTION

Probabilistic algorithms for parsing and disambiguation select the most probable analysis for a given sentence in accordance with a certain probability distribution. A fundamental property of such algorithms is thus the definition of the space of *possible sentence structures* that constitutes the domain of the probability distribution. Modern statistical parsers are often automatically derived from corpora of syntactically annotated sentences ("treebanks"). In this case, the "linguistic backbone" of the probabilistic grammar naturally depends on the convention for encoding syntactic structure that was used in annotating the corpus.

When different parsing and disambiguation algorithms are applied to the same treebank, their relative accuracies can be objectively assessed if the treebank is split into a training set (that is used to induce a grammar and its probabilities) and a test set (that provides a "gold standard" to assess the performance of the system). This is common practice now. In many cases, however, the linguistic significance of these evaluations may be questioned, since the test sets consist of phrase-structure trees, i.e., part-whole structures where all parts are contiguous chunks. Non-local syntactic relations are not represented in these trees; utterances in which such relations occur are therefore skipped or incorrectly annotated.

For certain practical applications this restriction may be harmless, but from a linguistic (and cognitive) viewpoint it cannot be defended. Since Chomsky's transformational-generative grammar, there have been many proposals for formal grammars with a less narrow scope. Some of these formalisms have been employed to annotate large corpora; in principle, they can thus be used in treebank grammars extracted from these corpora.

The Penn treebank, for instance, enriches its phrase-structure representations with "empty constituents" that share an index with the constituent that, from a transformational perspective, would be analyzed as originating in that position. Most grammars based on the Penn treebank ignore this information, but it was used by, e.g., Johnson (2002), Dienes and Dubey (2003), and Gabbard *et al.* (2006).

Another perspective on non-local syntactic dependencies generalizes the notion of a "syntactic constituent," in that it allows "dis-

continuous constituent structures," where a non-terminal node dom-
inates a lexical yield that consists of different non-contiguous parts
(McCawley 1982). Several German and Dutch treebanks have been
annotated in terms of discontinuous constituency, and some statistical parsers have been developed that use these treebanks. Also, phrase
structures with co-indexed traces can be converted into discontinuous constituent structures; the Penn treebank can therefore be transformed and used in the discontinuous constituency approach (Evang
and Kallmeyer 2011). Figure 1 shows an example of a tree with discontinuous constituents.

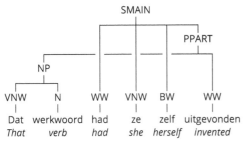

Figure 1:
A tree from the Dutch Alpino treebank
(van der Beek *et al.* 2002). PPART is a
discontinuous constituent (indicated with
crossing branches) due to its extraposed NP
object. Part-of-speech tags: VNW = pronoun,
N = noun, WW = verb, BW = adverb. The tags
also contain additional morphological features
not shown here that distinguish personal
pronouns from others, auxiliary verbs from
main verbs, etc.

It is an annotation choice to employ discontinuous constituents;
some treebanks elect not to model non-local phenomena, while others
may choose different mechanisms. For example, two German treebanks employ discontinuous constituents (Skut *et al.* 1997; Brants *et al.*
2002), while another German treebank does not (Telljohann *et al.*
2004, 2012). The annotation scheme of the latter treebank lacks information expressed in the former two. For instance, it cannot encode
the heads of non-local modifiers; with discontinuous constituents, a
modifier is a sibling of its head, regardless of their configuration.
On the other hand, the co-indexed traces of the Penn treebank provide more information than discontinuous constituents, because they
assume that constituents have been moved from somewhere else in
the tree and encode the original position. Discontinuous constituents
describe surface structure without making such assumptions. Some
phenomena that can be analyzed with discontinuous constituents are
extraposition, topicalization, scrambling, and parentheticals; cf. Maier
et al. (2014) for an overview of such phenomena in German.

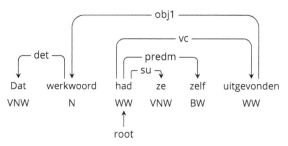

Figure 2: A dependency structure derived from the tree in Figure 1. The *obj1* arc makes this structure non-projective.

The notion of discontinuous constituents in annotation is useful to bridge the gap between the information represented in constituency and dependency structures. Constituency structures capture the hierarchical structure of phrases – which is useful for identifying re-usable elements; discontinuous constituents extend this to allow for arbitrary non-local relations that may arise due to such phenomena as extraposition and free word order. There is a close relation of discontinuous constituency to non-projectivity in dependency structures (Maier and Lichte 2011). Compare Figure 2, which shows a dependency structure for the constituency tree in Figure 1. Note that in this dependency structure, the edge labels are grammatical functions present in the original treebank, while the constituent labels in Figure 1 are syntactic categories. The dependency structure encodes the non-local relations within the discontinuous constituent. On the other hand, it does not represent the hierarchical grouping given by the NP and PPART constituents. By encoding both hierarchical and non-local information, trees with discontinuous constituents combine the advantages of constituency and dependency structures. We will also come back to grammatical function labels.

This paper is concerned with treebank-based parsing algorithms that accept discontinuous constituents. It takes as its point of departure work by Kallmeyer and Maier (2010, 2013) that represents discontinuous structures in terms of a string-rewriting version of Linear Context-Free Rewriting Systems (Section 3.1). In addition, we employ Tree-Substitution Grammar (TSG). We make the following contributions:

1. We discuss the notions of competence and performance in (computational) linguistics (Section 2). We argue that instead of focussing on the search for the formal (competence) grammar with the right capacity for natural language, we can consider performance aspects such as cognitive limitations and pruning strategies.

2. We show that Tree-Substitution Grammar can be applied to discontinuous constituents (Section 3.2) and that it is possible, using a transformation, to parse with a Tree-Substitution Grammar without having to write a separate parser for this formalism (Section 4.2).

3. We induce a tree-substitution grammar from a treebank (Section 5) using a method called Double-DOP (Sangati and Zuidema 2011). This method extracts a set of recurring tree fragments. We show that compared to another method which implicitly works with all possible fragments, this explicit method offers advantages in both accuracy and efficiency (Section 4.2.1, Section 9).

4. Fragments make it possible to treat discontinuous constituency as a statistical phenomenon within an encompassing context-free framework (Section 4.1, Section 7); this yields a considerable efficiency improvement without hurting accuracy (Section 9).

5. Finally, we present an evaluation on three languages. We employ manual state splits from previous work for improved performance (Section 8) and discuss methods and results for grammars that produce function tags in addition to phrasal labels (Section 8.3).

This work explores parsing discontinuous constituents with Linear Context-Free Rewriting Systems and Context-Free Grammar, as well as with and without the use of tree fragments through tree substitution. Figure 3 gives an overview of these systems and how they are combined in a coarse-to-fine pipeline (cf. Section 6.4).

2   THE DIVISION OF LABOR BETWEEN COMPETENCE AND PERFORMANCE

Traditionally, two aspects of language cognition have been distinguished: competence and performance (Chomsky 1965). Linguistic competence comprises a language user's "knowledge of language," usually described as a system of rules, while linguistic performance includes the details of the user's production and comprehension behavior. For a computational model, its syntactic competence defines the set of possible sentences that it can process in principle, and the structures it may assign to them, while its performance includes such

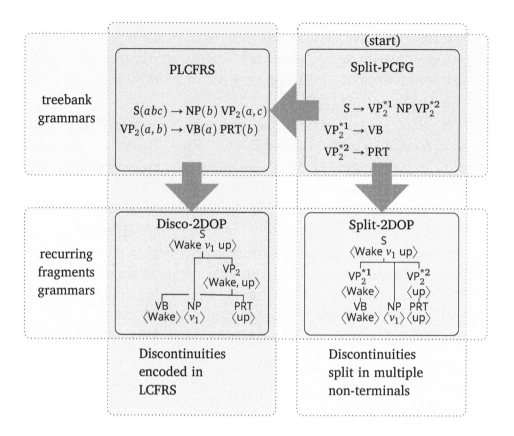

Figure 3: The systems explored in this work

aspects as disambiguation using occurrence frequencies of grammatical constructions. Thus, the choice of a formalism to describe the system's competence grammar depends on one's decisions on how syntax should be formalized. Regular and context-free grammars have
been argued to be too limited (Chomsky 1956; Shieber 1985), while
richer alternatives – context-sensitive and beyond – are considered
too powerful to allow for an efficient computational implementation; this applies to Transformational Grammar (Peters and Ritchie
1973), Lexical-Functional Grammar, and Head-Driven Phrase Structure Grammar (Trautwein 1995). We may therefore wish to strike a
balance and find a grammar formalism that is just powerful enough to
describe the syntax of natural language. Joshi (1985) proposes Mildly
Context-Sensitive grammars, which are beyond context-free, but avoid
the computational complexity that comes with the full class of context-
sensitive grammars. The first formalism developed in this framework
was Tree-Adjoining Grammar (TAG; Joshi 1985). There has been

work on automatic extraction of tree-adjoining grammars from corpora (Chiang 2000; Xia *et al.* 2001; Kaeshammer and Demberg 2012), and formal extensions such as multi-component TAG (Weir 1988; Schuler *et al.* 2000; Kallmeyer 2009). Linear Context-Free Rewriting Systems (LCFRSs), as employed in the work reported below, are instances of Mildly Context-Sensitive grammar. LCFRS appears to be a *lingua franca* among mildly context-sensitive formalisms, since several formalisms have been shown to be equivalent to it (Vijay-Shanker and Weir 1994).

Irrespective of whether one accepts the competence-performance dichotomy, a practical natural language system needs to deal with phenomena that depend on world knowledge reflected in language use (e.g., the fact that in *"eat pizza with a fork"*, *with a fork* is prototypically related to *eat* rather than to *pizza*). This has led to a statistical turn in computational linguistics, in which models are directly induced from treebanks (Scha 1990; Charniak 1996; Bod *et al.* 2003; Geman and Johnson 2004). If the end goal is to make an adequate model of language *performance,* there is actually no need to have a competence grammar which is 'just right.' Instead, we might reduce some of the formal complexity by encoding it in statistical patterns. Concretely, we can opt for a grammar formalism that deliberately overgenerates, and count on grammatical analyses having a higher probability of being selected during disambiguation. This operationalizes the idea of there being a spectrum between ungrammaticality, markedness, and felicity. In Section 4.1 we introduce an approximation of LCFRS that makes it possible to produce discontinuous constituents in cubic time using a context-free grammar, by encoding information in non-terminal labels. A probabilistic variant of the resulting grammar makes stronger independence assumptions than the equivalent LCFRS, but as a component in a larger statistical system this does not have to pose a problem.

In the debate about the context-freeness of language, cross-serial dependencies have played an important role (Huybregts 1976; Bresnan *et al.* 1982; Shieber 1985). Consider the following example in Dutch:

(1)   Jan zag dat Karel hem haar laat leren zwemmen.
       Jan saw that Karel him her   lets teach swim.
       'Jan saw that Karel lets him teach her to swim.'

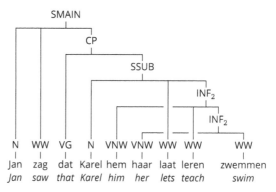

Figure 4: Cross-serial dependencies in Dutch expressed with discontinuous constituents

Ojeda (1988) gives an account using discontinuous constituents; cf. Figure 4. In Section 4.1 we show how such analyses may be produced by an overgenerating context-free grammar.

This is an instance of the more general idea of approximating rich formal models in formally weaker but statistically richer models, i.e., descriptive aspects of language that can be handled as a performance rather than a competence problem. Another instance of this is constituted by the various restricted versions of TAG, whose string languages form a proper subset of those of LCFRS. Restricted variants of TAG that generate context-free string languages are Tree-Insertion Grammar (Schabes and Waters 1995; Hoogweg 2003; Yamangil and Shieber 2012), and off-spine TAG (Swanson *et al.* 2013); TSG is an even more restricted variant of TAG in which the adjunction operation is removed altogether. These results suggest that there is a trade-off to be made in the choice of formalism. While on the one hand Mild Context-Sensitivity already aims to limit formal complexity to precisely what is needed for adequate linguistic description, a practical, statistical implementation presents further opportunities for constraining complexity.

Another performance aspect of language relevant for computational linguistics is pruning. While normally considered an implementation aspect made necessary by practical hardware limitations, finding linguistically and psychologically plausible shortcuts in language processing forms an interesting research question. Schuler *et al.* (2010) present a parser with human-like memory constraints based on a finite-state model. Although Roark *et al.* (2012) are not concerned with cognitive plausibility, they also work with finite-state methods and show that CFG parsing can be done in quadratic or even linear time with finite-state pruning methods.

As a specific example of a cognitive limitation relevant to parsing algorithms, consider center embedding. Karlsson (2007) reports from a corpus study that center embeddings only occur up to depth 3 in written language, and up to depth 2 in spoken language. If a statistical parser would take such cognitive limitations into account, many implausible analyses could be ruled out from the outset. More generally, it is worthwhile to strive for an explicit performance model that incorporates such cognitive and computational limitations as first class citizens.

In this work we do not go all the way to a finite-state model, but we do show that the non-local relations expressed in discontinuous constituents can be expressed in a context-free grammar model. We start with a mildly context-sensitive grammar formalism to parse discontinuous constituents, augmented with tree substitution. We then show that an approximation with context-free grammar is possible and effective. We find that the reduced independence assumptions and larger contexts taken into account as a result of tree substitution make it possible to capture non-local relations without going beyond context-free. Tree substitution thus increases the capabilities of the performance side without increasing the complexity of the competence side. A performance phenomenon that is modeled by this is that non-local relations are only faithfully produced as far as observed in the data.

3   GRAMMAR FORMALISMS

In this section we describe two formalisms related to discontinuous constituents; (string rewriting) Linear Context-Free Rewriting Systems and Discontinuous Tree-Substitution Grammar.

(String rewriting) Linear Context-Free Rewriting Systems (LCFRS; Vijay-Shanker *et al.* 1987) can produce such structures. An LCFRS generalizes CFG by allowing non-terminals to rewrite tuples of strings instead of just single, contiguous strings. This property makes LCFRS suitable for directly parsing discontinuous constituents (Kallmeyer and Maier 2010, 2013), as well as non-projective dependencies (Kuhlmann and Satta 2009; Kuhlmann 2013).

A tree-substitution grammar (TSG) provides a generalization of context-free grammar (CFG) that operates with larger chunks than just single grammar productions. A probabilistic TSG can be seen as a PCFG in which several productions may be applied at once, capturing structural relations between those productions. Tree-substitution grammars have numerous applications. They can be used for statistical parsing, such as with Data-Oriented Parsing (DOP; Scha 1990; Bod 1992; Bod *et al.* 2003; Bansal and Klein 2010; Sangati and Zuidema 2011) and Bayesian TSGs (O'Donnell *et al.* 2009; Post and Gildea 2009; Cohn *et al.* 2009, 2010; Shindo *et al.* 2012). Other applications include grammaticality judgements (Post 2011), multi-word expression identification (Green *et al.* 2011), stylometry (Bergsma *et al.* 2012; van Cranenburgh 2012b), and native language detection (Swanson and Charniak 2012).

Before defining these formalisms, we first define the tree structures they operate on. The notion of a "discontinuous tree" stems from a long linguistic tradition (Pike 1943, Sections 4.12–14; Wells 1947, Sections 55–62; McCawley 1982). It generalizes the usual notion of a phrase-structure tree in that it allows a non-terminal node to dominate a lexical span that consists of non-contiguous chunks. In our interpretation of this idea, it results in three formal differences:

1. A non-terminal with non-contiguous daughters does not have a non-arbitrary place in the left-to-right order with respect to its sibling nodes. Therefore, it is not obvious anymore that the left-to-right order of the terminals is to be described in terms of their occurrence in a tree with totally ordered branches. Instead, we employ trees with *unordered* branches, while every node is augmented with an explicit representation of its (ordered) yield.

2. An "ordinary" (totally ordered) tree has a contiguous string of leaf nodes as its yield. When we allow discontinuities, this property still applies to the (totally lexicalized) complete trees of complete sentences. But for tree fragments, it fails; their yields may contain gaps. In the general case, the yield of a discontinuous tree is thus a tuple of strings.

3. Extracting a fragment from a tree now consists of two steps:

   (a) Extracting a connected subset of nodes, and

(b) Updating the yield tuples of the nodes. In the yield tuple of every non-terminal leaf node, every element (a contiguous chunk of words) is replaced by a *terminal variable*. This replacement is percolated up the tree, to the yield tuples of all nodes. Different occurrences of the same word carry a unique index, to allow for the percolation to proceed correctly.

We now proceed to give a more formal definition of our notion of a discontinuous tree.

DEFINITION 1. A *discontinuous syntactic tree* is a rooted, unordered tree. Each node consists of a label and a yield. A yield is a tuple of strings composed of lexical items; the tuple of strings denotes a subsequence of the yield at the root of the tree. We write ⟨a b⟩ to denote a yield consisting of the contiguous sequence of lexical items 'a' and 'b', while ⟨a b, c⟩ denotes a yield containing 'a b' followed by 'c' with an intervening gap. Given a node X,

- the yield of X is composed of the terminals in the yields of the children of X;
- conversely, the yield of each child of X is a subsequence of the yield of X;
- the yields of siblings do not overlap.

Figure 5 shows a tree according to this definition in which discontinuities are visualized with crossing branches as before. The same tree is rendered in Figure 6, without crossing branches, to highlight the fact that the information about discontinuities is encoded in the yields of the tree nodes.

Figure 5: A discontinuous tree with yield tuples

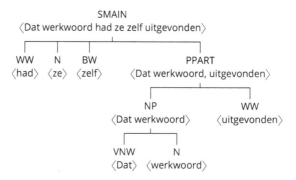

Figure 6: An equivalent representation of the tree in Figure 5, without crossing branches

DEFINITION 2. An *incomplete tree* is a discontinuous tree in which the yields may contain variables v_n with $n \in \mathbb{N}$ in addition to lexical items. Variables stand in for any contiguous string of lexical items. An incomplete tree contains 2 or more nodes, or a single node with only lexical items in its yield. A node without children whose yield consists solely of variables is called a *substitution site*.

An incomplete tree may be derived from an extracted tree fragment. The tree fragment may contain variables for substrings which needed to be distinguished in other parts of the tree, but only occur contiguously in the fragment. We reduce these strings of contiguous variables to single variables; i.e., we abstract fragments from their original context by reducing strings of variables that appear contiguously across the fragment into single variables (e.g. Figure 7).

Figure 7: Reducing variables in a fragment extracted from the tree in Figure 5

The *fan-out* of a non-terminal node equals the number of terminals in its yield that are not directly preceded by another terminal in the same yield; i.e., the number of contiguous substrings (components) of which the yield consists.[1] From here on we denote the fan-out of a discontinuous non-terminal with a subscript that is part of its label.

---

[1] Note that a distinction is often made between the *fan-out* of non-terminals in grammar productions, and the *block degree* of nodes of a syntactic tree (Maier and Lichte 2011; Kuhlmann 2013). Due to the fact that the productions of a TSG are trees, these notions coincide for our purposes.

3.1 *Linear Context-Free Rewriting Systems*

String-rewriting LCFRS can be seen as the discontinuous counterpart of CFG, and its probabilistic variant can be used to articulate a discontinuous treebank grammar. LCFRS productions differ from CFG productions in that they generate for a given non-terminal one or more strings at a time in potentially non-adjacent positions in the sentence. The number of these positions, the measure of discontinuity in a constituent, is called the fan-out. A CFG is an LCFRS with a maximum fan-out of 1. Together with the number of non-terminals on the right-hand side, the fan-out defines a hierarchy of grammars with increasing complexity, of which CFG is the simplest case. In this paper we use the simple RCG notation (Boullier 1998) for LCFRS. We focus on string-rewriting LCFRS and use the tree produced as a side-effect of a string's derivation as its syntactic analysis. It is possible to define an LCFRS that rewrites trees or graphs; however, the formalisms used in this paper are all expressible as string-rewriting LCFRSs.

DEFINITION 3. A string-rewriting LCFRS is a tuple $G = \langle N, T, V, P, S \rangle$. N and T are disjoint finite sets of non-terminals and terminals, respectively. A function $\varphi : N \rightarrow \{1, 2, \ldots, \}$ specifies the unique fan-out for every non-terminal symbol. V is a finite set of variables; we refer to the variables as x_j^i with $i, j \in \mathbb{N}$. S is the distinguished start symbol with $S \in N$ and $\varphi(S) = 1$. P is a finite set of productions, of the form:

$$A(\alpha_1, \ldots, \alpha_{\varphi(A)}) \rightarrow B_1(x_1^1, \ldots, x_{\varphi(B_1)}^1) \ldots B_r(x_1^r, \ldots, x_{\varphi(B_r)}^r)$$

for $r \geq 0$, where $A, B_1, \ldots, B_r \in N$, each $x_j^i \in V$ for $1 \leq i \leq r$, $1 \leq j \leq \varphi(B_i)$, and $\alpha_j \in (T \cup V)^+$ for $1 \leq j \leq \varphi(A)$. Observe that a component α_j is a concatenation of one or more terminals and variables.

The rank r refers to the number of non-terminals on the right-hand side of a production, while the fan-out φ of a non-terminal refers to the number of components it covers. A rank of zero implies a lexical production; in that case the right-hand side (RHS) is notated as ε implying no new non-terminals are produced (not to be confused with generating the empty string), and the left-hand side (LHS) argument is composed only of terminals.

Productions must be *linear* and *non-erasing*: if a variable occurs in a production, it occurs exactly once on the LHS, and exactly once on the RHS. A production is *monotone*[2] if for any two variables x_1 and x_2 occurring in a non-terminal on the RHS, x_1 precedes x_2 on the LHS iff x_1 precedes x_2 on the RHS. Due to our method of grammar extraction from treebanks, (cf. Section 3.1.1 below) all productions in this work are monotone and, except in some examples, at most binary ($r \leqslant 2$); lexical productions ($r = 0$) have fan-out 1 and introduce only a single terminal.

A production is *instantiated* when its variables are bound to spans such that for each component α_j of the LHS, the concatenation of the strings that its terminals and bound variables point to forms a contiguous, non-overlapping span in the input. In the remainder we will notate discontinuous non-terminals with a subscript indicating their fan-out.

When a sentence is parsed by an LCFRS, its derivation tree (Boullier 1998, Section 3.3; Kallmeyer 2010, pp. 115–117) is a discontinuous tree. Conversely, given a set of discontinuous trees, a set of productions can be extracted that generate those trees.

In a probabilistic LCFRS (PLCFRS), each production is associated with a probability and the probability of derivation is the product of the probabilities of its productions. Analogously to a PCFG, a PLCFRS may be induced from a treebank by using relative frequencies as probabilities (Maier and Søgaard 2008).

DEFINITION 4. The *language* of an LCFRS G is defined as follows (Kallmeyer and Maier 2013, pp. 92–93):

1. For every $A \in N$, we define the yield of A, $\text{yield}_G(A)$, as follows:

   (a) For every production $A(t) \to \varepsilon$ with $t \in T$, $\langle t \rangle \in \text{yield}_G(A)$

   (b) For every production

   $$A(\alpha_1,\ldots,\alpha_{\varphi(A)}) \to B_1(x_1^1,\ldots,x_{\varphi(B_1)}^1)\ldots B_r(x_1^r,\ldots,x_{\varphi(B_r)}^r)$$

   and all tuples $\tau_1 \in \text{yield}_G(B_1),\ldots,\tau_r \in \text{yield}_G(B_r)$:

   $$\langle f(\alpha_1),\ldots,f(\alpha_{\varphi(A)})\rangle \in \text{yield}_G(A)$$

   where f is defined as follows:
   i. $f(t) = t$ for all $t \in T$,

---

[2] This property is called *ordered* in the RCG literature.

    ii. $f(x_j^i) = \tau_i[j]$ for all $1 \leqslant i \leqslant r, 1 \leqslant j \leqslant \varphi(B_i)$, and

    iii. $f(ab) = f(a)f(b)$ for all $a, b \in (T \cup V)^+$.

   f is the *composition function* of the production.

  (c) Nothing else is in $\text{yield}_G(A)$.

 2. The language of G is then $L(G) = \text{yield}_G(S)$.

3.1.1   Extracting LCFRS productions from trees

LCFRS productions may be induced from a discontinuous tree, using a procedure described in Maier and Søgaard (2008). We extend this procedure to handle substitution sites, i.e., non-terminals with only variable terminals in their yield, but no lexical items; such nodes occur in tree fragments extracted from a treebank. The procedure is as follows:

Given a discontinuous tree, we extract a grammar production for each non-leaf non-terminal node. The label of the node forms the LHS non-terminal, and the labels of the nodes immediately dominated by it form the RHS non-terminals. The arguments of each RHS non-terminal are based on their yield tuples. Adjacent variables in the yield of the RHS non-terminals are collapsed into single variables and replaced on both LHS and RHS. Consider the tree fragment in Figure 7, which gives the following LCFRS production:

$$\text{SMAIN}(abcde) \rightarrow \text{PPART}(a, e) \, \text{WW}(b) \, \text{N}(c) \, \text{BW}(d)$$

Pre-terminals yield a production with their terminal as a direct argument to the pre-terminal, and an empty RHS. Substitution sites in a tree only appear on the RHS of extracted productions, since it is not known what they will expand to. See Figure 8 for examples of LCFRS productions extracted from a discontinuous tree.

3.2   *Discontinuous Tree-Substitution Grammar*

We now employ string-rewriting LCFRS, introduced in the previous section, to replace the CFG foundation of TSGs. Note that the resulting formalism directly rewrites elementary trees with discontinuous constituents, making it an instantiation of the more general notion of a tree-rewriting LCFRS. Tree-rewriting LCFRSs are more general because they allow other rewriting operations besides substitution. However, since we limit the operations in the formalism

$N = \{$SMAIN, PPART, NP, VNW, N, WW, BW$\}$

$T = \{$Dat, had, uitgevonden, werkwoord, ze, zelf$\}$

$V = \{a, b, c, d, e\}$

$\varphi = \{$SMAIN : 1, PPART : 2, NP : 1,

    VNW : 1, N : 1, WW : 1, BW : 1$\}$

$S = $ SMAIN

$P = \{$SMAIN$(abcde) \to$ WW(b) N(c) BW(d) PPART(a, e),

    PPART$(a, b) \to$ NP(a) WW(b),

    NP$(ab) \to$ VNW(a) N(b),

    VNW$($Dat$) \to \varepsilon$, N$($werkwoord$) \to \varepsilon$,

    WW$($had$) \to \varepsilon$, N$($ze$) \to \varepsilon$, BW$($zelf$) \to \varepsilon$,

    WW$($uitgevonden$) \to \varepsilon\}$

Figure 8: The LCFRS $G = \langle N, T, V, P, S \rangle$ extracted from the tree in Figure 5

to substitution, it remains possible to specify a direct mapping to a string-rewriting grammar, as we shall see in the next section. As noted before, a TSG can be seen as a TAG without the adjunction operation. A discontinuous TSG may be related to a special case of set-local multi-component TAG (Weir 1988; Kallmeyer 2009). A multi-component TAG is able to specify constraints that require particular elementary trees to apply together; this mechanism can be used to generate the non-local elements of discontinuous constituents.

The following definitions are based on the definition for continuous TSG in Sima'an (1997).

DEFINITION 5. A *probabilistic, discontinuous TSG* (PDTSG) is a tuple $\langle N, T, V, S, \mathscr{C}, P \rangle$, where N and T are disjoint finite sets that denote the set of non-terminal and terminal symbols, respectively; V is a finite set of variables; S denotes the start non-terminal; and $\mathscr{C}$ is a finite set of elementary trees. For all trees in $\mathscr{C}$ it holds that for each non-terminal, there is a unique fan-out; this induces a function $\varphi \subset N \times \{1, 2, \ldots\}$ with $\varphi(A)$ being the unique fan-out of $A \in N$. For convenience, we abbreviate $\varphi(\text{root}(t))$ for a tree t as $\varphi(t)$. The function P assigns a value $0 < P(t) \leqslant 1$ (probability) to each elementary tree t such that for every non-terminal $A \in N$, the probabilities of all elementary trees whose root node is labelled A sum to 1.

The tuple $\langle N, T, V, S, \mathscr{C} \rangle$ of a given PDTSG $\langle N, T, V, S, \mathscr{C}, P \rangle$ is called the DTSG underlying the PDTSG.

DEFINITION 6. *Substitution:* The substitution $A \circ B$ is defined iff the label of the left-most substitution site of A equals the label of the root node of B. The left-most substitution site of an incomplete tree A is the leaf node containing the first occurrence of a variable in the yield of the root of A. When defined, the result of $A \circ B$ equals a copy of the tree A with B substituted for the left-most substitution site of A. In the yield argument of A, each variable terminal is replaced with the corresponding component of one or more contiguous terminals from B. For example, given yield$(A) = \langle l_1 v_2, l_4 \rangle$ and yield$(B) = \langle l_2 l_3 \rangle$ where l_n is a lexical terminal and v_n a variable, yield$(A \circ B) = \langle l_1 l_2 l_3, l_4 \rangle$.

DEFINITION 7. A *left-most derivation* (derivation henceforth) d is a sequence of zero or more substitutions $T = (\dots (f_1 \circ f_2) \circ \dots) \circ f_m$, where $f_1, \dots, f_m \in \mathscr{C}, \text{root}(T) = \text{root}(f_1) = S, \varphi(T) = 1$ and T contains no substitution sites. The probability $P(d)$ is defined as:

$$P(f_1) \cdot \ldots \cdot P(f_m) = \prod_{i=1}^{m} P(f_i)$$

Refer to Figure 9 for an example.

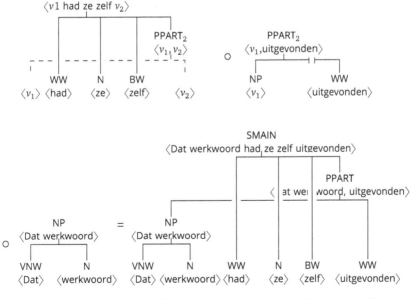

Figure 9: A discontinuous tree-substitution derivation of the tree in Figure 1. Note that in the first fragment, which has a discontinuous substitution site, the destination for the discontinuous spans is marked in advance, shown with variables (v_n) as placeholders.

DEFINITION 8. A *parse* is any tree which is the result of a derivation. A parse can have various derivations. Given the set $D(T)$ of derivations yielding parse T, the probability of T is defined as $\sum_{d \in D(T)} P(d)$.

4   GRAMMAR TRANSFORMATIONS

CFG, LCFRS, and DTSG can be seen as natural extensions of each other. This makes it possible to define transformations that help to make parsing more efficient. Specifically, we define simplified versions of these grammars that can be parsed efficiently, while their productions or labels map back to the original grammar.

4.1   *A CFG approximation of discontinuous LCFRS parsing*

Barthélemy *et al.* (2001) introduced a technique to guide the parsing of a range concatenation grammar (RCG) by a grammar with a lower parsing complexity. Van Cranenburgh (2012a) applies this idea to probabilistic LCFRS parsing and extends the method to prune unlikely constituents in addition to filtering impossible constituents.

The approximation can be formulated as a tree transformation instead of a grammar transformation. The tree transformation by Boyd (2007) encodes discontinuities in the labels of tree nodes.[3] The resulting trees can be used to induce a PCFG that can be viewed as an approximation to the corresponding PLCFRS grammar of the original, discontinuous treebank. We will call this a Split-PCFG.

DEFINITION 9. A Split-PCFG is a PCFG induced from a treebank transformed by the method of Boyd (2007); that is, discontinuous constituents have been split into several non-terminals, such that each new non-terminal covers a single contiguous component of the yield of the discontinuous constituent. Given a discontinuous non-terminal

---

[3] Hsu (2010) compares three methods for resolving discontinuity in trees: (*a*) node splitting, as applied here; (*b*) node adding, a simpler version of node splitting that does not introduce new non-terminal labels; and (*c*) node raising, the more commonly applied method of resolving discontinuity. While the latter two methods yield better performance, we use the node splitting approach because it provides a more direct mapping to discontinuous constituents, which, as we shall later see, makes it a useful source of information for pruning purposes.

X_n in the original treebank, the new non-terminals will be labelled X_n^{*m}, with m the index of the component, s.t. $1 \leqslant m \leqslant n$.

For example:

$$\text{LCFRS productions:}\ \ S(abc) \to NP(b)\ VP_2(a,c)$$
$$VP_2(a,b) \to VB(a)\ PRT(b)$$
$$\text{CFG approximation:}\ \ S \to VP_2^{*1}\ NP\ VP_2^{*2}$$
$$VP_2^{*1} \to VB$$
$$VP_2^{*2} \to PRT$$

In a post-processing step, PCFG derivations are converted to discontinuous trees by merging siblings marked with '*'. This approximation overgenerates compared to the respective LCFRS, i.e., it licenses a superset of the derivations of the respective LCFRS. For example, a component VP_2^{*1} may be generated without generating its counterpart VP_2^{*2}; such derivations can be filtered in post-processing. Furthermore, two components VP_2^{*1} and VP_2^{*2} may be generated which were extracted from different discontinuous constituents, such that their combination could not be generated by the LCFRS.[4] Another problem would occur when productions contain discontinuous constituents with the same label; the following two productions map to the same productions in the CFG approximation:

$$VP(adceb) \to VP_2(a,b)\ CNJ(c)\ VP_2(d,e)$$
$$VP(adcbe) \to VP_2(a,b)\ CNJ(c)\ VP_2(d,e)$$

However, such productions do not occur in any of the treebanks used in this work. The increased independence assumptions due to rewriting discontinuous components separately are more problematic, especially with nested discontinuous constituents. They necessitate the use of non-local statistical information to select the most likely structures, for instance by turning to tree-substitution grammar (cf. Section 2 above). (Note that the issue is not as problematic when the approximation is only used as a source of pruning information).

As a specific example of the transformation, consider the case of cross-serial dependencies. Figure 10 shows the parse tree for the

---

[4] A reviewer points out that if discontinuous rewriting is seen as synchronous rewriting (synchronous CFGs are equivalent to LCFRSs with fan-out 2), the split transformation is analogous to taking out the synchronicity.

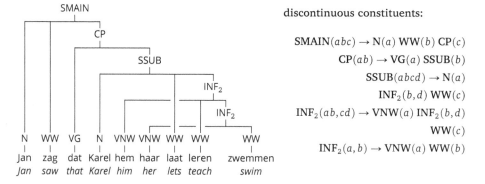

discontinuous constituents:

$$\text{SMAIN}(abc) \rightarrow \text{N}(a)\ \text{WW}(b)\ \text{CP}(c)$$
$$\text{CP}(ab) \rightarrow \text{VG}(a)\ \text{SSUB}(b)$$
$$\text{SSUB}(abcd) \rightarrow \text{N}(a)$$
$$\text{INF}_2(b,d)\ \text{WW}(c)$$
$$\text{INF}_2(ab,cd) \rightarrow \text{VNW}(a)\ \text{INF}_2(b,d)$$
$$\text{WW}(c)$$
$$\text{INF}_2(a,b) \rightarrow \text{VNW}(a)\ \text{WW}(b)$$

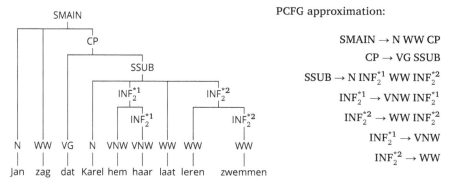

PCFG approximation:

$$\text{SMAIN} \rightarrow \text{N WW CP}$$
$$\text{CP} \rightarrow \text{VG SSUB}$$
$$\text{SSUB} \rightarrow \text{N INF}_2^{*1}\ \text{WW INF}_2^{*2}$$
$$\text{INF}_2^{*1} \rightarrow \text{VNW INF}_2^{*1}$$
$$\text{INF}_2^{*2} \rightarrow \text{WW INF}_2^{*2}$$
$$\text{INF}_2^{*1} \rightarrow \text{VNW}$$
$$\text{INF}_2^{*2} \rightarrow \text{WW}$$

Figure 10: Cross-serial dependencies in Dutch expressed with discontinuous constituents (top); and the same parse tree, after discontinuities have been encoded in node labels (bottom)

example sentence from the previous section, along with the grammar productions for it, before and after applying the CFG approximation of LCFRS. Note that in the approximation, the second level of INF nodes may be rewritten separately, and a context-free grammar cannot place the non-local constraint that each transitive verb should be paired with a direct object. On the other hand, through the use of tree substitution, an elementary tree may capture the whole construction of two verbs cross-serially depending on two objects, and the model needs only to prefer an analysis with this elementary tree. Once an elementary tree contains the whole construction, it no longer matters whether its internal nodes contain discontinuous constituents or indexed node labels, and the complexity of discontinuous rewriting is weakened to a statistical regularity.

A phenomenon which cannot be captured in this representation, not even with the help of tree-substitution, is recursive synchronous rewriting (Kallmeyer *et al.* 2009). Although this phenomenon is rare, it does occur in treebanks.

4.2   *TSG compression*

Using grammar transformations, it is possible to parse with a TSG without having to represent elementary trees in the chart explicitly, but instead work with a parser for the base grammar underlying the TSG (typically a CFG, in our case an LCFRS).

In this section we present such a transformation for an arbitrary discontinuous TSG to a string-rewriting LCFRS. We first look at well-established strategies for reducing a continuous TSG to a CFG, and then show that these carry over to the discontinuous case. Previous work was based on probabilistic TSG without discontinuity; this special case of PDTSG is referred to as PTSG.

4.2.1   Compressing PTSG to PCFG

Goodman (2003) gives a reduction to a PCFG for the special case of a PTSG based on all fragments from a given treebank and their frequencies. This reduction is stochastically equivalent to an all-fragments PTSG after the summation of probabilities from equivalent derivations; however, it does not admit parsing with TSGs consisting of arbitrary sets of elementary trees or assuming arbitrary probability models. Perhaps counter-intuitively, restrictions on the set of fragments increase the size of Goodman's reduction (e.g., depth restriction, Goodman 2003, p. 134). While Goodman (2003) gives instantiations of his reduction with various probability models, the limitation is that probability assignments of fragments have to be expressible as a composition of the weights of the productions in each fragment. Since each production in the reduction participates in numerous implicit fragments, it is not possible to adjust the probability of an individual fragment without affecting related fragments. We leave Goodman's reduction aside for now, because we would prefer a more general method.

A naive way to convert any TSG is to decorate each internal node of its elementary trees with a globally unique number, which can be removed from derivations in a post-processing step. Each elementary tree then contributes one or more grammar productions, and because of the unique labels, elementary trees will always be derived as a whole. However, this conversion results in a large number of non-terminals, which are essentially 'inert': they never participate in substitution but deterministically rewrite to the rest of their elementary tree.

A more compact transformation is used in Sangati and Zuidema (2011), which can be applied to arbitrary PTSGs, but adds a minimal number of new non-terminal nodes. Internal nodes are removed from elementary trees, yielding a flattened tree of depth 1. Each flattened tree is then converted to a grammar production. Each production and original fragment is stored in a backtransform table. This table makes it possible to restore the original fragments of a derivation built from flattened productions. Whenever two fragments would map to the same flattened production, a unary node with a unique identifier is added to disambiguate them. The weight associated with an elementary tree carries over to the first production it produces; the rest of the productions are assigned a weight of 1.

4.2.2   Compressing PDTSG to PLCFRS

The transformation defined by Sangati and Zuidema (2011) assumes that a sequence of productions can be read off from a syntactic tree, such as a standard phrase-structure tree that can be converted into a sequence of context-free grammar productions. Using the method for inducing LCFRS productions from syntactic trees given in Section 4.2.1, we can apply the same TSG transformation to discontinuous trees as well.

Due to the design of the parser we will use, it is desirable to have grammar productions in binarized form, and to separate phrasal and lexical productions. We therefore binarize the flattened trees with a left-factored binarization that adds unique identifiers to every intermediate node introduced by the binarization. In order to separate phrasal and lexical productions, a new POS tag is introduced for each terminal, which selects for that specific terminal. A sequence of productions is then read off from the transformed tree. The unique identifier in the first production is used to look up the original elementary tree in the backtransform table.[5]

Figure 11 illustrates the transformation of a discontinuous TSG. The middle column shows the productions after transforming each ele-

---

[5] Note that only this first production requires a globally unique identifier; to reduce the grammar constant, the other identifiers can be merged for equivalent productions.

Elementary tree	Productions	Weight

S
$\langle v_1 v_2 v_3 v_4$ uitgevonden $\rangle$

PPART$_2$
$\langle v_1$, uitgevonden $\rangle$

NP WW N BW WW
$\langle v_1 \rangle$ $\langle v_2 \rangle$ $\langle v_3 \rangle$ $\langle v_4 \rangle$ $\langle$uitgevonden $\rangle$

$S(ab) \rightarrow S^1(a) \, WW(b)$ f/f'
$S^1(ab) \rightarrow S^2(a) \, BW(b)$ 1
$S^2(ab) \rightarrow S^3(a) \, N(b)$ 1
$S^3(ab) \rightarrow NP(a) \, WW^4(b)$ 1
$WW^4(\text{uitgevonden}) \rightarrow \varepsilon$ 1

S
$\langle v1$ had ze zelf $v_2 \rangle$

PPART$_2$
$\langle v_1, v_2 \rangle$

WW N BW
$\langle v_1 \rangle \langle$had$\rangle$ $\langle$ze$\rangle$ $\langle$zelf$\rangle$ $\langle v_2 \rangle$

$S(abc) \rightarrow S^5_2(a,c) \, BW^6(b)$ f/f'
$S^5_2(ab,c) \rightarrow S^7_2(a,c) \, N(b)$ 1
$S^7_2(ab,c) \rightarrow PPART_2(a,c) \, WW^8(b)$ 1
$WW^8(\text{had}) \rightarrow \varepsilon$ 1
$N^7(\text{ze}) \rightarrow \varepsilon$ 1
$BW^6(\text{zelf}) \rightarrow \varepsilon$ 1

PPART$_2$
$\langle v_1,$uitgevonden$\rangle$

NP WW
$\langle v_1 \rangle$ $\langle$uitgevonden$\rangle$

$PPART_2(a,b) \rightarrow NP(a) \, WW^9(b)$ f/f'
$WW^9(\text{uitgevonden}) \rightarrow \varepsilon$ 1

Figure 11: Transforming a discontinuous tree-substitution grammar into an LCFRS and backtransform table. The elementary trees are extracted from the tree in Figure 1 with labels abbreviated. The first production of each fragment is used as an index to the backtransform table so that the original fragments in derivations can be reconstructed.

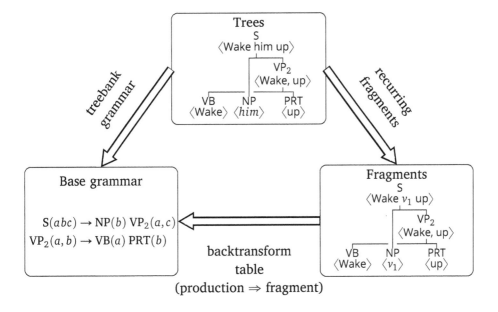

Figure 12: Diagram of the methods of grammar induction.

mentary tree. The rightmost column shows how relative frequencies can be used as weights, where f is the frequency of the elementary tree in the treebank, and f' is the frequency mass of elementary trees with the same root label. Note that the productions for the first elementary tree contain no discontinuity, because the discontinuous internal node is eliminated. Conversely, the transformation may also introduce more discontinuity, due to the binarization (but cf. Section 8.1 below).

Figure 12 presents an overview of the methods of grammar induction presented thus far, as well as the approach for finding recurring fragments that will be introduced in the next section.

5 INDUCING A TSG FROM A TREEBANK

In Data-Oriented Parsing the grammar is implicit in the treebank itself, and in principle all possible fragments from its trees can be used to derive new sentences. Grammar induction is therefore conceptually simple (even though the grammar may be very large), as there is no training or learning involved. This maximizes re-use of previous experience.

The use of all possible fragments allows for multiple derivations of the same tree; this spurious ambiguity is seen as a virtue in DOP, because it combines the specificity of larger fragments and the smoothing of smaller fragments. This is in contrast to parsimonious approaches which decompose each tree in the training corpus into a sequence of fragments representing a single derivation.

5.1   *Extracting recurring fragments*

Representing all possible fragments of a treebank is not feasible, since the number of fragments is exponential in terms of the number of nodes. A practical solution is to define a subset. A method called Double-DOP (2DOP; Sangati and Zuidema 2011) implements this without compromising on the principle of data-orientation. It restricts the fragment set to recurring fragments, i.e., fragments that occur in at least two different contexts. These are found by considering every pair of trees and extracting the largest tree fragments they have in common. It is feasible to do this exhaustively for the whole treebank. This is in contrast to the sampling of fragments in earlier DOP models (Bod 2001) and Bayesian TSGs. Since the space of fragments is enormous (that is, exponential in terms of sentence length), it stands to reason that a sampling approach will not discover all relevant fragments in a reasonable time frame.

Sangati *et al.* (2010) presents a tree-kernel method for extracting maximal recurring fragments that operates in quadratic time in terms of the number of nodes in the treebank. A faster version of this method was presented in van Cranenburgh (2014), which uses a linear average time tree kernel, and introduces the ability to handle discontinuous trees. We obtain a further increase in speed by implementing an inverted index with a compressed bitmap (Chambi *et al.* 2015).

5.2   *Discontinuous fragments*

The aforementioned fragment extraction algorithms can be adapted to support trees with discontinuous constituents. Instead of implementing a new version with data structures for discontinuous trees following Definitions 1 and 2, we apply a representation that makes it possible to add discontinuous trees as a special case.

In the representation, leaf nodes are decorated with indices indicating their ordering. Just as in Figure 6, a discontinuous tree may be represented as a continuous tree, as long as information about the yield is encoded somehow. We do this by storing indices as leaf nodes, which denote an ordering and refer to a separate list of tokens. This makes it possible to use the same data structures as for continuous trees, as long as the child nodes are kept in a canonical order (induced from the order of the lowest index of each child).

Indices are used not only to keep track of the order of lexical nodes in a fragment, but also for that of the contribution of substitution sites. This is necessary in order to preserve the configuration of the yield in the original sentence. When leaf nodes are compared, the indices stand in for the token at the sentence position referred to. After a fragment is extracted, any indices need to be canonicalized. The indices originate from the original sentence, but need to be decoupled from this original context. This process is analogous to how LCFRS productions are read off from a tree with discontinuous constituents, in which contiguous intervals of indices are replaced by variables.

The canonicalization of fragments is achieved in three steps, as defined in the pseudocode of Algorithm 1; Figure 13 illustrates the process. In the examples, substitution sites have spans denoted with inclusive *start:end* intervals, as extracted from the original parse tree, which are reduced to variables denoting contiguous spans whose relation to the other spans is reflected by their indices.

Algorithm 1 Canonicalizing discontinuous fragments.

INPUT: A tree fragment t with indexed terminals w_i or intervals $\langle i:j,\ldots\rangle$ as
  leaves $(0 \leqslant i < j < n)$
OUTPUT: A tree fragment with modified indices.
1: $k \leftarrow$ the smallest index in t
2: subtract k from each index in t
3: FOR ALL intervals $I = \langle i:j,\ldots\rangle$ of the substitution sites in t
4:     FOR ALL $i:j \in I$
5:         replace $i:j$ with i
6:         subtract $j - i$ from all indices k s.t. $k > j$
7: FOR ALL indices i in t
8:     IF the indices $i + 1$ and $i + 2$ are not in t
9:         $k \leftarrow$ the smallest index in t s.t. $k > i$
10:         subtract $k - i$ from all indices y s.t. $y > i$

---

1. Translate indices so that they start at 0; e.g.:

   WW   WW
   | ⇒ |
   uitgevonden$_5$ uitgevonden$_0$

2. Reduce spans of frontier non-terminals to length 1; move surrounding indices accordingly; e.g.:

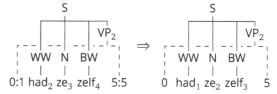

3. Compress gaps to length 1; e.g.:

   VP$_2$ VP$_2$
   NP   WW   ⇒   NP   WW
   | | | |
   0 uitgevonden$_5$ 0 uitgevonden$_2$

Figure 13: Canonicalization of fragments extracted from parse trees. These sample fragments have been extracted from the tree in Figure 1. The fragments are visualized here as discontinuous tree structures, but since the discontinuities are encoded in the indices of the yield, they can be represented in a standard bracketing format as used by the fragment extractor.

We will refer to the combination of Double-DOP with discontinuous constituents as Disco-2DOP. When recurring fragments are extracted from the Tiger treebank (cf. Section 8.1), we find that 10.4%

of fragment types contain a discontinuous node (root, internal, or substitution site). This can be contrasted with the observation that 30% of sentences in the Tiger treebank contain one or more discontinuous constituents, and that 20.9% of production types in the PLCFRS treebank grammar of Tiger contain a discontinuous non-terminal. On the other hand, when occurrence frequencies are taken into account, both the fragments and productions with discontinuities account for around 6.5% of the total frequency mass.

6   PARSING WITH PLCFRS AND PDTSG

After extracting fragments by means of the method of Section 5, we augment the set of fragments with all depth 1 fragments, in order to preserve complete coverage of the training set trees. Since depth 1 fragments are equivalent to single grammar productions, this ensures strong equivalence between the TSG and the respective treebank grammar.[6] We then apply the grammar transformation (cf. Section 4.2.1) to turn the fragments into productions. Productions corresponding to fragments are assigned a probability based on the relative frequency of the respective fragment; productions introduced by the transformation are given a probability of 1. For an example, please refer back to Figure 11.

We parse with the transformed grammar using the disco-dop parser (van Cranenburgh *et al.* 2011; van Cranenburgh 2012a). This is an agenda-based parser for PLCFRS based on the algorithm in Kallmeyer and Maier (2010, 2013), extended to produce *n*-best derivations (Huang and Chiang 2005) and exploit coarse-to-fine pruning (Charniak *et al.* 2006).

Parsing with LCFRS can be done with a weighted deduction system and an agenda-based parser. The deduction steps are given in Figure 14; for the pseudo-code of the parser see Algorithm 2, which is an extended version of the parser in Kallmeyer and Maier (2010, 2013) that obtains the complete parse forest as opposed to just the Viterbi derivation.

---

[6] Previous DOP work such as Zollmann and Sima'an (2005) adds all possible tree fragments up to depth 3. Preliminary experiments on 2DOP gave no improvement on performance, while tripling the grammar size; therefore we do not apply this in further experiments.

Lexical:
$$\frac{}{p : [A, \langle\langle w_i \rangle\rangle]}$$
$p : A(w_i) \to \varepsilon \in \mathcal{G}$

Unary:
$$\frac{x : [B, \alpha]}{p \cdot x : [A, \alpha]}$$
$p : A(\alpha) \to B(\alpha)$
is an instantiated rule
from $\mathcal{G}$

Binary:
$$\frac{x : [B, \beta], \; y : [C, \gamma]}{p \cdot x \cdot y : [A, \alpha]}$$
$p : A(\alpha) \to B(\beta) \, C(\gamma)$
is an instantiated rule
from $\mathcal{G}$

Goal:
$[S, \langle\langle w_1 \cdots w_n \rangle\rangle]$

Figure 14: Weighted deduction system for binarized LCFRS

In Section 6.1 we describe the probabilistic instantiation of DTSG and the criterion to select the best parse. Section 6.2 describes how derivations from the compressed TSG are converted back into trees composed of the full elementary trees. Section 6.4 describes how coarse-to-fine pruning is employed to make parsing efficient.

Algorithm 2 A probabilistic agenda-based parser for LCFRS.

INPUT: A sentence $w_1 \cdots w_n$, a grammar $\mathcal{G}$
OUTPUT: A chart $\mathcal{C}$ with Viterbi probabilities, a parse forest $\mathcal{F}$.
  1: initialize agenda $\mathcal{A}$ with all possible POS tags for input
  2: WHILE $\mathcal{A}$ not empty
  3:     $\langle I, x \rangle \leftarrow$ pop item with best score on agenda
  4:     add $\langle I, x \rangle$ to $\mathcal{C}$
  5:     FOR ALL $\langle I', z \rangle$ that can be deduced from $\langle I, x \rangle$ and items in $\mathcal{C}$
  6:         IF $I' \notin \mathcal{A} \cup \mathcal{C}$
  7:             enqueue $\langle I', z \rangle$ in $\mathcal{A}$
  8:         ELSE IF $I' \in \mathcal{A} \wedge z >$ score for I' in $\mathcal{A}$
  9:             update weight of I' in $\mathcal{A}$ to z
10:         add edge for I' to $\mathcal{F}$

6.1   *Probabilities and disambiguation*

Our probabilistic model uses the relative frequency estimate (RFE), which has shown good results with the Double-DOP model (Sangati and Zuidema 2011). The relative frequency of a fragment is the number of its occurrences, divided by the total number of occurrences of fragments with the same root node.

In DOP many derivations may produce the same parse tree, and it has been shown that approximating the most probable parse, which considers all derivations for a tree, yields better results than the most probable derivation (Bod 1995). To select a parse tree from a derivation forest, we compute tree probabilities on the basis of the 10,000 most probable DOP derivations, and select the tree with the largest probability. Although the algorithm of Huang and Chiang (2005) makes it is possible to extract the exact k-best derivations from a derivation forest, we apply pruning while building the forest.

6.2   *Reconstructing derivations*

After a derivation forest is obtained and a list of k-best derivations has been produced, the backtransform is applied to these derivations to recover their internal structure. This proceeds by doing a depth-first traversal of the derivations, and expanding each non-intermediate[7] node into a template of the original fragment. These templates are stored in a backtransform table indexed by the first binarized production of the fragment in question. The template fragment has its substitution sites marked, which are filled with values obtained by recursively expanding the children of the current constituent.

6.3   *Efficient discontinuous parsing*

We review several strategies for making discontinuous parsing efficient. As noted by Levy (2005, p. 138), the intrinsic challenge of discontinuous constituents is that a parser will generate a large number of potential discontinuous spans.

6.3.1   Outside estimates

Outside estimates (also known as context-summary estimates and figures-of-merit) are computed offline for a given grammar. During parsing they provide an estimate of the outside probability for a given constituent, i.e., the probability of a complete derivation with that constituent divided by the probability of the constituent. The estimate can be used to prioritize items in the agenda. Estimates were first introduced for discontinuous LCFRS parsing in Kallmeyer and Maier (2010, 2013). Their estimates are only applied up to sentences of 30 words. Beyond 30 words the table grows too large.

---

[7] An intermediate node is a node introduced by the binarization.

A different estimate is given by Angelov and Ljunglöf (2014), who succeed in parsing longer sentences and providing an A* estimate, which is guaranteed to find the best derivation.

6.3.2   Non-projective dependency conversion

Hall and Nivre (2008), Versley (2014), and Fernández-González and Martins (2015) apply a reversible dependency conversion to the Tiger treebank, and use a non-projective dependency parser to parse with the converted treebank. The method has the advantage of being fast due to the greedy nature of the arc-eager transition-based dependency parser that is employed. The parser copes with non-projectivity by reordering tokens during parsing. Experiments are reported on the full Tiger treebank without length restrictions.

6.3.3   Reducing fan-out

The most direct way of reducing the complexity of LCFRS parsing is to reduce the fan-out of the grammar.

Maier *et al.* (2012) introduces a linguistically motivated reduction of the fan-outs of the Negra and Penn treebanks to fan-out 2 (up to a single gap per constituent). This enables parsing of sentences of up to length 40.

Nederhof and Vogler (2014) introduce a method of synchronous parsing with an LCFRS and a definite clause grammar. A parameter allows the fan-out (and thus parsing complexity) of the LCFRS to be reduced. Experiments are reported on sentences of up to 30 words on a small section of the Tiger treebank.

6.3.4   Coarse-to-fine pruning

We will focus on coarse-to-fine pruning, introduced in Charniak *et al.* (2006) and applied to discontinuous parsing by van Cranenburgh (2012a), who reports parsing results on the Negra treebank without length restrictions. Compared to the previous methods, this method does not change the grammar, but adds several new grammars to be used as preprocessing steps. Compared to the outside estimates, this method exploits sentence-specific information, since pruning information is collected during parsing with the coarser grammars.

Pauls and Klein (2009) present a comparison of coarse-to-fine and (hierarchical A*) outside estimates, and conclude that except when near-optimality is required, coarse-to-fine is more effective as it prunes a larger number of unlikely constituents.

A similar observation is obtained from a comparison of the discontinuous coarse-to-fine method and the outside estimates of Angelov and Ljunglöf (2014): coarse-to-fine is faster with longer sentences (30 words and up), at the cost of not always producing the most likely derivation (Ljunglöf, personal communication).

6.4   *Coarse-to-fine pipeline*

In order to tame the complexity of LCFRS and DOP, we apply coarse-to-fine pruning. Different grammars are used in the sequel, each being an overgenerating approximation of the next. That is, a coarse grammar will generate a larger set of constituents than a fine grammar. Parsing with a coarser grammar is more efficient, and all constituents which can be ruled out as improbable with a coarser grammar can be discarded as candidates when parsing with the next grammar. A constituent is ruled improbable if it does not appear in the k-best derivations of a parse forest. We use the same setup as in van Cranenburgh (2012a); namely, we parse in three stages, using three different grammars:

1. Split-PCFG: A CFG approximation of the discontinuous treebank grammar; rewrites spans of discontinuous constituents independently.
2. PLCFRS: The discontinuous treebank grammar; rewrites discontinuous constituents in a single operation. A discontinuous span $X_n\langle x_1,\ldots,x_n\rangle$ is added to the chart only if all of $X_n^{*m}\langle x_m\rangle$ with $1 \leqslant m \leqslant n$ are part of the k-best derivations of the chart of the previous stage.
3. Disco-DOP: The discontinuous DOP grammar; uses tree fragments instead of individual productions from the treebank. A discontinuous span $X_n\langle x_1,\ldots,x_n\rangle$ is added to the chart only if $X_n\langle x_1,\ldots,x_n\rangle$ is part of the k-best derivations of the chart of the previous stage, or if X_n is an intermediate symbol introduced by the TSG compression.

The first stage is necessary because without pruning, the PLCFRS generates too many discontinuous spans, the majority of which are improbable or not even part of a complete derivation. The second stage is not necessary for efficiency but gives slightly better accuracy on discontinuous constituents.

For example, while parsing the sentence "Wake your friend up," the discontinuous VP "Wake ... up" may be produced in the PLCFRS stage. Before allowing this constituent to enter into the agenda and the chart, the chart of the previous stage is consulted to see if the two discontinuous components "Wake" and "up" were part of the k-best derivations. In the DOP stage, multiple elementary trees may be headed by this discontinuous constituent, and again they are only allowed on the chart if the previous stage produced the constituent as part of its k-best derivations.

The initial values for k are 10,000 and 50 for the PLCFRS and DOP grammar respectively. These values are chosen to be able to directly compare the new approach with the results in van Cranenburgh (2012a). However, experimenting with a higher value for k for the DOP stage has shown to yield improved performance. In other coarse-to-fine work the pruning criterion is based on a posterior threshold (e.g., Charniak *et al.* 2006; Bansal and Klein 2010); the k-best approach has the advantage that it does not require the computation of inside and outside probabilities.

For the initial PCFG stage, we apply beam search as in Collins (1999). The highest scoring item in each cell is tracked and only items up to 10,000 times less probable are allowed to enter the chart.

Experiments and results are described in Sections 8–9.

7   DISCONTINUITY WITHOUT LCFRS

The idea up to now has been to generate discontinuous constituents using formal rewrite operations of LCFRS. It should be noted, however, that the PCFG approximation used in the pruning stage reproduces discontinuities using information derived from the non-terminal labels. Instead of using this technique only as a crutch for pruning, it can also be combined with the use of fragments to obtain a pipeline that runs in cubic time. While the CFG approximation increases the independence assumptions for discontinuous constituents, the use of large fragments in the DOP approach can mitigate this increase. To create the CFG approximation of the discontinuous treebank grammar, the treebank is transformed by splitting discontinuous constituents into several non-terminal nodes (as explained in Section 4.1), after which grammar productions are extracted. This last step can also be replaced with fragment extraction to obtain a DOP grammar from the transformed treebank. We shall refer to this alternative approach as 'Split-2DOP.' The coarse-to-fine pipeline is now as follows:

1. Split-PCFG: A treebank grammar based on the CFG approximation of discontinuous constituents; rewrites spans of discontinuous constituents independently.
2. Split-2DOP grammar: tree fragments based on the same transformed treebank as above.

Since every discontinuous non-terminal is split up into a new non-terminal for each of its spans, the independence assumptions for that non-terminal in a probabilistic grammar are increased. While this representation is not sufficient to express the full range of nested discontinuous configurations, it appears adequate for the linguistic phenomena in the treebanks used in this work, since their trees can be unambiguously transformed back and forth into this representation. Moreover, the machinery of Data-Oriented Parsing mitigates the increase in independence assumptions through the use of large fragments. We can therefore parse using a DOP model with a context-free grammar as the symbolic backbone, and still recover discontinuous constituents.

8   EXPERIMENTAL SETUP

In this section we describe the experimental setup for benchmarking our discontinuous Double-DOP implementations on several discontinuous treebanks.

8.1   *Treebanks and preprocessing*

We evaluate on three languages: for German, we use the Negra (Skut *et al.* 1997) and Tiger (Brants *et al.* 2002) treebanks; for English, we use a discontinuous version of the Penn treebank (Evang and Kallmeyer 2011); and for Dutch, we use the Lassy (Van Noord 2009) and CGN (van der Wouden *et al.* 2002) treebanks; cf. Table 1. Negra and Tiger contain discontinuous annotations by design, as a strategy to cope with the relatively free word order of German. The discontinuous Penn treebank consists of the WSJ section in which traces have

Table 1: The discontinuous treebanks used in the experiments and the number of sentences used for development, training, and testing

Treebank	train (sentences)	dev (sentences)	test (sentences)
GERMAN			
Negra	18,602	1000	1000
	(#1–18,602)	(#19,603–20,602)	(#18,603–19,602)
Tiger	40,379 / 45,427	5048	5047
ENGLISH			
PTB: WSJ	39,832	1346	2416
DUTCH			
Lassy small	52,157	6520	6523
CGN	70,277	2000	2000

been converted to discontinuous constituents; we use the version used in Evang and Kallmeyer (2011, Sections 5.1–5.2) without restrictions on the transformations. The Lassy treebank is referred to as a dependency treebank but when discontinuity is allowed it can be directly interpreted as a constituency treebank. The *Corpus Gesproken Nederlands* (CGN, Spoken Dutch Corpus; van der Wouden *et al.* 2002) is a Dutch spoken language corpus with the same syntactic annotations. We use the syntactically annotated sentences from the Netherlands (i.e., without the Flemish part) of up to 100 tokens. The train-dev-test splits we employ are as commonly used for the Penn treebank: sec. 2–21, sec. 24, sec. 23, respectively. For Negra we use the one defined in Dubey and Keller (2003). For Tiger we follow Hall and Nivre (2008) who define sections 0–9 where sentence i belongs to section i mod 10, sec. 0 is used as test, sec. 1 as development, and 2–9 as training. When parsing the Tiger test set, the development set is added to the training set as well; while this is not customary, it ensures the results are comparable with Hall and Nivre (2008).

The same split is applied to the CGN treebank but with a single training set. For Lassy the split is our own.[8]

---

[8] The Lassy split derives from 80–10–10 partitions of the canonically ordered sentence IDs in each subcorpus (viz. dpc, WR, WS, and wiki). Canonically ordered refers to a 'version sort' where an identifier such as '2.12.a' is treated as a tuple of three elements compared consecutively.

For purposes of training we apply heuristics for head assignment (Klein and Manning 2003) and binarize the trees in the training sets head-outward with $h = 1$, $v = 1$ markovization; i.e., n-ary nodes are factored into nodes specifying an immediate sibling and parent. Note that for LCFRS, a binarization may increase the fan-out, and thus the complexity of parsing. It is possible to select the binarization in such a way as to minimize this complexity (Gildea 2010). However, experiments show that this increase in fan-out does not actually occur, regardless of the binarization strategy (van Cranenburgh 2012a). Head-outward means that constituents are binarized in a right-factored manner up until the head child, after which the rest of the binarization continues in a left-factored manner.

We add fan-out markers to guarantee unique fan-outs for non-terminal labels, e.g., $\{VP, VP_2, VP_3, \ldots\}$, which are removed again for evaluation.

For the Dutch and German treebanks, punctuation is not part of the syntactic annotations. This causes spurious discontinuities, as the punctuation interrupts the constituents dominating its surrounding tokens. Additionally, punctuation provides a signal for constituent boundaries, and it is useful to incorporate it as part of the rest of the phrase structures. We use the method described in van Cranenburgh (2012a): punctuation is attached to the highest constituent that contains a neighbor to its right. With this strategy there is no increase in the amount of discontinuity with respect to a version of the treebank with punctuation removed. The CGN treebank contains spoken language phenomena, including disfluencies such as interjections and repeated words. In preprocessing, we treat these as if they were punctuation tokens; i.e., they are moved to an appropriate constituent (as defined above) and are ignored in the evaluation.

The complexity of parsing with a binarized LCFRS is $O(n^{3\varphi})$ with φ the highest fan-out of the non-terminals in the grammar (Seki *et al.* 1991). For a given grammar, it is possible to give a tighter upper bound on the complexity of parsing. Given the unique fan-outs of non-terminals in a grammar, the number of operations it takes to apply a production is the sum of the fan-outs in the production (Gildea 2010):

$$c(p) = \varphi(A) + \sum_{i=1}^{r} \varphi(B_i)$$

The complexity of parsing with a grammar is then the maximum value of this measure for productions in the grammar. In our experiments we find a worst-case time complexity of $O(n^9)$ for parsing with the DOP grammars extracted from Negra and WSJ. The following sentence from Negra contributes a grammar production with complexity 9. The production is from the VP of *vorgeworfen*; bracketed words are from other constituents, indicating the discontinuities:

(2)   Den Stadtteilparlamentariern [ist] immer wieder ["Kirchturmpolitik"]
       The district-MPs   have always again   "parochialism"
       vorgeworfen [worden], weil   sie nicht über   die Grenzen   des
       accused   been,   because they not   beyond the boundaries of-the
       Ortsbezirks hinausgucken würden.
       local-district look-out   would.
       'Time and again, the district MPs have been accused of "parochialism" be-
       cause they would not look out beyond the boundaries of the local district.'

The complexities for Tiger and Lassy are $O(n^{10})$ and $O(n^{12})$ respectively, due to a handful of anomalous sentences; by discarding these sentences, a grammar with a complexity of $O(n^9)$ can be obtained with no or negligible effect on accuracy.

8.2   *Unknown words*

In initial experiments the parser is trained and evaluated on gold standard part-of-speech tags, as in previous experiments on discontinuous parsing. Later we show results when tags are assigned automatically with a simple unknown word model, based on the Stanford parser (Klein and Manning 2003). An open class threshold σ determines which tags are considered open class tags; tags that rewrite more than σ words are considered open class tags, and words they rewrite are open class words. Open class words in the training set that do not occur more than 4 times are replaced with signatures based on a list of features; words in the test set which are not part of the known words from the training set are replaced with similar signatures. The features are defined in the Stanford parser as *Model 4*, which is relatively language independent; cf. Table 2 for the list of features.[9] Signatures are formed by concatenating the names of features that apply

---

[9] This table is based on code from the Stanford parser (release 2014-08-27), specifically the method getSignature4 in the file EnglishUnknownWord-Model.java.

Table 2: Unknown word features, Stanford parser *Model 4*

Feature	Description
AC	All capital letters
SC	Initial capital, first word in sentence
C	Initial capital, other position
L, U	Has lower / upper case letter
S	No letters
N, n	All digits / one or more digits
H, P, C	Has dash / period / comma
x	Last character if letter and length > 3

to a word; e.g., 'forty-two' gives _UNK-L-H-o. A probability mass ϵ is assigned for combinations of known open class words with unseen tags. We use $\epsilon = 0.01$. We tuned σ on each training set to ensure that no closed class words are identified as open class words; for English and German we use $\sigma = 150$, and we use $\sigma = 100$ for Dutch.

8.3   *Function tags*

We investigated two methods of having the parser produce function tags in addition to the usual phrase labels. The first method is to train a separate discriminative classifier that adds function tags to parse trees in a post-processing step. This approach is introduced in Blaheta and Charniak (2000). We employed their feature set.

Another approach is to simply append the function tags to the non-terminal labels, resulting in, e.g., NP-SBJ and NP-OBJ for subject and object noun phrases. While this approach introduces sparsity and may affect the performance without function tags, we found this approach to perform best and therefore report results with this approach. Gabbard *et al.* (2006) and Fraser *et al.* (2013) use this approach as well. Compared to the classifier approach, it does not require any tuning, and the resulting model is fully generative. We apply this to the Tiger, WSJ, and Lassy treebanks.

The Penn treebank differs from the German and Dutch treebanks with respect to function tags. The Penn treebank only has function tags on selected non-terminals (never on preterminals) and each non-terminal may have several function tags from four possible categories; whereas the German and Dutch treebanks have a single function tag on most non-terminals. The tag set also differs considerably: the Penn treebank has 20 function tags, Lassy has 31, and Tiger has 43.

8.4   *Treebank refinements*

We apply a set of manual treebank refinements based on previous work. In order to compare the results on Negra with previous work, we do not apply the state splits when working with gold standard POS tags.

For Dutch and German we split the POS tags for the sentence-ending punctuation '.!?'. For all treebanks we add the feature 'year' to the preterminal label of tokens with numbers in the range 1900–2040, and replace the token with 1970. Other numbers are replaced with 000.

8.4.1   Tiger

For Tiger we apply the refinements described in Fraser *et al.* (2013). Since the Negra treebank is only partially annotated with morphological information, we do not apply these refinements to that treebank.

8.4.2   WSJ

We follow the treebank refinements of Klein and Manning (2003) for the Wall Street Journal section of the Penn treebank.

8.4.3   Lassy

The Lassy treebank contains fine-grained part-of-speech tags with morphological features. It is possible to use the full part-of-speech tags as the preterminal labels, but this introduces sparsity. We select a subset of features to add to the preterminal labels:

- nouns: proper/regular;
- verbs: auxiliary/main, finite/infinite;
- conjunctions: coordinating/subordinating;
- pronouns: personal/demonstrative;
- pre- vs. postposition.

Additionally, we percolate the feature identifying finite and infinite verbs to the parents and grandparents of the verb.

For multi-word units (MWU), we append the label of its head child. This helps distinguish MWUs as being nominal, verbal, prepositional, or otherwise.

The last two transformations are based on those for Tiger. Unary NPs are added for single nouns and pronouns in sentential, prepositional and infinitival constituents. For conjuncts, the function tag of the parent is copied. Both transformations can be reversed.

Since the CGN treebank uses a different syntax for the fine-grained POS tags, we do not apply these refinements to that treebank.

8.5 *Metrics*

We employ the exact match and Parseval measures (Black *et al.* 1992) as evaluation metrics. Both are based on bracketings that identify the label and yield of each constituent. The exact match is the proportion of sentences in which all labelled bracketings are correct. The Parseval measures consist of the precision, recall, and F-measure of the correct labelled bracketings averaged across the treebank. Since the POS accuracy is crucial to the performance of a parser and neither of the previous metrics reflect it, we also report the proportion of correct POS tags.

We use the evaluation parameters typically used with EVALB on the Penn treebank. Namely, the root node and punctuation are not counted towards the score (similar to COLLINS.prm,[10] except that we discount all punctuation, including brackets). Counting the root node as a constituent should not be done because it is not part of the corpus annotation and the parser is able to generate it without doing any work; when the root node is counted it inflates the F-score by several percentage points. Punctuation should be ignored because in the original annotation of the Dutch and German treebanks, punctuation is attached directly under the root node instead of as part of constituents. Punctuation can be re-attached using heuristics for the purposes of parsing, but evaluation should not be affected by this.

It is not possible to directly compare evaluation results from discontinuous parsing to existing state-of-the-art parsers that do not produce discontinuous constituents, since parses without discontinuous constituents contain a different set of bracketings; cf. Figure 15, which compares discontinuous bracketings to the bracketings extracted from a tree in which discontinuity has been resolved by attaching non-head siblings higher in the tree, as used in work on parsing Negra.

---

[10] This is part of the EVALB software, cf.

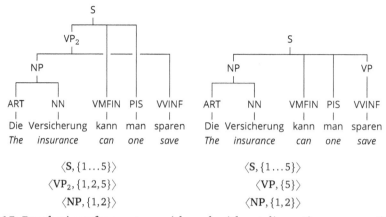

Figure 15: Bracketings from a tree with and without discontinuous constituents

Compared to an evaluation of bracketings without discontinuous constituents, an evaluation including discontinuous bracketings is more stringent. This is because bracketings are scored in an all-or-nothing manner, and a discontinuous bracketing includes non-local elements that would be scored separately when discontinuity is removed in a preprocessing step.

For function tags we use two metrics:

1. The non-null metric of Blaheta and Charniak (2000), which is the F-score of function tags on all correctly parsed bracketings. Since the German and Dutch treebanks include function tags on pre-terminals, we also include function tags on correctly tagged words in this metric.

2. A combined F-measure on bracketings of the form $\langle C, F, \text{span} \rangle$, where C is a syntactic category and F a function tag.

9   EVALUATION

This section presents an evaluation on three languages, and with respect to the use of function tags, tree fragments, pruning, and probabilities.

9.1   *Main results on three languages*

Table 3 lists the results for discontinuous parsing of three Germanic languages, with unknown word models. The cited works by Kallmeyer and Maier (2013) and Evang and Kallmeyer (2011) also use LCFRS

for discontinuity but employ a treebank grammar with relative frequencies of productions. Hall and Nivre (2008), Versley (2014), and
Fernández-González and Martins (2015) use a conversion to dependencies discussed in Section 6.3.2. For English and German our results
improve upon the best known discontinuous constituency parsing results. The new system achieves a 16% relative error reduction over the
previous best result for discontinuous parsing on sentences of size $\leqslant 40$
in the Negra test set. In terms of efficiency, the Disco-2DOP model is
more than three times as fast as the DOP reduction, taking about three
hours instead of ten on a single core. The grammar is also more compact: the Disco-2DOP grammar is only a third the size of that of the
DOP reduction, at 6 MB versus 18 MB compressed size.

Table 3 also includes results from van Cranenburgh and Bod
(2013) who do not add function tags to non-terminal labels nor apply the extensive treebank refinements described in Sections 8.3–8.4.
Although the refinements and some of the function tags would be ex-
pected to improve performance, the rest of the function tags increase
sparsity and consequently the resulting F-scores are slightly lower; but
this tradeoff seems to be justified in order to get parse trees with function tags. The results on CGN show a surprisingly high exact match
score. This is due to a large number of interjection utterances, e.g.,
"uhm."; since such sentences only consist of a root node and POS tags,
the bracketing F_1-score is not affected by this.

9.2   *Function tags*

Table 4 reports an evaluation including function tags. For these three
treebanks, the models reproduce most of the information in the original treebank. The following parts are not yet incorporated. The German and Dutch treebanks contain additional lexical information consisting of lemmas and morphological features. These could be added to
the non-terminal labels of the model or obtained from an external POS
tagger. Lastly, some non-terminals have multiple parents; these occur
in the German and Dutch treebanks and are referred to as secondary
edges.

9.3   *All-fragments vs. recurring fragments*

The original Disco-DOP model (van Cranenburgh *et al.* 2011) is based
on an all-fragments model, while Disco-2DOP is based on recurring

Table 3: Discontinuous parsing of three Germanic languages. POS is the part-of-speech tagging accuracy; F_1 is the labelled bracketing F_1-score; EX is the exact match score. Results marked with * use gold standard POS tags; those marked with † do not discount the root node and punctuation. NB: Kallmeyer and Maier (2013) and Evang and Kallmeyer (2011) use a different test set and length restriction. 'vanCraBod2013' refers to van Cranenburgh and Bod (2013), and 'FeMa2015' to Fernández-González and Martins (2015)

		DEV			TEST		
Treebank and parser	$\|w\|$	POS	F_1	EX	POS	F_1	EX
GERMAN							
Negra							
van Cranenburgh (2012a)*	⩽ 40	100	74.3	34.3	100	72.3	33.2
Kallmeyer and Maier (2013)*†	⩽ 30				100	75.8	
this work, Disco-2DOP*	⩽ 40	100	**77.7**	**41.5**	100	**76.8**	**40.5**
this work, Disco-2DOP	⩽ 40	96.7	76.4	39.2	96.3	74.8	38.7
Tiger							
Hall and Nivre (2008)	⩽ 40				97.0	75.3	32.6
Versley (2014)	⩽ 40				100	74.2	37.3
FeMa2015	⩽ 40					82.6	45.9
vanCraBod2013, Disco-2DOP	⩽ 40	97.6	78.7	40.5	97.6	78.8	40.8
this work, Disco-2DOP	⩽ 40	96.6	78.3	40.2	96.1	78.2	40.0
this work, Split-2DOP	⩽ 40	96.6	78.1	39.2	96.2	78.1	39.0
ENGLISH							
WSJ							
Evang and Kallmeyer (2011)*†	< 25				100	79.0	
vanCraBod2013, Disco-2DOP	⩽ 40	96.0	85.2	28.0	96.6	85.6	31.3
this work, Disco-2DOP	⩽ 40	96.1	**86.9**	**29.5**	96.7	**87.0**	**34.4**
this work, Split-2DOP	⩽ 40	96.1	86.7	**29.5**	96.7	87.0	33.9
DUTCH							
Lassy							
vanCraBod2013, Disco-2DOP	⩽ 40	94.1	**79.0**	**37.4**	94.6	**77.0**	**35.2**
this work, Disco-2DOP	⩽ 40	96.7	78.3	36.2	96.3	76.6	34.0
this work, Split-2DOP	⩽ 40	96.8	78.0	34.9	96.3	76.2	32.7
CGN							
this work, Disco-2DOP	⩽ 40	96.7	**72.6**	**64.1**	96.7	**73.0**	**63.8**
this work, Split-2DOP	⩽ 40	96.6	71.2	63.4	96.7	72.2	63.3

Table 4: Evaluation of function tags on sentences $\leqslant$ 40 words, test sets; F_1 scores as defined at the end of Section 8.5

Language, treebank	phrase labels	function tags	combined
German, Tiger	78.2	93.5	68.1
English, WSJ	87.0	86.3	82.5
Dutch, Lassy	76.6	92.8	70.0

fragments. Table 5 compares previous results of Disco-DOP to the new Disco-2DOP implementation. The second column shows the accuracy for different values of k, i.e., the number of coarse derivations that determine the allowed labelled spans for the fine stage. While increasing this value did not yield improvements using the DOP reduction, with Disco-2DOP there is a substantial improvement in performance, with $k = 5000$ yielding the best score among the handful of values tested. Figure 16 shows the average time spent in each stage using the latter model on WSJ. The average time to parse a sentence ($\leqslant$ 40 words) for this grammar is 7.7 seconds. Efficiency could be improved significantly by improving the PCFG parser using better chart representations such as packed parse forests and bit vectors (Schmid 2004).

Table 5: Comparing F-scores for the DOP reduction (implicit fragments) with Double-DOP (explicit fragments) on the Negra development set with different amounts of pruning (higher k means less pruning); gold standard POS tags

Model	$k = 50$ F_1	$k = 5000$ F_1
DOP reduction: disco-DOP	74.3	73.5
Double-DOP: disco-2DOP	76.3	**77.7**

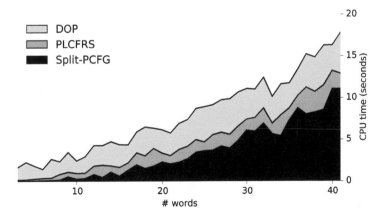

Figure 16: Average time spent in each stage for sentences by length; disco-2DOP, WSJ development set

9.4   *Effects of pruning*

The effects of pruning can be further investigated by comparing different levels of pruning. We first parse the sentences in the Negra development set that are up to 30 words long with a PLCFRS treebank grammar, with $k = 10,000$ and without pruning. Out of 897 sentences, the Viterbi derivation is pruned on only 14 occasions, while the pruned version is about 300 times faster.

Table 6 shows results for different levels of pruning on sentences of all lengths. For sentences of all lengths it is not feasible to parse with the unpruned PLCFRS. However, we can compare the items in the parse forest after pruning and the best derivation to the gold tree from the treebank. From the various measures, it can be concluded that the pruning has a large effect on speed and the number of items in the resulting parse forest, while having only a small effect on the quality of the parse (forest).

Table 6: Results for different levels of pruning; mean over 1000 sentences

	(PCFG)	$k = 100$	$k = 1000$	$k = 5000$	$k = 10,000$
CPU time (seconds)	2.461	0.128	0.193	0.444	0.739
Number of items in chart	69,570.5	207.6	282.7	378.2	436.5
Percentage of gold standard items in chart	94.7	94.2	97.2	98.1	98.4
F_1 score	69.3	69.8	69.9	69.9	69.8

9.5   *Without LCFRS*

Table 3 shows that the Disco-2DOP and Split-2DOP techniques have comparable performance, demonstrating that the complexity of LCFRS parsing can be avoided. Table 7 shows the performance in each step of the coarse-to-fine pipelines, with and without LCFRS. Surprisingly, the use of a formalism that explicitly models discontinuity as an operation does not give any improvement over a simpler model in which discontinuities are only modeled probabilistically by encoding them into labels and fragments. This demonstrates that given the use of tree fragments, discontinuous rewriting through LCFRS comes at a high computational cost without a clear benefit over CFG.

Table 7: Parsing discontinuous constituents is possible without LCFRS (Negra development set, gold standard POS tags; results are for Final stage)

Pipeline	F_1	EX%
Split-PCFG (no LCFRS, no TSG)	65.8	28.0
Split-PCFG $\Rightarrow$ PLCFRS (no TSG)	65.9	28.6
Split-PCFG $\Rightarrow$ PLCFRS $\Rightarrow$ 2DOP	77.7	41.5
Split-PCFG $\Rightarrow$ Split-2DOP (no LCFRS)	78.1	42.0

9.6 The role of probabilities

From the results it is clear that a probabilistic tree-substitution grammar is able to provide much better results than a simple treebank grammar. However, it is not obvious whether the improvement is specifically due to the more fine-grained statistics (i.e., frequencies of more specific events), or generally because of the use of larger chunks. A serendipitous discovery during development of the parser provides insight into this: during an experiment, the frequencies of fragments were accidentally permuted and assigned to different fragments, but the resulting decrease in performance was surprisingly low, from 77.7 to 74.1 F_1 – suggesting that most of the improvement over the 65.9 F_1 score of the PLCFRS treebank grammar comes from memorizing larger chunks, as opposed to statistical reckoning.

9.7 Previous work

Earlier work on recovering empty categories and their antecedents in the Penn treebank (Johnson 2002; Levy and Manning 2004; Gabbard *et al.* 2006; Schmid 2006; Cai *et al.* 2011) has recovered non-local dependencies by producing the traces and co-indexation as in the original annotation. If the results include both traces and antecedents (which holds for all but the last work cited), the conversion to discontinuous constituents of Evang and Kallmeyer (2011) could be applied to obtain a discontinuous F-score. Since this would require access to the original parser output, we have not pursued this.

As explained in Section 8.5, it is not possible to directly compare the results to existing parsers that do not produce discontinuous constituents. However, the F-measures do give a rough measure, since the majority of constituents are not discontinuous.

For English, there is a result with 2DOP by Sangati and Zuidema (2011) with an F_1 score of 87.9. This difference can be attributed to the absence of discontinuous bracketings, as well as their use of the Maximum Constituents Parse instead of the Most Probable Parse; the former optimizes the F-measure instead of the exact match score. Shindo *et al.* (2012) achieve an F_1 score of 92.9 with a Bayesian TSG that uses symbol refinement through latent variables (i.e., automatic state splitting).

For German, the best results without discontinuity and no length restriction are F_1 scores of 84.2 for Negra (Petrov 2010) and 76.8 for Tiger (Fraser *et al.* 2013; note that this result employs a different train-dev-test split than the one in this work).

10   CONCLUSION

We have shown how to parse with discontinuous tree-substitution grammars and presented a practical implementation. We employ a fragment extraction method that finds recurring structures in treebanks efficiently, and supports discontinuous treebanks. This enables a data-oriented parsing implementation that employs a compact, efficient, and accurate model for discontinuous parsing in a generative model that improves upon previous results for this task.

Surprisingly, it turns out that the formal power of LCFRS is not necessary to describe discontinuity, since equivalent results can be obtained with a probabilistic tree-substitution grammar in which non-local relations are encoded in the non-terminal labels. In other words, it is feasible to produce discontinuous constituents without invoking mild context-sensitivity.

We have presented parsing results on three languages. Compared to previous work on statistical parsing, our models are linguistically richer. In addition to discontinuous constituents, our models also reproduce function tags from the treebank. While there have been previous results on reproducing non-local relations or function tags, this work reproduces both using models derived straightforwardly from treebanks, while exploiting ready-made treebank transformations for improved performance.

ACKNOWLEDGMENTS

We are grateful to Kilian Evang for supplying the discontinuous Penn treebank, to the reviewers for detailed comments, and to Dave Carter and Adam Przepiórkowski for copy-editing suggestions.

This work is supported by the Computational Humanities Program of the Royal Netherlands Academy of Arts and Sciences, as part of The Riddle of Literary Quality.

REFERENCES

Krasimir ANGELOV and Peter LJUNGLÖF (2014), Fast statistical parsing with parallel multiple context-free grammars, in *Proceedings of EACL*, pp. 368–376, http://aclweb.org/anthology/E14-1039.

Mohit BANSAL and Dan KLEIN (2010), Simple, accurate parsing with an all-fragments grammar, in *Proceedings of ACL*, pp. 1098–1107, http://aclweb.org/anthology/P10-1112.

François BARTHÉLEMY, Pierre BOULLIER, Philippe DESCHAMP, and Éric DE LA CLERGERIE (2001), Guided parsing of range concatenation languages, in *Proceedings of ACL*, pp. 42–49, http://aclweb.org/anthology/P01-1007.

Shane BERGSMA, Matt POST, and David YAROWSKY (2012), Stylometric analysis of scientific articles, in *Proceedings of NAACL*, pp. 327–337, http://aclweb.org/anthology/N12-1033.

Ezra BLACK, John LAFFERTY, and Salim ROUKOS (1992), Development and evaluation of a broad-coverage probabilistic grammar of English-language computer manuals, in *Proceedings of ACL*, pp. 185–192, http://aclweb.org/anthology/P92-1024.

Don BLAHETA and Eugene CHARNIAK (2000), Assigning function tags to parsed text, in *Proceedings of NAACL*, pp. 234–240, http://aclweb.org/anthology/A00-2031.

Rens BOD (1992), A computational model of language performance: data-oriented parsing, in *Proceedings COLING*, pp. 855–859, http://aclweb.org/anthology/C92-3126.

Rens BOD (1995), The problem of computing the most probable tree in data-oriented parsing and stochastic tree grammars, in *Proceedings of EACL*, pp. 104–111, http://aclweb.org/anthology/E95-1015.

Rens BOD (2001), What is the minimal set of fragments that achieves maximal parse accuracy?, in *Proceedings of ACL*, pp. 69–76, http://aclweb.org/anthology/P01-1010.

Rens BOD, Remko SCHA, and Khalil SIMA'AN, editors (2003), *Data-Oriented Parsing*, The University of Chicago Press.

Pierre BOULLIER (1998), Proposal for a natural language processing syntactic backbone, Technical Report RR-3342, INRIA-Rocquencourt, Le Chesnay, France, http://www.inria.fr/RRRT/RR-3342.html.

Adriane BOYD (2007), Discontinuity revisited: An improved conversion to context-free representations, in *Proceedings of the Linguistic Annotation Workshop*, pp. 41–44, http://aclweb.org/anthology/W07-1506.

Sabine BRANTS, Stefanie DIPPER, Silvia HANSEN, Wolfgang LEZIUS, and George SMITH (2002), The Tiger treebank, in *Proceedings of the workshop on treebanks and linguistic theories*, pp. 24–41, http://www.bultreebank.org/proceedings/paper03.pdf.

Joan BRESNAN, Ronald M. KAPLAN, Stanley PETERS, and Annie ZAENEN (1982), Cross-serial dependencies in Dutch, *Linguistic Inquiry*, 13(4):613–635.

Shu CAI, David CHIANG, and Yoav GOLDBERG (2011), Language-independent parsing with empty elements, in *Proceedings of ACL-HLT*, pp. 212–216, http://aclweb.org/anthology/P11-2037.

Samy CHAMBI, Daniel LEMIRE, Owen KASER, and Robert GODIN (2015), Better bitmap performance with Roaring bitmaps, *Software: Practice and Experience*, ISSN 1097-024X, doi:10.1002/spe.2325, http://arxiv.org/abs/1402.6407, to appear.

Eugene CHARNIAK (1996), Tree-bank grammars, in *Proceedings of the National Conference on Artificial Intelligence*, pp. 1031–1036.

Eugene CHARNIAK, Mark JOHNSON, M. ELSNER, J. AUSTERWEIL, D. ELLIS, I. HAXTON, C. HILL, R. SHRIVATHS, J. MOORE, M. POZAR, *et al.* (2006), Multilevel coarse-to-fine PCFG parsing, in *Proceedings of NAACL-HLT*, pp. 168–175, http://aclweb.org/anthology/N06-1022.

David CHIANG (2000), Statistical parsing with an automatically-extracted tree adjoining grammar, in *Proceedings of ACL*, pp. 456–463, http://aclweb.org/anthology/P00-1058.

Noam CHOMSKY (1956), Three models for the description of language, *IRE Transactions on Information Theory*, 2(3):113–124.

Noam CHOMSKY (1965), *Aspects of the Theory of Syntax*, MIT press.

Trevor COHN, Phil BLUNSOM, and Sharon GOLDWATER (2010), Inducing tree-substitution grammars, *The Journal of Machine Learning Research*, 11(Nov):3053–3096.

Trevor COHN, Sharon GOLDWATER, and Phil BLUNSOM (2009), Inducing compact but accurate tree-substitution grammars, in *Proceedings of NAACL-HLT*, pp. 548–556, http://aclweb.org/anthology/N09-1062.

Michael COLLINS (1999), *Head-driven statistical models for natural language parsing*, Ph.D. thesis, University of Pennsylvania.

Peter DIENES and Amit DUBEY (2003), Deep syntactic processing by combining shallow methods, in *Proceedings of ACL*, pp. 431–438, http://aclweb.org/anthology/P03-1055.

Amit DUBEY and Frank KELLER (2003), Probabilistic parsing for German using sister-head dependencies, in *Proceedings of ACL*, pp. 96–103, http://aclweb.org/anthology/P03-1013.

Kilian EVANG and Laura KALLMEYER (2011), PLCFRS parsing of English discontinuous constituents, in *Proceedings of IWPT*, pp. 104–116, http://aclweb.org/anthology/W11-2913.

Daniel FERNÁNDEZ-GONZÁLEZ and André F. T. MARTINS (2015), Parsing as reduction, in *Proceedings of ACL*, pp. 1523–1533, http://aclweb.org/anthology/P15-1147.

Alexander FRASER, Helmut SCHMID, Richárd FARKAS, Renjing WANG, and Hinrich SCHÜTZE (2013), Knowledge sources for constituent parsing of German, a morphologically rich and less-configurational language, *Computational Linguistics*, 39(1):57–85, http://aclweb.org/anthology/J13-1005.

Ryan GABBARD, Mitchell MARCUS, and Seth KULICK (2006), Fully parsing the Penn treebank, in *Proceedings of NAACL-HLT*, pp. 184–191, http://aclweb.org/anthology/N06-1024.

Stuart GEMAN and Mark JOHNSON (2004), Probability and statistics in computational linguistics, a brief review, in Mark JOHNSON, Sanjeev P. KHUDANPUR, Mari OSTENDORF, and Roni ROSENFELD, editors, *Mathematical foundations of speech and language processing*, pp. 1–26, Springer.

Daniel GILDEA (2010), Optimal parsing strategies for linear context-free rewriting systems, in *Proceedings of NAACL-HLT*, pp. 769–776, http://aclweb.org/anthology/N10-1118.

Joshua GOODMAN (2003), Efficient parsing of DOP with PCFG-reductions, in Bod *et al.* (2003), pp. 125–146.

Spence GREEN, Marie-Catherine DE MARNEFFE, John BAUER, and Christopher D. MANNING (2011), Multiword expression identification with tree substitution grammars: A parsing tour de force with French, in *Proceedings of EMNLP*, pp. 725–735, http://aclweb.org/anthology/D11-1067.

Johan HALL and Joakim NIVRE (2008), Parsing discontinuous phrase structure with grammatical functions, in Bengt NORDSTRÖM and Aarne RANTA, editors, *Advances in Natural Language Processing*, volume 5221 of *Lecture Notes in Computer Science*, pp. 169–180, Springer, http://dx.doi.org/10.1007/978-3-540-85287-2_17.

Lars HOOGWEG (2003), Extending DOP with insertion, in Bod *et al.* (2003), pp. 317–335.

Yu-Yin HSU (2010), Comparing conversions of discontinuity in PCFG parsing, in *Proceedings of Treebanks and Linguistic Theories*, pp. 103–113, http://hdl.handle.net/10062/15954.

Liang HUANG and David CHIANG (2005), Better k-best parsing, in *Proceedings of IWPT*, pp. 53–64, NB corrected version on author homepage: http://www.cis.upenn.edu/~lhuang3/huang-iwpt-correct.pdf.

Marinus A.C. HUYBREGTS (1976), Overlapping dependencies in Dutch, *Utrecht Working Papers in Linguistics*, 1:24–65.

Mark JOHNSON (2002), A simple pattern-matching algorithm for recovering empty nodes and their antecedents, in *Proceedings of ACL*, pp. 136–143, http://aclweb.org/anthology/P02-1018.

Aravind K. JOSHI (1985), How much context sensitivity is necessary for characterizing structural descriptions: Tree adjoining grammars, in David R. DOWTY, Lauri KARTTUNEN, and Arnold M. ZWICKY, editors, *Natural language parsing: Psychological, computational and theoretical perspectives*, pp. 206–250, Cambridge University Press, New York.

Miriam KAESHAMMER and Vera DEMBERG (2012), German and English treebanks and lexica for tree-adjoining grammars, in *Proceedings of LREC*, pp. 1880–1887, http://www.lrec-conf.org/proceedings/lrec2012/pdf/398_Paper.pdf.

Laura KALLMEYER (2009), A declarative characterization of different types of multicomponent tree adjoining grammars, *Research on Language and Computation*, 7(1):55–99.

Laura KALLMEYER (2010), *Parsing Beyond Context-Free Grammars*, Cognitive Technologies, Springer.

Laura KALLMEYER and Wolfgang MAIER (2010), Data-driven parsing with probabilistic linear context-free rewriting systems, in *Proceedings of COLING*, pp. 537–545, http://aclweb.org/anthology/C10-1061.

Laura KALLMEYER and Wolfgang MAIER (2013), Data-driven parsing using probabilistic linear context-free rewriting systems, *Computational Linguistics*, 39(1):87–119, http://aclweb.org/anthology/J13-1006.

Laura KALLMEYER, Wolfgang MAIER, and Giorgio SATTA (2009), Synchronous rewriting in treebanks, in *Proceedings of IWPT*, http://aclweb.org/anthology/W09-3810.

Fred KARLSSON (2007), Constraints on multiple centre-embedding of clauses, *Journal of Linguistics*, 43(2):365–392.

Dan KLEIN and Christopher D. MANNING (2003), Accurate unlexicalized parsing, in *Proceedings of ACL*, volume 1, pp. 423–430, http://aclweb.org/anthology/P03-1054.

Marco KUHLMANN (2013), Mildly non-projective dependency grammar, *Computational Linguistics*, 39(2):355–387, http://aclweb.org/anthology/J13-2004.

Marco KUHLMANN and Giorgio SATTA (2009), Treebank grammar techniques for non-projective dependency parsing, in *Proceedings of EACL*, pp. 478–486, http://aclweb.org/anthology/E09-1055.

Roger LEVY (2005), *Probabilistic models of word order and syntactic discontinuity*, Ph.D. thesis, Stanford University.

Roger LEVY and Christopher D. MANNING (2004), Deep dependencies from context-free statistical parsers: correcting the surface dependency approximation, in *Proceedings of ACL*, pp. 327–334, http://aclweb.org/anthology/P04-1042.

Wolfgang MAIER, Miriam KAESHAMMER, Peter BAUMANN, and Sandra KÜBLER (2014), Discosuite – A parser test suite for German discontinuous structures, in *Proceedings of LREC*, http://www.lrec-conf.org/proceedings/lrec2014/pdf/230_Paper.pdf.

Wolfgang MAIER, Miriam KAESHAMMER, and Laura KALLMEYER (2012), PLCFRS parsing revisited: Restricting the fan-out to two, in *Proceedings of TAG*, volume 11, http://wolfgang-maier.net/pub/tagplus12.pdf.

Wolfgang MAIER and Timm LICHTE (2011), Characterizing discontinuity in constituent treebanks, in *Proceedings of Formal Grammar 2009*, pp. 167–182, Springer.

Wolfgang MAIER and Anders SØGAARD (2008), Treebanks and mild context-sensitivity, in *Proceedings of Formal Grammar 2008*, pp. 61–76.

James D. McCAWLEY (1982), Parentheticals and discontinuous constituent structure, *Linguistic Inquiry*, 13(1):91–106, http://www.jstor.org/stable/4178261.

Mark-Jan NEDERHOF and Heiko VOGLER (2014), Hybrid grammars for discontinuous parsing, in *Proceedings of COLING*, pp. 1370–1381, http://aclweb.org/anthology/C14-1130.

Timothy J. O'DONNELL, Joshua B. TENENBAUM, and Noah D. GOODMAN (2009), Fragment grammars: Exploring computation and reuse in language, Technical Report MIT-CSAIL-TR-2009-013, MIT CSAIL, http://hdl.handle.net/1721.1/44963.

Almerindo E. OJEDA (1988), A linear precedence account of cross-serial dependencies, *Linguistics and Philosophy*, 11(4):457–492.

Adam PAULS and Dan KLEIN (2009), Hierarchical search for parsing, in *Proceedings of NAACL-HLT*, pp. 557–565, http://aclweb.org/anthology/N09-1063.

P. Stanley PETERS and R. W. RITCHIE (1973), On the generative power of transformational grammars, *Information Sciences*, 6:49–83, http://dx.doi.org/10.1016/0020-0255(73)90027-3.

Slav PETROV (2010), Products of random latent variable grammars, in *Proceedings of NAACL-HLT*, pp. 19–27, http://aclweb.org/anthology/N10-1003.

Kenneth L. PIKE (1943), Taxemes and immediate constituents, *Language*, 19(2):65–82, http://www.jstor.org/stable/409840.

Matt POST (2011), Judging grammaticality with tree substitution grammar derivations, in *Proceedings of the ACL-HLT 2011*, pp. 217–222, http://aclweb.org/anthology/P11-2038.

Matt POST and Daniel GILDEA (2009), Bayesian learning of a tree substitution grammar, in *Proceedings of the ACL-IJCNLP 2009 Conference, Short Papers*, pp. 45–48, http://aclweb.org/anthology/P09-2012.

Brian ROARK, Kristy HOLLINGSHEAD, and Nathan BODENSTAB (2012), Finite-state chart constraints for reduced complexity context-free parsing pipelines, *Computational Linguistics*, 38(4):719–753, http://aclweb.org/anthology/J12-4002.

Federico SANGATI and Willem ZUIDEMA (2011), Accurate parsing with compact tree-substitution grammars: Double-DOP, in *Proceedings of EMNLP*, pp. 84–95, http://aclweb.org/anthology/D11-1008.

Federico SANGATI, Willem ZUIDEMA, and Rens BOD (2010), Efficiently extract recurring tree fragments from large treebanks, in *Proceedings of LREC*, pp. 219–226, http://dare.uva.nl/record/371504.

Remko SCHA (1990), Language theory and language technology; competence and performance, in Q.A.M. DE KORT and G.L.J. LEERDAM, editors, *Computertoepassingen in de Neerlandistiek*, pp. 7–22, LVVN, Almere, the Netherlands, original title: Taaltheorie en taaltechnologie; competence en performance. English translation: http://iaaa.nl/rs/LeerdamE.html.

Yves SCHABES and Richard C. WATERS (1995), Tree insertion grammar: cubic-time, parsable formalism that lexicalizes context-free grammar without changing the trees produced, *Computational Linguistics*, 21(4):479–513, http://aclweb.org/anthology/J95-4002.

Helmut SCHMID (2004), Efficient parsing of highly ambiguous context-free grammars with bit vectors, in *Proceedings of COLING '04*, http://aclweb.org/anthology/C04-1024.

Helmut SCHMID (2006), Trace prediction and recovery with unlexicalized PCFGs and slash features, in *Proceedings of COLING-ACL*, pp. 177–184, http://aclweb.org/anthology/P06-1023.

William SCHULER, Samir ABDELRAHMAN, Tim MILLER, and Lane SCHWARTZ (2010), Broad-coverage parsing using human-like memory constraints, *Computational Linguistics*, 36(1):1–30, http://aclweb.org/anthology/J10-1001.

William SCHULER, David CHIANG, and Mark DRAS (2000), Multi-component TAG and notions of formal power, in *Proceedings of ACL*, pp. 448–455, http://aclweb.org/anthology/P00-1057.

Hiroyuki SEKI, Takahashi MATSUMURA, Mamoru FUJII, and Tadao KASAMI (1991), On multiple context-free grammars, *Theoretical Computer Science*, 88(2):191–229.

Stuart M. SHIEBER (1985), Evidence against the context-freeness of natural language, *Linguistics and Philosophy*, 8:333–343.

Hiroyuki SHINDO, Yusuke MIYAO, Akinori FUJINO, and Masaaki NAGATA (2012), Bayesian symbol-refined tree substitution grammars for syntactic parsing, in *Proceedings of ACL*, pp. 440–448, http://aclweb.org/anthology/P12-1046.

Khalil SIMA'AN (1997), Efficient Disambiguation by means of stochastic tree substitution grammars, in D. JONES and H. SOMERS, editors, *New Methods in Language Processing*, pp. 178–198, UCL Press, UK.

Wojciech SKUT, Brigitte KRENN, Thorsten BRANTS, and Hans USZKOREIT (1997), An annotation scheme for free word order languages, in *Proceedings of ANLP*, pp. 88–95, http://aclweb.org/anthology/A97-1014.

Ben SWANSON, Elif YAMANGIL, Eugene CHARNIAK, and Stuart SHIEBER (2013), A context free TAG variant, in *Proceedings of the ACL*, pp. 302–310, http://aclweb.org/anthology/P13-1030.

Benjamin SWANSON and Eugene CHARNIAK (2012), Native language detection with tree substitution grammars, in *Proceedings of ACL*, pp. 193–197, http://aclweb.org/anthology/P12-2038.

Heike TELLJOHANN, Erhard HINRICHS, and Sandra KÜBLER (2004), The Tüba-D/Z Treebank: Annotating German with a context-free backbone, in *Proceedings of LREC*, pp. 2229–2235, http://www.lrec-conf.org/proceedings/lrec2004/pdf/135.pdf.

Heike TELLJOHANN, Erhard W HINRICHS, Sandra KÜBLER, Heike ZINSMEISTER, and Kathrin BECK (2012), Stylebook for the Tübingen treebank of written German (TüBa-D/Z), technical report, Seminar für Sprachwissenschaft, Universität Tübingen, Germany, http://www.sfs.uni-tuebingen.de/fileadmin/static/ascl/resources/tuebadz-stylebook-1201.pdf.

Marten H. TRAUTWEIN (1995), *Computational pitfalls in tractable grammar formalisms*, Ph.D. thesis, University of Amsterdam, http://www.illc.uva.nl/Research/Publications/Dissertations/DS-1995-15.text.ps.gz.

Andreas VAN CRANENBURGH (2012a), Efficient parsing with linear context-free rewriting systems, in *Proceedings of EACL*, pp. 460–470, corrected version: http://andreasvc.github.io/eacl2012corrected.pdf.

Andreas VAN CRANENBURGH (2012b), Literary authorship attribution with phrase-structure fragments, in *Proceedings of CLFL*, pp. 59–63, revised version: http://andreasvc.github.io/clfl2012.pdf.

Andreas VAN CRANENBURGH (2014), Extraction of phrase-structure fragments with a linear average time tree kernel, *Computational Linguistics in the Netherlands Journal*, 4:3–16, ISSN 2211-4009, http://www.clinjournal.org/sites/default/files/01-Cranenburgh-CLIN2014.pdf.

Andreas VAN CRANENBURGH and Rens BOD (2013), Discontinuous parsing with an efficient and accurate DOP model, in *Proceedings of IWPT*, pp. 7–16, http://www.illc.uva.nl/LaCo/CLS/papers/iwpt2013parser_final.pdf.

Andreas VAN CRANENBURGH, Remko SCHA, and Federico SANGATI (2011), Discontinuous data-oriented parsing: A mildly context-sensitive all-fragments grammar, in *Proceedings of SPMRL*, pp. 34–44, http://aclweb.org/anthology/W11-3805.

Leonoor VAN DER BEEK, Gosse BOUMA, Robert MALOUF, and Gertjan VAN NOORD (2002), The Alpino dependency treebank, *Language and Computers*, 45(1):8–22.

Ton VAN DER WOUDEN, Heleen HOEKSTRA, Michael MOORTGAT, Bram RENMANS, and Ineke SCHUURMAN (2002), Syntactic analysis in the spoken Dutch corpus (CGN), in *Proceedings of LREC*, pp. 768–773, http://www.lrec-conf.org/proceedings/lrec2002/pdf/71.pdf.

Gertjan VAN NOORD (2009), Huge parsed corpora in Lassy, in *Proceedings of TLT7*, LOT, Groningen, The Netherlands.

Yannick VERSLEY (2014), Experiments with easy-first nonprojective constituent parsing, in *Proceedings of SPMRL-SANCL 2014*, pp. 39–53, http://aclweb.org/anthology/W14-6104.

K. VIJAY-SHANKER and David J. WEIR (1994), The equivalence of four extensions of context-free grammars, *Theory of Computing Systems*, 27(6):511–546.

K. VIJAY-SHANKER, David J. WEIR, and Aravind K. JOSHI (1987), Characterizing structural descriptions produced by various grammatical formalisms, in *Proceedings of ACL*, pp. 104–111, http://aclweb.org/anthology/P87-1015.

David J. WEIR (1988), *Characterizing mildly context-sensitive grammar formalisms*, Ph.D. thesis, University of Pennsylvania, http://repository.upenn.edu/dissertations/AAI8908403/.

Rulon S. WELLS (1947), Immediate constituents, *Language*, 23(2):81–117, http://www.jstor.org/stable/410382.

Fei XIA, Chung-Hye HAN, Martha PALMER, and Aravind JOSHI (2001), Automatically extracting and comparing lexicalized grammars for different languages, in *Proceedings of IJCAI*, pp. 1321–1330.

Elif YAMANGIL and Stuart SHIEBER (2012), Estimating compact yet rich tree insertion grammars, in *Proceedings of ACL*, pp. 110–114, http://aclweb.org/anthology/P12-2022.

Andreas ZOLLMANN and Khalil SIMA'AN (2005), A consistent and efficient estimator for data-oriented parsing, *Journal of Automata Languages and Combinatorics*, 10(2/3):367–388, http://staff.science.uva.nl/~simaan/D-Papers/JALCsubmit.pdf.

Permissions

All chapters in this book were first published in JLM, by Institute of Computer Science of the Polish Academy of Sciences; hereby published with permission under the Creative Commons Attribution License or equivalent. Every chapter published in this book has been scrutinized by our experts. Their significance has been extensively debated. The topics covered herein carry significant findings which will fuel the growth of the discipline. They may even be implemented as practical applications or may be referred to as a beginning point for another development.

The contributors of this book come from diverse backgrounds, making this book a truly international effort. This book will bring forth new frontiers with its revolutionizing research information and detailed analysis of the nascent developments around the world.

We would like to thank all the contributing authors for lending their expertise to make the book truly unique. They have played a crucial role in the development of this book. Without their invaluable contributions this book wouldn't have been possible. They have made vital efforts to compile up to date information on the varied aspects of this subject to make this book a valuable addition to the collection of many professionals and students.

This book was conceptualized with the vision of imparting up-to-date information and advanced data in this field. To ensure the same, a matchless editorial board was set up. Every individual on the board went through rigorous rounds of assessment to prove their worth. After which they invested a large part of their time researching and compiling the most relevant data for our readers.

The editorial board has been involved in producing this book since its inception. They have spent rigorous hours researching and exploring the diverse topics which have resulted in the successful publishing of this book. They have passed on their knowledge of decades through this book. To expedite this challenging task, the publisher supported the team at every step. A small team of assistant editors was also appointed to further simplify the editing procedure and attain best results for the readers.

Apart from the editorial board, the designing team has also invested a significant amount of their time in understanding the subject and creating the most relevant covers. They scrutinized every image to scout for the most suitable representation of the subject and create an appropriate cover for the book.

The publishing team has been an ardent support to the editorial, designing and production team. Their endless efforts to recruit the best for this project, has resulted in the accomplishment of this book. They are a veteran in the field of academics and their pool of knowledge is as vast as their experience in printing. Their expertise and guidance has proved useful at every step. Their uncompromising quality standards have made this book an exceptional effort. Their encouragement from time to time has been an inspiration for everyone.

The publisher and the editorial board hope that this book will prove to be a valuable piece of knowledge for researchers, students, practitioners and scholars across the globe.

List of Contributors

Olúgbénga O. Akinadé and Ọdẹ́túnjí A. Ọdẹ́jọbí
Computing and Intelligent Systems Research Group Awólọwọ University Ilé-Ifẹ, Nigeria Department of Computer Science and Engineering Ọbáfẹ́mi Awólọ́wọ̀ University Ilé-Ifẹ, Nigeria

Peter R. Sutton and Hana Filip
Heinrich Heine University Düsseldorf

Stergios Chatzikyriakidis
Centre for Linguistic Theory and Studies in Probability (CLASP), Department of Philosophy, Linguistics and Theory of Science, University of Gothenburg; Open University of Cyprus

Mathieu Lafourcade
LIRMM, University of Montpellier

Lionel Ramadier
Radiology Dept. CHU Montpellier

Manel Zarrouk
National University of Ireland, Galway

Mehrnoosh Sadrzadeh
School of Electronic Engineering and Computer Science, Queen Mary University of London

Reinhard Muskens
Department of Philosophy, Tilburg University

Andreas van Cranenburgh
Huygens ING, Royal Netherlands Academy of Arts and Sciences
Institute for Logic, Language and Computation, University of Amsterdam

Remko Scha and Rens Bod
Institute for Logic, Language and Computation, University of Amsterdam

Index

Printed in the USA
CPSIA information can be obtained
at www.ICGtesting.com
JSHW051358221024
72173JS00006B/1313